Praise for *The Tr*

MW00613071

"Barbara Smith is visionary, courageous, and insightful. Her work provides a crucial challenge to all of us."—Dr. Cornel West

"A feminist writer and theorist . . . Smith's writing frequently reaches strident polemicist peaks, but just as frequently, stretches of sublime prose translate her crystalline intellect to the page, exciting both mind and senses."—*Publishers Weekly*

"At every moment of serious political crisis—and no thinking person can argue that ours is not such a moment—certain writers step forward with words that seem to ring from the very heart of history. Barbara Smith is certainly one of these writers, and her new book—electrifying, thought-provoking, illuminating, eloquent, harsh, and funny—is essential reading. Whether you agree with everything she says is not important; the essays in this book will revivify your heart and mind and reawaken a passion for activism and for justice."—Tony Kushner

"A provocative collection of impassioned essays written from a radical gay African American feminist perspective. . . . This manifesto is always challenging and often convincing."—*Kirkus Reviews*

"In these essays, Smith explores several explosive issues, among them sexual politics, racism and women's studies, and homophobia." —*Library Journal*

"*The Truth That Never Hurts* provides a universal message about struggle, resistance, and freedom, grounded within a Black lesbian feminist critique of America's culture and politics. The cogently written essays represent a cross section of Smith's work over the past twenty years and the first book dedicated exclusively to her own writing. Focusing on race, feminism, and the politics of sexuality, Smith provides an alternative lens to view the world by making connections between systems of oppression and offering suggestions for social change."—*Washington Blade*

"Barbara Smith's uncompromising intelligence helped invent the politics of intersection that grounds progressive thinking today. These essays deliver trenchant analysis from one of the most original, astute, and practical thinkers in the gay, lesbian, bisexual, and transgender movement."—Urvashi Vaid, director of the Policy Institute, National Gay and Lesbian Task Force

"As a Black lesbian feminist activist and scholar, Smith is a highly respected voice of conscience who speaks discomforting but necessary truths about the interlocking nature of oppressions within American culture and institutions. These landmark essays . . . show Smith challenging academic, political, and community organizations to expand their missions in order to include persons who have been perennially at the margins of our society. . . . Recommended."—*MultiCultural Review*

"Smith's book is an excellent example of powerful, introspective writing that challenges readers to reexamine their stance on complex issues concerning race and gender."—*Bloomsbury Review*

"Smith has provided us with a collection of erudite and profoundly moving writings [that are] smart, incisive, and instructive. There is no stone that Smith has left unturned. From homophobia in the Black community to police brutality to racism in the women's movement to Black women and anti-Semitism . . . Barbara Smith has explained the linkages among the multiplicity of oppressions facing Blacks in general and Black lesbians in particular."—*Journal of Lesbian Studies*

"The ancestors are surely ecstatic about the diligence, courage, passion, and good humor exhibited in *The Truth That Never Hurts*. This is a landmark work from a pioneering activist who has always kept the faith."—Evelyn C. White, editor of *The Black Women's Health Book*

"Sobering in what it has to tell us, *The Truth That Never Hurts* forces us to face those truths that disrupt the placid surfaces of our lives. A personal/political odyssey that documents some of the most critical moments in the last three decades of our national life, Smith's book forces us to new levels of awareness. Her piercing eye and uncompromising search for human justice for all make this volume a must-read for everyone who cares about the future."—Nellie Y. McKay, coeditor of *The Norton Anthology of African American Literature*

The Truth That Never Hurts

The Truth That Never Hurts

Writings on Race, Gender, and Freedom

25th Anniversary Edition

Barbara Smith

RUTGERS UNIVERSITY PRESS
NEW BRUNSWICK, CAMDEN, AND NEWARK, NEW JERSEY
LONDON AND OXFORD

Rutgers University Press is a department of Rutgers, The State University of
New Jersey, one of the leading public research universities in the nation. By publishing
worldwide, it furthers the University's mission of dedication to excellence
in teaching, scholarship, research, and clinical care.

25th Anniversary Edition 2024
ISBN 978-1-9788-3904-5 (paperback)
ISBN 978-1-9788-3905-2 (hardcover)

First published in 1998

Library of Congress Cataloging-in-Publication Data
Smith, Barbara, 1946–
p. cm.
Includes bibliographical references.
ISBN 0-8135-2573-X (cloth) — ISBN 0-8135-2761 (pbk.)
1. Afro-American women—Civil rights. 2. Lesbian feminism—United States.
3. American literature—Afro-American authors—History and criticism.
4. Afro-American women authors. 5. Afro-American lesbians. 6. United
States—Race relations. 7. Racism—United States. 8. Smith, Barbara, 1946– I. Title.
E 185.86.S635 1999   98-18668
305.42-dc21   CIP

A British Cataloging-in-Publication record for this
book is available from the British Library.

rutgersuniversitypress.org

In memory of Joseph F. Beam, Lucretia M. Diggs, and Isabelle Bell

For my family:

William Beall
Barbara Beall
Linda Brodie Chase
Sandra Brodie
Jason Morgan Edwards
Iris Hayes
Joan S. Laughlin
Mascha Oehlmann
Beverly Smith
Judith McDaniel
Vickie Smith

Contents

Acknowledgments   ix

Introduction   xiii

A Note on Citations   xxi

I. Toward a Black Feminist Criticism

Toward a Black Feminist Criticism   3

The Souls of Black Women   27

Sexual Politics and the Fiction of Zora Neale Hurston   33

Naming the Unnameable: The Poetry of Pat Parker   49

The Truth That Never Hurts: Black Lesbians
    in Fiction in the 1980s   57

We Must Always Bury Our Dead Twice: A Tribute
    to James Baldwin   97

African American Lesbian and Gay History:
    An Exploration   105

II. Between a Rock and a Hard Place

Racism and Women's Studies   123

The Tip of the Iceberg   129

The Rodney King Verdict   133

Ain't Gonna Let Nobody Turn Me Around:
    Reflections on the Hill-Thomas Hearings   139

Homophobia: Why Bring It Up?   147

The NEA Is the Least of It   153

Blacks and Gays: Healing the Great Divide   165

Between a Rock and a Hard Place: Relationships
    between Black and Jewish Women   177

III. Working for Liberation and Having a Damn Good Time

Chicago Firsthand: A Distortion of Reality   207

Working for Liberation and Having a Damn Good Time   213

Doing It from Scratch: The Challenge of
    Black Lesbian Organizing   221

Where's the Revolution?   235

Where's the Revolution? Part II   245

IV. A Rose

A Rose   253

Organizations to Contact   277

Selected Bibliography   285

Acknowledgments

Throughout the years many individuals have helped me to fulfill the dream of writing. Without their encouragement, technical expertise, criticism, and material and moral support, I would not have been able to continue. Although I cannot mention each person by name here, my appreciation is, nonetheless, heartfelt.

I am especially grateful to Ed Roberson, Nancy Hoffman, Doris Grumbach, and Cynthia Rich, who provided inspiration and demonstrated confidence in my work early on. The founding editors of *Conditions* magazine, Jan Clausen, Irena Klepfisz, Rima Shore, and especially Elly Bulkin, offered me the opportunity not only to contribute regularly, but also to introduce them to other writers. Michelle Cliff and Adrienne Rich, as individuals and as editors of *Sinister Wisdom*, were extremely supportive to me in myriad ways.

Coediting *But Some of Us Are Brave* with Akasha (Gloria) Hull and Patricia Bell-Scott was an experience of true sisterhood and began professional collaborations and friendships which continue to this day.

When I lived in Brooklyn from 1981 to 1984, I was fortunate to be a part of a community of women writers whose commitment to their craft, generosity, and humor were so important to me. Among them were Dorothy Allison, Toi Derricotte, Alexis De Veaux, Jewelle Gomez, Amber Hollibaugh, Audre Lorde, Cherríe Moraga,

Joan Nestle, and Grace Paley. During this period, I also studied with the novelist Nicholasa Mohr, an invaluable experience upon which I continue to draw.

I have been fortunate to have had the opportunity to take time away to write as the result of several artist residencies. I would like to thank the Millay Colony for the Arts, the Hambidge Center for the Arts and Sciences, Yaddo, Blue Mountain Center, and the Berkshire Forum Writer's Retreat for supporting my work in this way. A residency at the Windcall retreat for political and social activists in 1993 enabled me to begin work on *The Truth That Never Hurts*.

Without the efforts of the Kitchen Table: Women of Color Press Transition Team under the leadership of Jaime Grant, director of the Union Institute Center for Women, I would not have been able to relinquish my responsibilities as publisher and to devote the majority of my time to writing. I owe each team member a huge debt.

I would like to express my sincerest appreciation to my literary agents, Charlotte Sheedy and Neeti Madan, whose expert guidance has played a significant role in my becoming a full-time writer. I also wish to thank Neeti for her terrific help in finding the right home for this book.

My participation in the Bunting Institute of Radcliffe College's 1997 Publications Day, expertly organized by Lyn O'Conor, was extremely helpful in putting me in initial contact with Rutgers University Press.

It has been a joy to work with Rutgers. Their high level of professionalism and the respect extended to me as an author are, in my experience, rare. I would especially like to thank Susannah A. Driver for her precision, insight, and care in copy editing my manuscript, which made this a better book. I extend my greatest thanks to my editor, Leslie Mitchner, for recognizing the value of this project from the very beginning, for her excellent suggestions and criticisms, and for the remarkably loving spirit she brings to all aspects of her work.

There have been many friends whose faith and love I rely upon. Your creativity, intelligence, integrity, and passion for justice not only provide models for my own writing, but in many cases have built the movements out of which this writing comes. My love and deepest appreciation go to each of you, especially for being there in the darkest hours.

Introduction

In Robert Altman's film *Kansas City*, Blondie, a working-class white woman, kidnaps the wife of a well-connected politician in order to secure her husband's safe return from the hands of a powerful Black gangster. The film is set in the 1930s. When Blondie sneaks into the Western Union office where she is employed, she runs into the Black cleaning woman, Addie. Blondie warns Addie not to say anything about having seen her.

Addie replies, "Oh, nobody's gonna ask me anything. They never do." Her lines are delivered with resignation and perhaps a tinge of anger.

Later in the film, Blondie happens to run into Addie on the street. Addie has just come from voting. Addie tells her, "There's a lot of folks down there at the Western Union been looking for you." Blondie asks, "What did you tell 'em?" Addie says, "Nothing. 'Cause nobody didn't ask me nothing. But they were asking everybody else." This time there is less resignation and more acid in Addie's tone. This time she is dressed nicely in hat, topcoat, and pocketbook instead of a maid's uniform. She is also standing on the street in her own community.

When I saw these scenes, I was amazed that Altman would call attention to a Black woman's silencing and invisibility, that he would have a Black woman character actually comment upon her own submerged voice. What struck me most about Addie's remarks is that her frustration at the nonrecognition of her intelligence, emotions, personhood illuminates the most important reasons that I write.

"Nobody's gonna ask me anything. They never do."

In the last days of the twentieth century, Black women are still seldom asked. Racism is what happens to Black men. Sexism is what happens to white women. When public discourse occurs about race, gender, sexuality, class, or whether the speed limit should be raised to sixty-five, Black women's opinions generally are not sought.

But in my writing, I have found a way to "answer" even when no one asks. In 1977, for example, few people were dying to know about Black women writers and certainly not about Black lesbian ones, but I wrote "Toward a Black Feminist Criticism" anyway. Because of my political activism, I have been able to use writing to raise questions, to criticize the status quo, to open up dialogue, to imagine something better, and always, I hope, to shake things up. I love not having to get permission to write what I believe. Even if no one ever reads it, I can still write it.

Writing for me has become synonymous with power, the power to shape reality and to share that reality with others. It is very hard work. I often say that there has hardly ever been a project I have undertaken that at some point, usually near the beginning of sitting down to write, I do not regret having agreed to do it. But that feeling always evaporates as the writing takes hold and then there is what can only be described as joy. I am so glad I found writing, or perhaps that it found me. I had little idea when I began what it would come to mean.

I think my desire to write came first from my love of reading. I thought books were magic and always devoured print. Luckily, books were plentiful in my home, especially since my Aunt LaRue worked as a clerk-typist at the main branch of the Cleveland Public Library and as an employee could bring home unlimited quantities of books and magazines with no due dates.

By the time I reached junior high school I had begun to enjoy writing. My seventh-grade English teacher took the carefully written and designed autobiographies that my sister, Beverly, and I had done to a teachers' convention in the summer to show off our work. I wrote in my diary and eagerly took the journalism course that would allow me to work on our school newspaper in ninth grade. I also had started to study cello in elementary school and liked playing in the orchestra. When I got to high school, after participating in the orchestra my first year, I had to decide whether to concentrate upon music or the high school newspaper. The newspaper won hands down.

High school was not easy for me, a shy, "too smart" adolescent whose mother had died several years before. Two things saved it. One was my wonderful Advanced Placement history teacher, Albert J. Carroll, who among the many gifts he provided helped me to hone my research skills and analytical writing. The other was the newspaper. Working on the *John Adams Journal* was terrific. Our journalism teacher, Virginia Follin, would probably have pursued a career as a professional journalist if there had been more opportunities for women of her generation other than being assigned to the women's page. She loved what she did and held us up to quite professional standards. After all, pages from the *Journal* appeared as teaching models in our journalism textbook. The newspaper regularly won Medalist, the highest award in the Columbia Scholastic Press Association's annual national competition. We had a tradition to uphold.

I loved that we got to stay late after school on most nights, writing, figuring out headlines, doing layouts, as well as laughing, eating, and talking with other members of the staff, several of whom became close friends of mine. By this time I knew that writing was centrally important to me. If my high school had had a literary magazine, I undoubtedly would have joined it, but it did not, so my first immersion in writing outside of class work was on the newspaper.

When I entered Mount Holyoke College in 1965, I had no idea what I would eventually do to earn a living, but I did know how much I wanted to write. I was constantly trying to make up my mind between declaring either an English or a sociology major. (Sociology was the only discipline in which one could study Black Americans, albeit almost always as examples of social pathology.) In the second semester of my sophomore year I took three writing courses at one time: "Exposition," "Description," and "Short Story." I wanted to write both fiction and essays, like my hero, James Baldwin. Unfortunately the white male poet and rising literary star who taught short story that year gave me very little encouragement. In fact I was humiliated by his response to my work.

After that course I dejectedly decided that since I did not have what it took to be a writer I would settle for second best and prepare myself to teach literature. This discouragement about my work of course occurred in the context of my being one of a tiny number of Black students at a highly élite white institution. I often wonder what might have happened with my fiction if I had gotten support at that critical juncture as opposed to dismissal.

During my senior year I designed an interdepartmental major in sociology and English and began an intensive independent study of Black writers, who were of course not taught in any of the department's offerings. My English advisor, Richard Johnson, and my sociology advisor, Marjorie Childers, offered wonderful support and greatly helped build my confidence in my ability to do challenging academic work. My grounding in sociology, especially in social theory, which began during my junior year at the New School for Social Research, had a major impact upon my later ability to write political analysis of issues that had been previously unexplored. In graduate school I continued to read Black literature on my own and never stopped thinking about writing. I assumed that mine would be a traditional academic career and that my writing would be done primarily for scholarly journals.

The feminist movement altered my expectations about everything. As I got more involved in the movement in the early 1970s I found new feminist and women's studies journals to which I could send my work. Gradually, I also found other women writers who provided mentoring and networks of support. Before the women's movement, I had often considered my situation as a writer impossible. I believed a writer should tell the truth and I knew that I was hiding something. During the late 1960s and early 1970s I was haunted by the question of my sexuality. I spent so much energy hiding my lesbian feelings even from myself. I wondered if I were really to commit myself to writing, what in the world would I write about, since there was this central fact of my existence that I was not able to reveal. Coming out in the mid-1970s was a crucial factor in finding my voice. Since so much of my work has focused upon Black lesbian as well as all Black women's experience, it is unnerving to imagine what kind of stunted career I would have had if I had not come out.

Although I was out by the time I met Audre Lorde in 1976, knowing her was signally important to my survival and growth as a writer. My involvement in Black feminist organizing, especially the Combahee River Collective, my work to build Black women's studies, and my academic training and personal immersion in literature were all elements that made it possible for me to write.

In 1974 I had an experience which significantly shaped the direction my career would take. I had become good friends with a woman I met in a consciousness raising group in Boston whose father, I learned, was editor-in-chief of the *National Observer*. The *Observer* was a highly regarded national weekly newspaper, owned by Dow Jones, which also owned *The Wall Street Journal*. There was an opening on the newspaper for book review editor, which I learned about from my friend, who had already told her father about me. After a series of interviews, I was hired. I relocated to Washington with serious misgivings, but also with excitement about having a full-time writing job. I was the only Black writer on staff and my senior editor made it clear that he did not think I should have gotten the job. My friend's father had great faith in me, however. Thus began six of the most difficult months of my life.

I stayed at the newspaper from May through November, but when I left I had learned a valuable lesson. I decided that never again would I put myself in the position of having to make my writing conform to someone else's standards or beliefs. Without fully knowing it at the time, I was committing myself to publishing most of my writing in alternative, independent publications, which usually only paid contributors in copies, but whose politics were much more compatible with my own.

In the mid-1970s, while a member of the Modern Language Association Commission on the Status of Women in the Profession, I conceptualized an anthology on Black women's studies that became *All the Women Are White, All the Blacks Are Men, But Some of Us Are Brave*, coedited with Akasha (Gloria) Hull and Patricia Bell-Scott (1982). The editors of *Conditions* invited me to guest edit a Black women's issue of the magazine, *Conditions: Five*, which I did with Lorraine Bethel (1979). In the early 1980s I decided that I wanted *Conditions: Five* to become permanently available as a book and edited *Home Girls: A Black Feminist Anthology* (1983). In 1984 I coauthored *Yours in Struggle: Three Feminist Perspectives on Anti-Semitism and Racism* with Elly Bulkin and Minnie Bruce Pratt. I loved working on each of these projects and looked forward to continuing to do other books, including a collection of my own short fiction to which I had finally returned.

In 1980, however, as a result of a series of conversations with Audre Lorde about the need for women of color to have our own autonomous publishing resource, I became with her one of the founders of Kitchen Table: Women of Color Press. By 1984 most of the women who had initiated the Press had moved on. I still believed strongly that it was critical for women of color to have our own writing outlets. Most women of color and lesbian of color periodicals that began during this period published for a few months or years and then disappeared. We had pledged from the outset that Kitchen Table would be an institution, which meant that it needed to last.

I had never wanted to run the Press, but to concentrate instead upon publicity and promotion. In 1984 an administrator was hired to coordinate Kitchen Table's daily operations and I moved from Brooklyn to Albany. I did Kitchen Table work at home and commuted to New York several times a month to work at the Press's office. In 1986, however, I found myself moving the by-then-bankrupt business to Albany and starting again from scratch. I genuinely believed in the Press's mission and did everything humanly possible to keep it alive. The level of rigorous, unpaid labor it required had a definite impact upon my writing. In early 1995, after fifteen years, I was able to relinquish my responsibilities as publisher and return to my own work.

Even during what I now refer to as "the Kitchen Table years," I never stopped writing and publishing my work. Much of the writing collected here was written in early morning hours, on weekends, or at the ends of twelve-hour days following my tasks as publisher. I could not earn a living from my work for Kitchen Table, nor from my writing, but scraped by on whatever I earned from speaking engagements and occasional part-time teaching jobs. I think it is important to know the material conditions under which my writing has been done, difficult conditions which many artists, especially ones who are poor, working class, and people of color, share.

I have dreamed of completing a collection of my own writing for many years. My work as a publisher was the primary obstacle. It has been frustrating to know that even those who are quite familiar with my work have not read all of it and that new generations of readers have had even less access to it. In the autumn of 1993 I was invited to spend several weeks at Windcall, a beautiful retreat for "burnt out" activists outside of Bozeman, Montana. There were no expectations whatsoever about how residents spent their time, but I was eager to begin the work of conceptualizing this book. In 1995, after leaving the Press, I was able to return to it.

I have selected these "Writings on Race, Gender, and Freedom" from dozens of essays, articles, and reviews. I picked the writing I felt was the strongest and most representative of my career. The first section, "Toward a Black Feminist Criticism," includes writing about literature and an essay about my more recent involvement in history. The second section, "Between a Rock and a Hard Place," includes articles that explore those issues that divide communities from each other, especially racism, homophobia, and anti-Semitism. The third section, "Working for Liberation and Having a Damn Good Time," includes writing about solutions to oppression and injustices, that is, organizing for economic, political, and social change. The fourth section, "A Rose," was written to conclude the collection and explores issues I often address in my work from a more personal perspective.

It feels very fitting to complete this book near the end of my fiftieth year. It is the best possible way I can imagine to celebrate my first half century. I often tell my friends that I would love to have another fifty years (goddesses willing) because there are so many other books I want to write.

A Note on Citations

The original footnotes and bibliographic references for these articles have been retained, although some of the publication information has changed. The Selected Bibliography provides publication information for books frequently cited in the text that was current as of the 1998 printing.

I

Toward a Black
Feminist Criticism

In early 1977 the editors of the new lesbian feminist literary magazine, *Conditions*, invited me to write an essay about Black women writers. Although they offered several suggestions for what I might cover, I felt that it was absolutely necessary to provide a general analytical framework for approaching this just beginning field. Black women writers, especially Black lesbian writers, were virtually invisible in the context of women's literary studies and were also included in only token numbers, if at all, in the context of Black studies. The *Conditions* editors agreed to my plans and "Toward a Black Feminist Criticism," which appeared in *Conditions: Two*, began an extremely fruitful relationship with the magazine which continued until it ceased publication in 1989.

Of all the things I have written, "Toward a Black Feminist Criticism" probably has been the most immediately catalytic. It started people thinking differently. In fact, when I was completing it in July 1977, a colleague who was also beginning to work on Black women writers was visiting me in Boston. She would look over my shoulder as I sat at the typewriter and offer valuable criticism and moral support. At one point she asked me if I really believed that there was a Black women's literary tradition, as I asserted in the essay, and I told her, "Yes," I definitely did.

"Toward a Black Feminist Criticism" has probably been more widely reprinted than any of my other work. In 1985 Elaine Showalter, one of the feminist scholars I criticized, had the integrity and grace to include it in her collection *The New Feminist Criticism: Essays on Women, Literature, and Theory*.

The most controversial aspect of the essay was my reading of Toni Morrison's novel *Sula*. Some thought my discussion of a lesbian subtext was on the mark and others,
including Morrison, thought that I was seeing something
that was not there. My perspective about *Sula* was influenced by the bold new ideas of 1970s lesbian feminism.
Lesbian feminist activists and theorists pointed out that the
dominant heterosexist regime so often obscured actual
erotic connections between women that it was important
to intuit the possibility of lesbian existence in order to claim
our history and our lives. "Toward a Black Feminist Criticism" reflects the era in which it was created and is widely
read and taught to this day.

Toward a Black Feminist Criticism

For all my sisters, especially Beverly and Demita

I do not know where to begin. Long before I tried to write this I realized that I was attempting something unprecedented, something dangerous, merely by writing about Black women writers from a feminist perspective and about Black lesbian writers from any perspective at all. These things have not been done. Not by white male critics, expectedly. Not by Black male critics. Not by white women critics who think of themselves as feminists. And most crucially not by Black women critics, who, although they pay the most attention to Black women writers as a group, seldom use a consistently feminist analysis or write about Black lesbian literature. All segments of the literary world—whether establishment, progressive, Black, female, or lesbian—do not know, or at least act as if they do not know, that Black women writers and Black lesbian writers exist.

For whites, this specialized lack of knowledge is inextricably connected to their not knowing in any concrete or politically transforming way that Black women of any description dwell in this place. Black women's existence, experience, and culture and the brutally complex systems of oppression which shape these are in the "real world" of white and/or male consciousness beneath consideration, invisible, unknown.

This invisibility, which goes beyond anything that either Black men or white women experience and tell about in their writing, is one reason it is so difficult for me to know where to start. It seems overwhelming to break such a massive silence. Even more numbing, however, is the realization that so many of the women who will read this have not yet noticed us missing either from their reading matter, their politics, or their lives. It is galling that ostensible feminists and acknowledged lesbians have been so oblivious to the implications of any womanhood that is not white womanhood and that they have yet to struggle with the deep racism in themselves that is at the source of their ignorance.

I think of the thousands and thousands of books, magazines, and articles which have been devoted, by this time, to the subject of women's writing and I am filled with rage at the fraction of those pages that mention Black and other Third World women. I finally do not know how to begin because in 1977 I want to be writing this for a Black feminist publication, for Black women who know and love these writers as I do and who, if they do not yet know their names, have at least profoundly felt the pain of their absence.

The conditions that coalesce into the impossibilities of this essay have as much to do with politics as with the practice of literature. Any discussion of Afro-American writers can rightfully begin with the fact that for most of the time we have been in this country we have been categorically denied not only literacy but the most minimal possibility of a decent human life. In her landmark essay, "In Search of Our Mothers' Gardens," Alice Walker discloses how the political, economic, and social restrictions of slavery and racism have historically stunted the creative lives of Black women.[1]

At the present time I feel that the politics of feminism have a direct relationship to the state of Black women's literature. A viable, autonomous Black feminist movement in this country would open up the space needed for the exploration of Black women's lives and the creation of consciously Black woman-identified art. At the same time a redefinition of the goals and strategies of the white feminist movement would lead to much-needed change in the focus and content of what is now generally accepted as women's culture.

I want to make in this essay some connections between the politics of Black women's lives, what we write about, and our situation as artists. In order to do this I will look at how Black women have been viewed critically by outsiders, demonstrate the necessity for Black feminist criticism, and try to understand what the existence or non-existence of Black lesbian writing reveals about the state of Black women's culture and the intensity of *all* Black women's oppression.

The role that criticism plays in making a body of literature rec-ognizable and real hardly needs to be explained here. The necessity for nonhostile and perceptive analysis of works written by persons outside the "mainstream" of white/male cultural rule has been proven by the Black cultural resurgence of the 1960s and 1970s and by the even more recent growth of feminist literary scholar-ship. For books to be real and remembered they have to be talked about. For books to be understood they must be examined in such a way that the basic intentions of the writers are at least considered. Because of racism Black literature has usually been viewed as a discrete subcategory of American literature, and there have been Black critics of Black literature who did much to keep it alive long before it caught the attention of whites. Before the advent of spe-cifically feminist criticism in this decade, books by white women, on the other hand, were not clearly perceived as the cultural mani-festation of an oppressed people. It took the surfacing of the sec-ond wave of the North American feminist movement to expose the fact that these works contain a stunningly accurate record of the impact of patriarchal values and practice upon the lives of women, and more significantly, that literature by women provides essential insights into female experience.

In speaking about the current situation of Black women writers, it is important to remember that the existence of a feminist move-ment was an essential precondition to the growth of feminist litera-ture, criticism, and women's studies, which focused at the beginning almost entirely upon investigations of literature. The fact that a par-allel Black feminist movement has been much slower in evolving cannot help but have impact upon the situation of Black women writers and artists and explains in part why during this very same period we have been so ignored.

There is no political movement to give power or support to those who want to examine Black women's experience through studying our history, literature, and culture. There is no political presence that demands a minimal level of consciousness and respect from those who write or talk about our lives. Finally, there is not a developed body of Black feminist political theory whose assumptions could be used in the study of Black women's art. When Black women's books are dealt with at all, it is usually in the context of Black literature, which largely ignores the implications of sexual politics. When white women look at Black women's works they are of course ill equipped to deal with the subtleties of racial politics. A Black feminist approach to literature that embodies the realization that the politics of sex as well as the politics of race and class are crucially interlocking factors in the works of Black women writers is an absolute necessity. Until a Black feminist criticism exists we will not even know what these writers mean. The citations from a variety of critics which follow prove that without a Black feminist critical perspective not only are books by Black women misunderstood, they are destroyed in the process.

Jerry H. Bryant, *The Nation*'s white male reviewer of Alice Walker's *In Love & Trouble: Stories of Black Women*, wrote in 1973:

> The subtitle of the collection, "Stories of Black Women," is probably an attempt by the publisher to exploit not only black subjects but feminine ones. There is nothing feminist about these stories, however.[2]

Blackness and feminism are to his mind mutually exclusive and peripheral to the act of writing fiction. Bryant of course does not consider that Walker might have titled the work herself, nor did he apparently read the book, which unequivocally reveals the author's feminist consciousness.

In *The Negro Novel in America*, a book that Black critics recognize as one of the worst examples of white racist pseudoscholarship, Robert Bone cavalierly dismisses Ann Petry's classic, *The Street*. He perceives it to be "a superficial social analysis" of how slums victimize their Black inhabitants. He further objects:

> It is an attempt to interpret slum life in terms of *Negro* experience, when a larger frame of reference is required. As Alain Locke has observed, "*Knock on Any Door* is superior to *The Street* because it designates class and environment, rather than mere race and environment, as its antagonist."[3]

Neither Robert Bone nor Alain Locke, the Black male critic he cites, can recognize that *The Street* is one of the best delineations in literature of how sex, race, *and* class interact to oppress Black women.

In her review of Toni Morrison's *Sula* for the *New York Times Book Review* in 1973, putative feminist Sara Blackburn makes similarly racist comments:

> Toni Morrison is far too talented to remain only a marvelous recorder of the black side of provincial American life. If she is to maintain the large and serious audience she deserves, she is going to have to address a riskier contemporary reality than this beautiful but nevertheless distanced novel. *And if she does this, it seems to me that she might easily transcend that early and unintentionally limiting classification "black woman writer" and take her place among the most serious, important and talented American novelists now working.*[4] (Italics mine)

Recognizing Morrison's exquisite gift, Blackburn unashamedly asserts that Morrison is "too talented" to deal with mere Black folk, particularly those double nonentities, Black women. In order to be accepted as "serious," "important," "talented," and "American," she must obviously focus her efforts upon chronicling the doings of white men.

The mishandling of Black women writers by whites is paralleled more often by their not being handled at all, particularly in feminist criticism. Although Elaine Showalter in her review essay on

literary criticism for *Signs* states that "the best work being produced today [in feminist criticism] is exacting and cosmopolitan,"
her essay is neither. If it were, she would not have failed to mention
a single Black or Third World woman writer, whether "major" or
"minor," to cite her questionable categories. That she also does not
even hint that lesbian writers of any color exist renders her pur-
ported overview virtually meaningless. Showalter obviously thinks
that the identities of being Black and female are mutually exclusive, as this statement illustrates:

> Furthermore, there are other literary subcultures (black American
> novelists, for example) whose history offers a precedent for femi-
> nist scholarship to use.[5]

The idea of critics like Showalter *using* Black literature is chilling,
a case of barely disguised cultural imperialism. The final insult is
that she footnotes the preceding remark by pointing readers to
works on Black literature by white males Robert Bone and Roger
Rosenblatt!

Two recent works by white women, Ellen Moers's *Literary
Women: The Great Writers* and Patricia Meyer Spacks's *The Female
Imagination*, evidence the same racist flaw.[6] Moers includes the
names of four Black and one Puertorriqueña writer in her seventy
pages of bibliographical notes and does not deal at all with Third
World women in the body of her book. Spacks refers to a comparison between Negroes (*sic*) and women in Mary Ellmann's *Thinking
about Women* under the index entry "blacks, women and." "*Black
Boy* (Wright)" is the preceding entry. Nothing follows. Again there
is absolutely no recognition that Black and female identity ever
coexist, specifically in a group of Black women writers. Perhaps one
can assume that these women do not know who Black women writers are, that like most Americans they have little opportunity to
learn about them. Perhaps. Their ignorance seems suspiciously selec-
tive, however, particularly in the light of the dozens of truly obscure
white women writers they are able to unearth. Spacks was herself

employed at Wellesley College at the same time that Alice Walker was there teaching one of the first courses on Black women writers in the country.

I am not trying to encourage racist criticism of Black women writers like that of Sara Blackburn, to cite only one example. As a beginning I would at least like to see in print white women's acknowledgment of the contradictions of who and what are being left out of their research and writing.[7]

Black male critics can also *act* as if they do not know that Black women writers exist and are, of course, hampered by an inability to comprehend Black women's experience in sexual as well as racial terms. Unfortunately there are also those who are as virulently sexist in their treatment of Black women writers as their white male counterparts. Darwin Turner's discussion of Zora Neale Hurston in his *In a Minor Chord: Three Afro-American Writers and Their Search for Identity* is a frightening example of the near assassination of a great Black woman writer.[8] His descriptions of her and her work as "artful," "coy," "irrational," "superficial," and "shallow" bear no relationship to the actual quality of her achievements. Turner is completely insensitive to the sexual political dynamics of Hurston's life and writing.

In a recent interview the notoriously misogynist writer Ishmael Reed comments in this way upon the low sales of his newest novel:

> But the book only sold 8000 copies. I don't mind giving out the figure: 8000. Maybe if I was one of those young *female* Afro-American writers that are so hot now, I'd sell more. You know, fill my books with ghetto women who can *do no wrong.* . . . But come on, I think I could have sold 8000 copies by myself.[9]

The politics of the situation of Black women are glaringly illuminated by this statement. Neither Reed nor his white male interviewer has the slightest compunction about attacking Black women in print. They need not fear widespread public denunciation since Reed's statement is in perfect agreement with the values of a society that

hates Black people, women, and Black women. Finally the two of
them feel free to base their actions on the premise that Black women
are powerless to alter either their political or their cultural oppression.

In her introduction to "A Bibliography of Works Written by
American Black Women" Ora Williams quotes some of the reactions
of her colleagues toward her efforts to do research on Black women:

> Others have reacted negatively with such statements as, "I really
> don't think you are going to find very much written," "Have 'they'
> written anything that is any good?" and, "I wouldn't go overboard
> with this woman's lib thing." When discussions touched on the pos-
> sibility of teaching a course in which emphasis would be on the lit-
> erature by Black women, one response was, "Ha, ha. That will
> certainly be the most nothing course ever offered!"[10]

A remark by Alice Walker capsulizes what all the preceding
examples indicate about the position of Black women writers and
the reasons for the damaging criticism about them. She responds
to her interviewer's question, "Why do you think that the black
woman writer has been so ignored in America? Does she have even
more difficulty than the black male writer, who perhaps has just
begun to gain recognition?" Walker replies:

> There are two reasons why the black woman writer is not taken as
> seriously as the black male writer. One is that she's a woman. Crit-
> ics seem unusually ill-equipped to intelligently discuss and analyze
> the works of black women. Generally, they do not even make the
> attempt; they prefer, rather, to talk about the lives of black women
> writers, not about what they write. And, since black women writers
> are not—it would seem—very likable—until recently they were
> the least willing worshippers of male supremacy—comments
> about them tend to be cruel.[11]

A convincing case for Black feminist criticism can obviously be
built solely upon the basis of the negativity of what already exists.
It is far more gratifying, however, to demonstrate its necessity by

showing how it can serve to reveal for the first time the profound subtleties of this particular body of literature.

Before suggesting how a Black feminist approach might be used to examine a specific work, I will outline some of the principles that I think a Black feminist critic could use. Beginning with a primary commitment to exploring how both sexual and racial politics and Black and female identity are inextricable elements in Black women's writings, she would also work from the assumption that Black women writers constitute an identifiable literary tradition. The breadth of her familiarity with these writers would have shown her that not only is theirs a verifiable historical tradition that parallels in time the tradition of Black men and white women writing in this country, but that thematically, stylistically, aesthetically, and conceptually Black women writers manifest common approaches to the act of creating literature as a direct result of the specific political, social, and economic experience they have been obliged to share. The way, for example, that Zora Neale Hurston, Margaret Walker, Toni Morrison, and Alice Walker incorporate the traditional Black female activities of root-working, herbal medicine, conjure, and midwifery into the fabric of their stories is not mere coincidence, nor is their use of specifically Black female language to express their own and their characters' thoughts accidental. The use of Black women's language and cultural experience in books *by* Black women *about* Black women results in a miraculously rich coalescing of form and content and also takes their writing far beyond the confines of white/male literary structures. The Black feminist critic would find innumerable commonalities in works by Black women.

Another principle which grows out of the concept of a tradition and which would also help to strengthen this tradition would be for the critic to look first for precedents and insights in interpretation within the works of other Black women. In other words she would think and write out of her own identity and not try to graft the ideas or methodology of white/male literary thought upon the precious materials of Black women's art. Black feminist criticism would by definition be highly innovative, embodying the daring spirit of the works themselves. The Black feminist critic would be constantly aware of the political implications of her work and would assert the connections between it and the political situation of all Black women. Logically developed, Black feminist criticism would owe its existence to a Black feminist movement while at the same time contributing ideas that women in the movement could use.

Black feminist criticism applied to a particular work can overturn previous assumptions about it and expose for the first time its actual dimensions. At the "Lesbians and Literature" discussion at the 1976 Modern Language Association convention Bertha Harris suggested that if in a woman writer's work a sentence refuses to do what it is supposed to do, if there are strong images of women and if there is a refusal to be linear, the result is innately lesbian literature. As usual, I wanted to see if these ideas might be applied to the Black women writers that I know and quickly realized that many of their works were, in Harris's sense, lesbian. Not because women are "lovers," but because they are the central figures, are positively portrayed and have pivotal relationships with one another. The form and language of these works are also nothing like what white patriarchal culture requires or expects.

I was particularly struck by the way in which Toni Morrison's novels *The Bluest Eye* and *Sula* could be explored from this new perspective.[12] In both works the relationships between girls and women are essential, yet at the same time physical sexuality is overtly expressed only between men and women. Despite the apparent heterosexuality of the female characters, I discovered in rereading *Sula* that it works as a lesbian novel not only because of the passionate friendship between Sula and Nel but because of Morrison's consistently critical stance toward the heterosexual institutions of male-female relationships, marriage, and the family. Consciously or not, Morrison's work poses both lesbian and feminist questions about Black women's autonomy and their impact upon each other's lives.

Sula and Nel find each other in 1922 when each of them is twelve, on the brink of puberty and the discovery of boys. Even as awakening sexuality "clotted their dreams," each girl desires "a someone" obviously female with whom to share her feelings. Morrison writes:

> For it was in dreams that the two girls had met. Long before Edna Finch's Mellow House opened, even before they marched through the chocolate halls of Garfield Primary School . . . they had already made each other's acquaintance in the delirium of their noon dreams. They were solitary little girls whose loneliness was so profound it intoxicated them and sent them stumbling into Technicolored visions that always included a presence, a someone who, quite like the dreamer, shared the delight of the dream. When Nel, an only child, sat on the steps of her back porch surrounded by the high silence of her mother's incredibly orderly house, feeling the neatness pointing at her back, she studied the poplars and fell easily into a picture of herself lying on a flower bed, tangled in her own hair, waiting for some fiery prince. He approached but never quite arrived. But always, watching the dream along with her, were some smiling sympathetic eyes. Someone as interested as she herself in the flow of her imagined hair, the thickness of the mattress of flowers, the voile sleeves that closed below her elbows in gold-threaded cuffs.
>
> Similarly, Sula, also an only child, but wedged into a household of throbbing disorder constantly awry with things, people, voices and the slamming of doors, spent hours in the attic behind a roll of linoleum galloping through her own mind on a gray-and-white horse tasting sugar and smelling roses in full view of someone who shared both the taste and the speed.
>
> So when they met, first in those chocolate halls and next through the ropes of the swing, they felt the ease and comfort of old friends. Because each had discovered years before that they were neither white nor male, and that all freedom and triumph was forbidden to them, they had set about creating something else to be. Their meeting was fortunate, for it let them use each other to grow on. Daughters of distant mothers and incomprehensible fathers (Sula's because he was dead; Nel's because he wasn't),

they found in each other's eyes the intimacy they were looking for.
(Pp. 51–52)

As this beautiful passage shows, their relationship, from the very beginning, is suffused with an erotic romanticism. The dreams in which they are initially drawn to each other are actually complementary aspects of the same sensuous fairy tale. Nel imagines a "fiery prince" who never quite arrives while Sula gallops like a prince "on a gray-and-white horse."[13] The "real world" of patriarchy requires, however, that they channel this energy away from each other to the opposite sex. Lorraine Bethel explains this dynamic in her essay "Conversations with Ourselves: Black Female Relationships in Toni Cade Bambara's *Gorilla, My Love* and Toni Morrison's *Sula*":

> I am not suggesting that Sula and Nel are being consciously sexual, or that their relationship has an overt lesbian nature. I am suggesting, however, that there is a certain sensuality in their interactions that is reinforced by the mirror-like nature of their relationship. Sexual exploration and coming of age is a natural part of adolescence. Sula and Nel discover men together, and though their flirtations with males are an important part of their sexual exploration, the sensuality that they experience in each other's company is equally important.[14]

Sula and Nel must also struggle with the constrictions of racism upon their lives. The knowledge that "they were neither white nor male" is the inherent explanation of their need for each other. Morrison depicts in literature the necessary bonding that has always taken place between Black women for the sake of barest survival. Together the two girls can find the courage to create themselves.

Their relationship is severed only when Nel marries Jude, an unexceptional young man who thinks of her as "the hem—the tuck and fold that hid his raveling edges" (p. 83). Sula's inventive wildness cannot overcome social pressure or the influence of Nel's parents who "had succeeded in rubbing down to a dull glow any sparkle or splutter she had" (p. 83). Nel falls prey to convention while Sula escapes it. Yet at the wedding which ends the first phase of their relationship, Nel's final action is to look past her husband toward Sula,

> a slim figure in blue, gliding, with just a hint of a strut, down the path towards the road. . . . Even from the rear Nel could tell that it was Sula and that she was smiling; that something deep down in that litheness was amused. (P. 85)

When Sula returns ten years later, her rebelliousness full blown, a major source of the town's suspicions stems from the fact that although she is almost thirty, she is still unmarried. Sula's grandmother, Eva, does not hesitate to bring up the matter as soon as she arrives. She asks:

> "When you gone to get married? You need to have some babies. It'll settle you. . . . Ain't no woman got no business floatin' around without no man." (P. 92)

Sula replies: "I don't want to make somebody else. I want to make myself" (p. 92). Self-definition is a dangerous activity for any woman to engage in, especially a Black one, and it expectedly earns Sula pariah status in Medallion.

Morrison clearly points out that it is the fact that Sula has not been tamed or broken by the exigencies of heterosexual family life which most galls the others:

> Among the weighty evidence piling up was the fact that Sula did not look her age. She was near thirty and, unlike them, had lost no teeth, suffered no bruises, developed no ring of fat at the waist or pocket at the back of her neck. (P. 115)

In other words she is not a domestic serf, a woman run down by obligatory childbearing or a victim of battering. Sula also sleeps with the husbands of the town once and then discards them,

needing them even less than her own mother did for sexual grati-
fication and affection. The town reacts to her disavowal of patriarchal values by becoming fanatically serious about their own family
obligations, as if in this way they might counteract Sula's radical
criticism of their lives.

Sula's presence in her community functions much like the presence of lesbians everywhere to expose the contradictions of supposedly "normal" life. The opening paragraph of the essay "The
Woman-Identified Woman" has amazing relevance as an explanation of Sula's position and character in the novel. It asks:

> What is a lesbian? A lesbian is the rage of all women condensed to
> the point of explosion. She is the woman who, often beginning at
> an extremely early age, acts in accordance with her inner compul-
> sion to be a more complete and freer human being than her
> society—perhaps then, but certainly later—cares to allow her.
> These needs and actions, over a period of years, bring her into
> painful conflict with people, situations, the accepted ways of
> thinking, feeling and behaving, until she is in a state of continual
> war with everything around her, and usually with herself. She may
> not be fully conscious of the political implications of what for her
> began as personal necessity, but on some level she has not been able
> to accept the limitations and oppression laid on her by the most
> basic role of her society—the female role.[15]

The limitations of the *Black* female role are even greater in a racist and sexist society, as is the amount of courage it takes to challenge them. It is no wonder that the townspeople see Sula's
independence as imminently dangerous.

Morrison is also careful to show the reader that despite their
years of separation and their opposing paths, Nel and Sula's relationship retains its primacy for each of them. Nel feels transformed
when Sula returns and thinks:

> It was like getting the use of an eye back, having a cataract
> removed. Her old friend had come home. Sula. Who made her

laugh, who made her see old things with new eyes, in whose presence she felt clever, gentle and a little raunchy. (P. 95)

Laughing together in the familiar "rib-scraping" way, Nel feels "new, soft and new" (p. 98). Morrison uses here the visual imagery which symbolizes the women's closeness throughout the novel.

Sula fractures this closeness, however, by sleeping with Nel's husband, an act of little import according to her system of values. Nel, of course, cannot understand. Sula thinks ruefully:

Nel was the one person who had wanted nothing from her, who had accepted all aspects of her. Now she wanted everything, and all because of *that*. Nel was the first person who had been real to her, whose name she knew, who had seen as she had the slant of life that made it possible to stretch it to its limits. Now Nel was one of *them*. (Pp. 119–120)

Sula also thinks at the realization of losing Nel about how unsatisfactory her relationships with men have been and admits:

She had been looking all along for a friend, and it took her a while to discover that a lover was not a comrade and could never be—for a woman. (P. 121)

The nearest that Sula comes to actually loving a man is in a brief affair with Ajax and what she values most about him is the intellectual companionship he provides, the brilliance he "allows" her to show.

Sula's feelings about sex with men are also consistent with a lesbian interpretation of the novel. Morrison writes:

She went to bed with men as frequently as she could. It was the only place where she could find what she was looking for: *misery and the ability to feel deep sorrow.* . . . During the lovemaking she found and needed to find the cutting edge. When she left off cooperating with her body and began to assert herself in the act, particles of strength gathered in her like steel shavings drawn to a spacious magnetic center, forming a tight cluster that nothing, it seemed, could break. *And there was utmost irony and outrage in lying under someone, in a position of surrender, feeling her own abiding strength and limitless power. . . .* When her partner disengaged himself, she looked up at him in wonder trying to recall his name . . . waiting impatiently for him to turn away . . . *leaving her to the postcoital privateness in which she met herself, welcomed herself, and joined herself in matchless harmony.* (Pp. 122–123; italics mine)

Sula uses men for sex which results, not in communion with them, but in her further delving into self.

Ultimately the deepest communion and communication in the novel occurs between two women who love each other. After their last painful meeting, which does not bring reconciliation, Sula thinks as Nel leaves her:

"So she will walk on down that road, her back so straight in that old green coat . . . thinking how much I have cost her and never remember the days when we were two throats and one eye and we had no price." (P. 147)

It is difficult to imagine a more evocative metaphor for what women can be to each other, the "pricelessness" they achieve in refusing to sell themselves for male approval, the total worth that they can only find in each other's eyes.

Decades later the novel concludes with Nel's final comprehension of the source of the grief that has plagued her from the time her husband walked out:

"All that time, all that time, I thought I was missing Jude." And the loss pressed down on her chest and came up into her throat. "We was girls together," she said as though explaining something. "O Lord, Sula," she cried, "girl, girl, girlgirlgirl."

It was a fine cry—loud and long—but it had no bottom and it had no top, just circles and circles of sorrow. (P. 174)

Again Morrison exquisitely conveys what women, Black women, mean to each other. This final passage verifies the depth of Sula and Nel's relationship and its centrality to an accurate interpretation of the work.

Sula is an exceedingly lesbian novel in the emotions expressed, in the definition of female character, and in the way that the politics of heterosexuality are portrayed. The very meaning of lesbianism is being expanded in literature, just as it is being redefined through politics. The confusion that many readers have felt about *Sula* may well have a lesbian explanation. If one sees Sula's inexplicable "evil" and nonconformity as the evil of not being male-identified, many elements in the novel become clear. The work might be clearer still if Morrison had approached her subject with the consciousness that a lesbian relationship was at least a possibility for her characters. Obviously Morrison did not *intend* the reader to perceive Sula and Nel's relationship as inherently lesbian. However, this lack of intention only shows the way in which heterosexist assumptions can veil what may logically be expected to occur in a work. What I have tried to do here is not to prove that Morrison wrote something that she did not, but to point out how a Black feminist critical perspective at least allows consideration of this level of the novel's meaning.

In her interview in *Conditions: One* Adrienne Rich talks about unconsummated relationships and the need to reevaluate the meaning of intense yet supposedly nonerotic connections between women. She asserts:

> We need a lot more documentation about what actually happened: I think we can also imagine it, because we know it happened—we know it out of our own lives.[16]

Black women are still in the position of having to "imagine," discover, and verify Black lesbian literature because so little has been written from an avowedly lesbian perspective. The near nonexistence of Black lesbian literature which other Black lesbians and I so deeply feel has everything to do with the politics of our lives, the total suppression of identity that all Black women, lesbian or not, must face. This literary silence is again intensified by the unavailability of an autonomous Black feminist movement through which we could fight our oppression and also begin to name ourselves.

In a speech, "The Autonomy of Black Lesbian Women," Wilmette Brown comments upon the connection between our political reality and the literature we must invent:

> Because the isolation of Black lesbian women, given that we are superfreaks, given that our lesbianism defies both the sexual identity that capital gives us and the racial identity that capital gives us, the isolation of Black lesbian women from heterosexual Black women is very profound. Very profound. I have searched throughout Black history, Black literature, whatever, looking for some women that I could see were somehow lesbian. Now I know that in a certain sense they were all lesbian. But that was a very painful search.[17]

Heterosexual privilege is usually the only privilege that Black women have. None of us have racial or sexual privilege, almost none of us have class privilege; maintaining "straightness" is our last resort. Being out, particularly out in print, is the final renunciation of any claim to the crumbs of "tolerance" that nonthreatening "ladylike" Black women are sometimes fed. I am convinced that it is our lack of privilege and power in every other sphere that allows so few Black women to make the leap that many white women, particularly writers, have been able to make in this decade, not merely because they are white or have economic leverage, but because they have had the strength and support of a movement behind them.

As Black lesbians we must be out not only in white society but in the Black community as well, which is at least as homophobic. That the sanctions against Black lesbians are extremely high is well illustrated in this comment by Black male writer Ishmael Reed. Speaking about the inroads that whites make into Black culture, he asserts:

> In Manhattan you find people actively trying to impede intellectual debate among Afro-Americans. The powerful "liberal/radical/existentialist" influences of the Manhattan literary and drama establishment speak through tokens, like for example that ancient notion of the *one* black ideologue (who's usually a Communist), the *one* black poetess (who's usually a feminist lesbian).[18]

To Reed, "feminist" and "lesbian" are the most pejorative terms he can hurl at a Black woman and totally invalidate anything she might say, regardless of her actual politics or sexual identity. Such accusations are quite effective for keeping in line Black women writers who are writing with integrity and strength from any conceivable perspective, but especially ones who are actually feminist and lesbian. Unfortunately Reed's reactionary attitude is all too typical. A community which has not confronted sexism, because a widespread Black feminist movement has not required it to, has likewise not been challenged to examine its heterosexism. Even at this moment I am not convinced that one can write explicitly as a Black lesbian and live to tell about it.

Yet there are a handful of Black women who have risked everything for truth. Audre Lorde, Pat Parker, and Ann Allen Shockley have at least broken ground in the vast wilderness of works that do not exist.[19] Black feminist criticism will again have an essential role not only in creating a climate in which Black lesbian writers can survive, but in undertaking the total reassessment of Black literature and literary history needed to reveal the Black woman-identified women that Wilmette Brown and so many of us are looking for.

Although I have concentrated here upon what does not exist and what needs to be done, a few Black feminist critics have already begun this work. Gloria T. Hull at the University of Delaware has discovered in her research on Black women poets of the Harlem Renaissance that many of the women who are considered "minor" writers of the period were in constant contact with each other and provided both intellectual stimulation and psychological support for each other's work. At least one of these writers, Angelina Weld Grimké, wrote many unpublished love poems to women. Lorraine Bethel, a recent graduate of Yale College, has done substantial work on Black women writers, particularly in her senior essay, "This Infinity of Conscious Pain: Blues Lyricism and Hurston's Black Female Folk Aesthetic and Cultural Sensibility in *Their Eyes Were Watching God*," in which she brilliantly defines and uses the principles of Black feminist criticism. Elaine Scott at the State University of New York at Old Westbury is also involved in highly creative and politically resonant research on Hurston and other writers.

The fact that these critics are young and, except for Hull, unpublished merely indicates the impediments we face. Undoubtedly there are other women working and writing whom I do not even know, simply because there is no place to read them. As Michele Wallace states in her article "A Black Feminist's Search for Sisterhood":

> We exist as women who are Black who are feminists, each stranded for the moment, working independently because there is not yet an environment in this society remotely congenial to our struggle—[or our thoughts].[20]

I only hope that this essay is one way of breaking our silence and our isolation, of helping us to know each other.

Just as I did not know where to start I am not sure how to end. I feel that I have tried to say too much and at the same time have left too much unsaid. What I want this essay to do is lead everyone who reads it to examine *everything* that they have ever thought and believed about feminist culture and to ask themselves how their thoughts connect to the reality of Black women's writing and lives. I want to encourage in white women, as a first step, a sane accountability to all the women who write and live on this soil. I want most of all for Black women and Black lesbians somehow not to be so alone. This last will require the most expansive of revolutions as well as many new words to tell us how to make this revolution real. I finally want to express how much easier both my waking and my sleeping hours would be if there were one book in existence that would tell me something specific about my life. One book based in Black feminist and Black lesbian experience, fiction or nonfiction. Just one work to reflect the reality that I and the Black women whom I love are trying to create. When such a book exists then each of us will not only know better how to live, but how to dream.

1977

Notes

1. Alice Walker, "In Search of Our Mothers' Gardens," *Ms.*, May 1974, and *Southern Exposure* 4, no. 4, *Generations: Women in the South* (Winter 1977): 60–64.

2. Jerry H. Bryant, "The Outskirts of a New City," *The Nation*, November 12, 1973, 502.

3. Robert Bone, *The Negro Novel in America* (New Haven, Conn.: Yale University Press, 1958), 180. *Knock on Any Door* is a novel by Black writer Willard Motley.

4. Sara Blackburn, "You Still Can't Go Home Again," *New York Times Book Review*, December 30, 1973, 3.

5. Elaine Showalter, "Literary Criticism," Review Essay, *Signs* 1 (Winter 1975): 460, 445.

6. Ellen Moers, *Literary Women: The Great Writers* (Garden City, N.Y.: Anchor Books, 1977); Patricia Meyer Spacks, *The Female Imagination* (New York: Avon Books, 1976).

7. An article by Nancy Hoffman, "White Women, Black Women: Inventing an Adequate Pedagogy," *Women's Studies Newsletter* 5 (Spring 1977): 21–24, gives valuable insights into how white women can approach the writing of Black women.

8. Darwin T. Turner, *In a Minor Chord: Three Afro-American Writers and Their Search for Identity* (Carbondale and Edwardsville: Southern Illinois University Press, 1971).

9. John Domini, "Roots and Racism: An Interview with Ishmael Reed," *Boston Phoenix*, April 5, 1977, 20.

10. Ora Williams, "A Bibliography of Works Written by American Black Women," *College Language Association Journal* 15 (March 1972): 355.

There is an expanded, book-length version of this bibliography: *American Black Women in the Arts and Social Sciences: A Bibliographic Survey* (Metuchen, N.J.: Scarecrow Press, 1973; rev. and expanded ed., 1978).

11. John O'Brien, ed., *Interviews with Black Writers* (New York: Liveright, 1973), 201.

12. Toni Morrison, *The Bluest Eye* (1970; reprint ed., New York: Pocket Books, 1972, 1976) and *Sula* (New York: Alfred A. Knopf, 1974). All subsequent references to this work will be designated in the text.

13. My sister, Beverly Smith, pointed out this connection to me.

14. Lorraine Bethel, "Conversations with Ourselves: Black Female Relationships in Toni Cade Bambara's *Gorilla, My Love* and Toni Morrison's *Sula*," unpublished paper written at Yale University, 1976, 47 pp. Bethel has worked from a premise similar to mine in a much more developed treatment of the novel.

15. New York Radicalesbians, "The Woman-Identified Woman," in *Lesbians Speak Out* (Oakland, Calif.: Women's Press Collective, 1974), 87.

16. Elly Bulkin, "An Interview with Adrienne Rich: Part I," *Conditions: One*, no. 1 (April 1977): 62.

17. Wilmette Brown, "The Autonomy of Black Lesbian Women," manuscript of speech delivered July 24, 1976, in Toronto, Canada, 7.

18. Domini, "Roots and Racism," 18.

19. Audre Lorde, *New York Head Shop and Museum* (Detroit: Broadside Press, 1974); *Coal* (New York: W. W. Norton, 1976); *Between Our Selves* (Point Reyes, Calif.: Eidolon Editions, 1976); *The Black Unicorn* (New York: W. W. Norton, 1978).

Pat Parker, *Child of Myself* (Oakland, Calif.: Women's Press Collective, 1972 and 1974); *Pit Stop* (Oakland, Calif.: Women's Press Collective, 1973); *Womanslaughter* (Oakland, Calif.: Diana Press, 1978); *Movement in Black* (Oakland, Calif.: Diana Press, 1978).

Ann Allen Shockley, *Loving Her* (Indianapolis: Bobbs-Merrill, 1974).

There is at least one Black lesbian writers' collective, Jemima, in New York. They do public readings and have available a collection of their poems.

20. Michele Wallace, "A Black Feminist's Search for Sisterhood," *Village Voice*, July 28, 1975, 7.

This review of Alice Walker's *In Love & Trouble: Stories of Black Women*, published in the February 1974 issue of *Ms.*, was my first work to appear in a national publication. As a young writer, I was extremely excited to write for this groundbreaking, high-profile feminist magazine. I got the assignment because my sister, Beverly Smith, worked at *Ms.* at the time. Although she was not on the editorial staff, she was aware that the white writer who had been assigned the review had done an unacceptable job and that, close to their deadline, the editors were searching for someone who could write another review immediately. My sister told them about me and I got the assignment.

I had been familiar with Alice's work for several years and had just taught her poetry collection *Revolutionary Petunias* in my first Black women's literature course during the autumn of 1973. This was the first of many reviews I wrote for both Black and feminist journals; however, I did not get another assignment from *Ms.* until 1990 when the magazine became advertising-free and Robin Morgan became editor-in-chief.

That same fall, I was also fortunate to meet Ann Petry, one of the novelists I most admired. She wrote a kind note to me about the review and said that she especially liked that I concluded by stating the need for both "Black *and* feminist goals." Her encouragement meant a great deal to me both as a writer and politically during a period when most Black women dismissed feminism as irrelevant to their lives.

The Souls of Black Women

In 1966 Langston Hughes commented on one of Alice Walker's short stories, "Neither you nor I have ever read a story like 'To Hell with Dying' before. At least, I do not think you have." Hughes's early recognition of the uniqueness of Walker's artistic voice is equally applicable to the twelve other stories in Walker's new book, *In Love & Trouble: Stories of Black Women*. This collection would be an extraordinary literary work if its only virtue were the fact that the author sets out consciously to explore with honesty the textures and terrors of Black women's lives. Attempts to penetrate the myths surrounding Black women's experiences are so pitifully rare in Black, feminist, or American writing that each shred of truth about these experiences constitutes a breakthrough. The fact that Walker's perceptions, style, and artistry are also consistently high makes her work a treasure, particularly for those of us whom her writing describes.

Blood and violence seem the everyday backdrop to her characters' lives—a violence all the more chilling because it is so understated. It affects the ten-year-old girl who discovers a lynched man's headless body just as surely and ruinously as it destroys the middle-aged wife trapped in a loveless marriage or the ancient Black woman ousted from a white house of worship.

Even as a Black woman, I found the cumulative impact of these stories devastating. I questioned the quantity of pain in these sisters' lives and also wondered why none of the men and women were able to love each other. Women love their men, but they are neither loved nor understood in return. The affective relationships are between mother and child or between Black woman and Black woman. The only successful "romance" is in "To Hell with Dying"; it flowers between the young girl narrator and the lonely, grandfatherly Mr. Sweet.

I soon realized, however, that the reason these stories saddened me so much was because of their truthfulness. For every one of Walker's fictional women I knew or had heard of a real woman whose fate was all too similar. Harsh as these stories seem, they describe the kind of pain that can be described only by one who has shared it and has recognized its victims as real. Because Walker tells each story from the point of view of the character herself, we share the inner life of persons who have been dismissed as superdominant matriarchs or bitches by both white sociologists and together "revolutionary" brothers alike.

Many of these stories deal with marriage, and Walker leaves no doubt that it can be as problematic and trying an institution for Black females as for white ones. In "Roselily" she describes a marriage contracted out of material practicality, which the bride begins to question even while the wedding service is being spoken:

> She blinks her eyes. Remembers she is finally being married, like other girls. Like other girls, women? Something strains upward behind her eyes. She thinks of the something as a rat trapped, cornered, scurrying to and fro in her head, peering through the windows of her eyes. She wants to live for once. But doesn't know quite what that means. Wonders if she has ever done it. If she ever will.

Roselily's one comfort is the respectability that her Muslim husband will offer her, an unmarried mother of four. Whether there will ever be anything personal between the two of them is left unanswered.

"'Really, *Doesn't* Crime Pay?'" provides a more complete account of the isolation between two married people. Through the pages of the wife's journal, we learn that she writes obsessively, although no one has ever valued her work. Her dull husband, Ruel, reacts to her literary activity: "'No wife of mine is going to embarrass me with a lot of foolish, vulgar stuff.'" He suggests that she have a baby or go shopping, instead of writing and being so peculiar.

She does shop, spending hours every day purchasing expensive cosmetics and anointing herself with them, all of which Walker describes in minute detail. The woman's earlier entries reveal, however, that she did not always acquiesce, that she has had an affair with a young writer who left her and also stole her work. Her lover offered her not only the first sexual pleasure she had known, but also the chance for escape. When he disappeared, she unsuccessfully attempted to kill her husband, suffered a mental breakdown, and then returned with seeming willingness to the life of conspicuous consumption Ruel has willed for her. But there is a final turn to this tale: the woman's passive rebelliousness as she secretly undermines her husband's plan to have a child by taking the Pill. Walker writes:

> I wait, beautiful and perfect in every limb, cooking supper as if my life depended on it. Lying unresisting on his bed like a drowned body washed to shore. But he is not happy. For he knows now that I intend to do nothing but say yes until he is completely exhausted.

At the point of mutual exhaustion she plans to "leave him and this house . . . forever without once looking back."

In the most searing marriage story, "Her Sweet Jerome," a middle-aged hairdresser masochistically pampers her cute little school-teacher husband, although he beats her or, at best, ignores her. She continues to spoil him nevertheless until she finds out that she has a rival. After searching futilely for the other woman, she discovers that Jerome has been won over by the dozens of Black revolutionary books he has stacked under their bed. She sets the bed and books on fire and watches them burn "in hopeless jubilation." The story ends with her, trapped in a corner of the room, screaming as much from her inner emotional pain as from the outer fire.

Marriages between partners with differing educational backgrounds have been the source of real tensions in the Black community, although it has often been the Black woman who has had more formal training than her husband. Walker takes this social fact and shapes it into personal tragedy so that more of us will understand. It is not strange that so many of her women are deranged, when one considers their actual options.

Another complex set of interrelationships which Walker explores is that between the races. The stories "The Welcome Table," "The Revenge of Hannah Kemhuff," "Strong Horse Tea," and "The Flowers" all reveal the cruel toll that racial hostility exerts upon Black women particularly and upon Black people generally.

Undoubtedly the collection's most nightmarish story is "The Child Who Favored Daughter," in which both racial and sexual oppression combine to annihilate the characters emotionally and physically. The male protagonist has suffered terribly in the past because his sister betrayed him and her race by loving a white man. Her punishment for this transgression is the most dire mental and physical illness as well as torture at the hands of her own family. The brother thinks:

> That she had given herself to the lord of his own bondage was what galled him! And that she was cut down so! He could not forgive her the love she gave that knew nothing of master and slave. For though her own wound was a bitter one and in the end fatal, he bore a hurt throughout his life that slowly poisoned him. In a world where innocence and guilt became further complicated by questions of color and race, he felt hesitant and weary of living as though all the world were out to trick him.

His bitterness leads him to treat women, especially the ones who love him, with contempt and cruelty.

> His own wife, beaten into a cripple to prevent her from returning the imaginary overtures of the white landlord, killed herself while she was still young enough and strong enough to escape him. But

she left a child, a girl, a daughter; a replica of Daughter, his dead sister. A replica in every way.

Both his sister and his own child are beautiful women who are destroyed by their beauty, because it attracts the white males who use them, then cast them aside. Walker describes the young girl as a "slight, pretty flower that grows on any ground; and flowers pledge no allegiance to banners of any man." Physical loveliness can be a destructive element in a Black woman's life, because it enhances her chance of being a racial-sexual victim.

I believe that the worst results of racism in this country have been to subvert the most basic human relationships among Black men, women, and children and to destroy their individual psyches. It is on this level of interpersonal experience that Walker succeeds in illuminating Black women's lives. Some of her characters are damaged by material poverty, but what they suffer from most often is emotional destitution. These portraits are not pretty. When the reality is prettier, as a result of the implementation of Black *and* feminist goals and values, the stories will be prettier too.

1974

In 1974 I became the first woman of color appointed to the Modern Language Association's Commission on the Status of Women in the Profession. The Commission, founded in 1968, was very instrumental in building the new field of women's studies nationwide. My term on the Commission began in January 1975 and in December 1974 I attended my first MLA convention, in New York City. It was here that I met my longtime colleague, coauthor, and friend, Akasha (Gloria) Hull. There were only a handful of Black women among the thousands in attendance and no papers were delivered concerning Black women's literature in either women's studies or Black studies sessions.

As a new member of the Commission, I was determined that there would be programming about Black women writers at the next MLA. At the 1975 convention in San Francisco, there were two sessions: "Black Women Writers: Strategies for Criticism," which I chaired, and a seminar on Zora Neale Hurston, chaired by Hortense E. Thornton, where I presented this essay as a talk. Hurston eventually became recognized as a major U.S. writer, whose works are widely read and taught. In 1975, however, few were familiar with her and her books were frequently out of print.

The Radical Teacher, which is still active in Cambridge, Massachusetts, published this essay in 1978. The following editors' note, which accompanied the article, provides historical context about the building of Black women's studies and illustrates how crucial alternative, grassroots efforts were to this work.

The editors write:

This essay is a companion piece to the author's "Toward a Black Feminist Criticism" (*Radical Teacher* no. 7) and to Gloria Hull's "Rewriting Afro-American Literature: A Case for Black Women Writers" (*Radical Teacher* no. 6). All three are part of a collective effort to develop a Black feminist criticism. They are, as well, an attempt to recover important works which have been excluded from the American literary canon, and make them available to the curriculum. *Radical Teacher* no. 9 will have more about Hurston. We hope these essays will mark the beginning of a continuing effort. Readers are encouraged to send us their contributions to this important task.

Sexual Politics and the
Fiction of Zora Neale Hurston

Before beginning to look at Hurston's works themselves I would like to tell how I got involved with Zora Neale Hurston. I read her novel, *Their Eyes Were Watching God*, in 1972 when I was searching for a paper topic for a women's literature seminar. I was entranced by the lyricism of her work and her ability to evoke complex psychological realities using seemingly simple language. I read her autobiography, *Dust Tracks on a Road*, in preparation for teaching the novel in my first Black women writers course in 1973 and was pleased to find that my students shared my enthusiasm about Hurston's writing.

I became deeply interested in Hurston, however, early in 1974 while reading Darwin Turner's *In a Minor Chord: Three Afro-American Writers and Their Search for Identity*. I was actually reading Turner's book to get biographical information on Jean Toomer and only read his section on Hurston because of my prior interest in her. To use an expression that Zora used herself: "What did I do that for?" The title, "Zora Neale Hurston: The Wandering Minstrel," was not very promising, but I was not prepared for the contempt and sarcasm that followed.

As far as Turner was concerned Hurston could do nothing right. She was neither a good writer nor a good anthropologist. She had the audacity never to live in the same place for more than three years. He described her and her work as "artful," "coy," "irrational," "superficial," and "shallow." Never had I read a scholarly article so obviously infused with personal dislike. I did not recognize in Turner's words the spirit of the woman whose writing I so much admired. I began to recall the terms in which Langston Hughes had described Hurston in *The Big Sea*, and became more and more curious to know what Hurston was really like, wondered what she had done to make people so angry at her. In the back of my mind was the suspicion that the very qualities they did not approve of in her might be the same ones that made me respect her.

I am not convinced that I will ever know the whole story behind the enigma of Hurston's reputation, but I do believe that sexual politics play a significant role in this problem: the sexual politics both of her living and of her writing.

In an interview with John O'Brien, novelist and poet Alice Walker was asked, "Why do you think that the black woman writer has been so ignored in America? Does she have even more difficulty than the black male writer, who perhaps has just begun to gain recognition?" Walker answered:

> There are two reasons why the black woman writer is not taken as seriously as the black male writer. One is that she's a woman. Critics seem unusually ill-equipped to intelligently discuss and analyze the works of black women. Generally they do not even make the attempt; they prefer rather to talk about the lives of black women writers, not about what they write. And, since black women writers are not—it would seem—very likable—until recently they were the least willing worshippers of male supremacy—comments about them tend to be cruel. (*Interviews with Black Writers*, ed. John O'Brien)

Walker went on to describe Nathan Huggins's negative treatment of Hurston in his work *Harlem Renaissance*. The fact that Hurston not only did not worship male supremacy, but was also skeptical concerning claims of Black racial superiority would be sufficient to make her *persona non grata* in the Black literary community. As far as racial politics were concerned Hurston can fairly be described as individualistic and conservative, yet her insights into sexual politics indicate that she was inherently a feminist, a radical stance for a Black woman in any era. Her downplaying of racial differences combined with her personal assertiveness as a woman no doubt made her an anomaly to many of the Harlem Renaissance figures she encountered. Her capacity to get along with white people seemingly without serious psychic damage probably did not endear her to her fellow artists either. In his introduction to *Dust Tracks on a Road*, Larry Neal describes Hurston as:

> one of the most publicly flamboyant personalities of the Harlem literary movement. She was very bold and outspoken—an attractive woman who had learned how to survive with native wit. She approached life as a series of encounters and challenges; most of these she overcame without succumbing to the maudlin bitterness of many of her contemporaries.

Consider the adjectives "bold" and "outspoken" in contrast to the traditional expectation of passivity in women, even women writers. Consider why, as obscured as Hurston's career has been, she is the single woman whose name often surfaces in connection with the Renaissance group, having published more works than any Black woman writer who preceded her and more than most of those who came after.

It is sexual politics, not skill, that kept Hurston unknown while her age peer Richard Wright became the "father" of modern Black literature. It may well have been sexual politics that contributed to her poor reputation among her male contemporaries. It is the delineation of sexual politics in her fiction that has contributed to critical disapproval. And it is her generally pro-female view of sexual politics that makes her work so meaningful to contemporary women readers.

Much of Hurston's fiction focuses upon marriage and family life. *Jonah's Gourd Vine* (1934) is closely based upon the author's family and the sometimes rocky relationship between her own parents. *Moses, Man of the Mountain* (1939) although focused upon the

Biblical character reveals a sensitivity to women's identity. *Their Eyes Were Watching God* (1937), Hurston's master work, chronicles the heroine's marriages, two unsuccessful and one successful. Hurston's last novel, *Seraph on the Suwanee* (1948), also focuses on the main character's marital relationship. Two short stories, "Sweat" and "The Gilded Six Bits," portray the misunderstanding and hatred of two married couples. Hurston is often criticized for being apolitical because she does not write traditional protest or portray interracial conflict. Yet one can only consider her apolitical if the political ramifications of relationships between the sexes are completely ignored.

Hurston chose a male main character, John Pearson, for her first novel, *Jonah's Gourd Vine*; however, she invests a great deal of emotional energy in portraying his wife, Lucy, and the course of their marriage. In language which characteristically combines the beauty of poetry and folk idiom Hurston describes Lucy's feelings. She writes that "The blue sky looked all wrinkled to Lucy thru the tears." On her deathbed Lucy says to a friend:

> "Don't worry 'bout me, Sister Clarke. Ah done been in sorrow's kitchen and Ah done licked out all de pots. Ah done died in grief and been buried in de bitter waters, and Ah done rose agin from de dead lak Lazarus. Nothin' kin touch mah soul no mo'."

Lucy is the victim of the traditional double standard that frees men and bridles women, a standard that determines a great deal more than sexual mores and that Hurston repeatedly calls into question. It doesn't matter that John is a well-known preacher. He cannot leave the women alone and only reaps the disapproval of his congregation after countless affairs. He becomes quite furious, however, at even the hint that Lucy might one day become involved with someone else. John excuses his actions by saying, "Don't tell me 'bout dem trashy women Ah lusts after once in uh while. Dey's less dan leaves uh grass.'" John placates Lucy by telling her that she is the only woman he has ever loved, whatever evidence she sees to the contrary.

Lucy dies an early and unhappy death, emotionally abandoned by John who soon falls on evil days without her. His success has actually been the result of Lucy's prodding and advice and once she is gone he flounders. He marries an evil woman named Hattie, supposedly because she has had roots worked against him. By the time he comes to his senses his stock is so low in the Sanford community he must leave town. John gets his second chance in life when he meets and marries Sally, a woman with the same kind of intelligence and resourcefulness as Lucy. Unfortunately he falls from grace one more time on a return visit to Sanford. Driving home to Sally, lost in repentant thought, he is run over by a train.

Hurston ends John's life in the same way her own father's ended, by an unexpected accident. Just as in the novel too it is Zora's mother who inspired the family to reach for better things, to "jump at de sun." Her father, on the other hand, seemed more resigned to the racial and economic status quo. Hurston writes in her autobiography that although she idolized her father, "I was Mama's child. I knew that she had not always been happy and I wanted to know just how sad he was that night," that is, the night her mother died.

Zora's strong identification with her mother and her lifelong sorrow at her early death partially explain why Lucy is such a compelling presence in *Jonah's Gourd Vine*. Hurston always displays a great ability to evoke her female characters' inner lives, even when she chooses a male protagonist, and it is only when she chooses a Black woman persona that her full artistic powers come into play.

Moses, Man of the Mountain, Hurston's third novel, published in 1939, does not provide much material for an analysis of sexual politics in her works. Moses is a true hero; his marriage to Zipporah is idyllic and calm. The work is an epic with larger-than-life concerns instead of Hurston's usual focus upon domestic relationships. The portrayal of Moses's sister Miriam, however, is fascinating because Hurston once again exhibits her sensitivity to a woman's psyche.

Miriam is constantly aware of her low status as a Hebrew slave and longs for a better life. When she is a little girl watching Moses by the river, she sees the princess's royal party and hungrily admires all their richness and finery. She thinks: "'Royalty is a wonderful thing. It sure is a fine happening. It ought to be so that everybody that wanted to could be a queen.'" Hurston is quick to point out, however, that a queen's lot is not all that advantageous. She writes:

> Inside the palace also was the Pharaoh's widowed daughter who was not expected to do any more than she did. She must lend her support to the female robes of state. She must lend her ears to the sounds of mighty words boiling out of futile men. She must bear something in male form, for after all that is what she was born for—a passageway for boy children.

The pharaoh's daughter is as much victim of patriarchal rule as the lowliest slave woman.

Miriam never realizes her dream of being a queen. Instead she becomes a prophetess, reluctantly recognized by Moses as a leader during the liberation of the children of Israel. Hurston explains that Miriam is a bitter, lonely woman who never marries. The resentment that Miriam feels toward Moses's beautiful wife, Zipporah, mirrors the way Black women have traditionally felt toward white women and high yellow beauties.

> She looked again and saw well-cared for hands and feet of Zipporah, and looked at her own gnarled fists and her square feet all twisted and coarsened by slavery, and almost snarled out loud. She, Miriam, had had so little in her life and now this place she had won by hard work and chance was being taken from her by the looks of a Prince's daughter who hadn't done anything but deck herself to come here and bewitch the eyes of foolish women! Miriam boiled with anger and a sense of injustice.

When Miriam initiates a whispering campaign against Zipporah she is punished with leprosy. Although she recovers physically after seven days, she is a broken woman. There is the implication that because Miriam is exceptional, not conforming to the traditional female role, she is destined to be unhappy. Yet it is obvious that she has Hurston's sympathy and ultimately Moses's respect. At her death Moses considers Miriam's contribution to the Exodus.

> He wondered if she had not been born if he would have been standing here in the desert of Zin. In fact, he wondered if the Exodus would have taken place at all. . . . He doubted it. . . . A mighty thing had happened in the world through the stumblings of a woman who couldn't see where she was going. She needed a big tomb so the generations that come after would know her and remember.

Hurston once more makes the point that it is the invisible work of women that often accounts for the successful deeds of men. In Biblical times a woman had few choices. She could be an idle queen or independent and an outcast. The only proper role was that of wife. In *Their Eyes Were Watching God* Hurston questions these assumptions still in force some two thousand years later.

Hurston's second novel is one of the most miraculous books written in English. Not because of its lushness of language, the depth of its characterization, nor its ennobling treatment of Black love. All of these qualities and more make it great, but what makes it miraculous is that it is one of a handful of books in existence that take Black women seriously. Janie is one of the finest characters in American fiction. In *Their Eyes Were Watching God* Hurston makes it absolutely clear that there is nothing innately wrong with being a Black woman, that it is neither a form of physical disorder nor a moral disease.

It is also clear that she is writing directly from the heart. Hurston explains: "I wrote *Their Eyes Were Watching God* in Haiti. It was dammed up in me, and I wrote it under internal pressure in seven weeks. I wish that I could write it again" (*Dust Tracks on a Road*). The novel was conceived while the author was herself involved in a very significant relationship and it captures both the passion and the difficulties she was experiencing.

Taking Black women seriously in the novel means for one thing that Janie's life is seen as inherently valuable. There is the assumption that she has the right to search for happiness and freedom, however she may define them. Hurston writes:

> She was sixteen. She had glossy leaves and bursting buds and she wanted to struggle with life but it seemed to elude her. Where were the singing bees for her? Nothing on the place nor in her grandma's house answered her. She searched as much of the world as she could from the top of the front steps and then went on down to the front gate and leaned over to gaze up and down the road. Looking, waiting, breathing short with impatience. Waiting for the world to be made.

Janie must wait for years and go through two unhappy marriages before she meets a man who recognizes who she is and does not infringe upon her sense of self. Hurston is fully aware of the fundamental oppressiveness of traditional marriage, yet she also has a deep understanding of what the institution represents to women who were formerly enslaved.

Nanny's speech in which she justifies marrying Janie off to the unappealing Logan Killicks amazingly documents how both racism and sexism have undermined Black women's lives. She explains:

> "Honey, de white man is de ruler of everything as fur as Ah been able to find out. . . . So de white man throw down de load and tell de nigger man tuh pick it up. He pick it up because he have to, but he don't tote it. He hand it to his womenfolks. De nigger woman is de mule uh de world so fur as Ah can see. Ah been prayin fuh it tuh be different wid you. Lawd, Lawd, Lawd!"

Nanny speaks of her unrealized hopes to do something outstanding, transferred first to her daughter and then to her granddaughter, Janie: "'Ah wanted to preach a great sermon about colored women sittin' on high, but they wasn't no pulpit for me.'" It should be noted that this is a "sermon" that has yet to be preached.

Nanny then recalls both sexual abuse by her master and physical abuse by her master's wife. Despite the fact that she has not recovered from childbirth Nanny is forced to run away to save her baby and herself. After years of struggling alone to raise and educate her daughter her hopes are again smashed because of sexual violence. Nanny continues:

> "But one day she didn't come home at de usual time and Ah waited and waited but she never come all dat night. Ah took a lantern and went round askin' everybody but nobody ain't seen her. De next mornin' she come crawlin' in on her hands and knees. A sight to see. Dat school teacher had done hid her in de woods all night long and he had done raped mah baby and run on off just before day."

She ends this moving monologue by saying that she doesn't want men white or Black to make a "spit cup" out of Janie It will be safer for Janie to belong to one man so that she can be protected from all the rest. Janie marries Logan Killicks and makes a painful discovery. Hurston writes: "She knew now that marriage did not make love. Janie's first dream was dead, so she became a woman."

When the prosperous looking Jody Starks happens along the road and talks prettily to her, he seems to offer a means of escape. Janie runs off with him, filled with hopes of recapturing her romantic dreams. Unfortunately Starks's one-dimensional goal is the obtaining of money and power. Janie soon discovers that she is merely one of his possessions, a beautiful status symbol. Jody also turns out to be an unregenerate male supremacist who takes every opportunity to squelch and humiliate his wife. When he is elected mayor of the all-Black town of Eatonville the crowd invites Janie to say a few words. Before she can open her mouth, however, Jody interrupts:

> "Thank yuh fuh yo' compliments, but mah wife don't know nothin' 'bout no speech-makin'. Ah never married her for nothin' lak dat. She's uh woman and her place is in de home."

Janie finds that the restrictions that Jody imposes upon her in the name of pampering make her life intolerable. Despite her place being in the home she is required to work in the store where Jody berates her interminably, makes her tie up her hair and won't let her participate in the talk, games, and storytelling.

Jody's arrogance knows no bounds. During an altercation over a misplaced bill he says, "All you got tuh do is mind me. How come you can't do lak Ah tell yuh?'" Janie retorts, "'You sho loves to tell me whut to do, but Ah can't tell you nothin' Ah see!'" Jody informs her:

> "Dat's 'cause you need tellin'. . . . It would be pitiful if Ah didn't. Somebody got to think for women and chillun and chickens and cows. I god, they sho don't think none theirselves."

The only way for Janie to keep peace is to keep silent. Even so she cannot escape his verbal and even physical intimidation.

Only when Jody is on his deathbed can she express all the things that she has held in for so long:

> "You done lived wid me for twenty years and you don't half know me atall. And you could have but you was so busy worshippin' de works of yo' own hands and cuffin' folks around in their minds till you didn't see uh whole heap uh things yuh could have. . . . Listen, Jody, you ain't de Jody Ah run off down de road wid. You'se what's left after he died. Ah run off tuh keep house wid you in uh wonderful way. But you wasn't satisfied wid me de way Ah was. Naw! Mah own mind had tuh be squeezed and crowded out tuh make room for yours in me."

Janie's fate is a common and a bitter one and her last words to her husband are hardly retribution for his abuse. Nevertheless Darwin Turner considers this "one of the crudest scenes which . . . [Hurston] ever wrote," and rationalizes, "Never was his conduct so cruel as to deserve the vindictive attack which Janie unleashes while he is dying. For Janie, the behavior seems grotesquely out of character." An example of Jody's not so cruel behavior occurs when Janie makes a dinner not to his liking and he slaps her "until she had a ringing sound in her ears." It seems strange to call a woman's expression of pain and assertion of her right to be treated humanly grotesque. Sexual politics are unquestionably at variance here, Zora Neale Hurston's versus the male critic's.

Janie ultimately experiences a few years of happiness with Teacake, who works with her to build an egalitarian relationship. With him Janie gets to do the many things Jody never permitted, even activities as simple as playing checkers and going fishing. Teacake is not obsessed with material success or status, but desires instead to create a full and happy life. He compliments Janie's deep spirituality and she finally becomes the "glossy leaved" person she was meant to be at sixteen. The most significant activity that Janie and Teacake share is working side by side harvesting vegetables on the Florida muck. The issue of work was no doubt much on Hurston's mind since it was conflict over her career that caused her to part with her lover. Hurston very effectively criticizes the bourgeois division of labor in marriage, particularly as it is appropriated by Black people. Janie explains her distaste for living on a pedestal before she marries Teacake.

> "Ah done lived Grandma's way, now Ah means tuh live mine. . . . She was borned in slavery time when folks dat is black folks didn't sit down anytime dey felt lak it. So sittin' on porches lak de white madam looked lak uh mighty fine thing tuh her. Dat's whut she wanted for me—don't keer whut it cost. Git up on uh high chair and sit dere. She didn't have time tuh think what tuh do after you got up on de stool uh do nothin'. De object wuz tuh git dere. So Ah got up on de high stool lak she told me, but Pheoby, Ah done nearly languished tuh death up dere. Ah felt like de world wuz cryin' extry and Ah ain't read de common news yet."

Unfortunately Janie's idyllic relationship with Teacake ends abruptly with Teacake's nightmarish death. Janie returns to Eatonville to live out the rest of her days in peace, knowing that she has achieved what few women have, a meaningful love without loss of self-esteem.

Eleven years later in her last novel, *Seraph on the Suwanee* (1948), Hurston appears to have abandoned her passionate advocacy of equality in marriage. Indeed she does not seem deeply involved with the novel at all. Larry Neal suggests that "she may have intended it as a better-than-average pot-boiler," which may also explain her choice of poor white characters. Arvay and Jim Meserve have a marriage that is constantly strained because Arvay's deep inferiority complex will not let her believe that Jim is truly committed to her. Jim is a very hard worker and eventually becomes successful financially, raising Arvay to a station in life she never expected to reach and is not sure she deserves. He is also rather loud and domineering, though not so obnoxious as Jody Starks. Arvay finally fixes things up between them by becoming properly worshipful of Jim and all he has done for her. Jim reciprocates by assuring her that she belongs on the pedestal he has built for her. It is hard to believe that Hurston took seriously their closing dialogue.

> "So you're planted here now forever. You're going to do just what I say do, and you had better not let me hear you part your lips in a grumble. Do you hear me, Arvay?"
>
> "Yes, Jim, I hear you." . . . Her job was mothering. What more could any woman want and need? . . . She was serving and meant to serve.

Whenever a Black author deals with white characters there is always the potential for satire. Certainly Hurston had stated elsewhere that the kind of marriage in which the woman waited on the man and was rewarded by being treated like a queen was not anything that Black folk should strive for. It is tragic that this was to be the last work of Hurston's career, that there would be nothing else containing the fullness and honesty of *Their Eyes Were Watching God*, no other work to tell us more of what this extraordinary writer thought and felt.

June Jordan, in an article titled "On Richard Wright and Zora Neale Hurston: Notes Toward a Balancing of Love and Hatred" (*Black World*, August 1974), explains why Hurston's literary contributions have been so belittled:

> But: because Zora Neale Hurston was a woman, and because we have been misled into devaluating the functions of Black affirmation, her work has been derogated as romantic/the natural purview of a woman (*i.e.*, unimportant), "personal" (not serious) in its scope, and assessed as *sui generis*, or idiosyncratic accomplishment of no lasting reverberation or usefulness.

Jordan points out that contrary to this negative evaluation, "*Their Eyes Were Watching God* is the prototypical novel of affirmation; it is the most successful, convincing and exemplary novel of Blacklove that we have. Period." It is also a sensitive evocation of a Black woman's consciousness and the concrete embodiment of the feminist truism that "the personal is political." Only when a heightened understanding of the way in which sexual politics affects Black women's lives emerges will the gifts of an artist like Zora Neale Hurston be fully understood and the ironies of her life fully mourned.

1975/1978

This review of two books and a recording by Pat Parker (1944–1989) appeared in *Conditions: Three* (following the publication of "Toward a Black Feminist Criticism" in *Conditions: Two*). Pat's poetry is the first explicitly Black lesbian writing I remember reading. Originally published in chapbooks by Shameless Hussy Press and The Women's Press Collective of Oakland, California, her work and Audre Lorde's provided a lifeline for me and for many other Black lesbians fortunate enough to find it.

Pat's was a unique poetic voice, influenced as much by the Black Arts Movement of the 1960s and 1970s as by the directness and self-revelation of early lesbian feminism. She was a seasoned political organizer who worked in a variety of movements and accurately described herself as a revolutionary. I was privileged to know her. I chose to include this piece so that others might discover her gifts as well.

My assertion that "Parker writes the poems that only a Black feminist dyke can write" might be considered "essentialist" in the postmodern era. In that time and place, however, when so few Black women had the courage to be out as feminists, let alone as lesbians, the experiences and perspectives of "sister outsiders" led directly to the creation of a new kind of literature.

Naming the Unnameable

The Poetry of Pat Parker

What does a Black lesbian poet write about when it would seem that our very preservation depends upon our ability to keep silent, to not bring up the many layers of our oppression? What kinds of things are finally said when we name the unnameable?

Pat Parker's writing provides some initial answers. One of a handful of Black women writers who acknowledge their lesbian identity, Parker gives us poetry which is woman-identified, feminist, and stunningly brave. "My lover is a woman," she declares at the opening of *Pit Stop*, and we know from that point on there will be no half-stepping.

All poetry quoted in this review appears in *Movement in Black: The Collected Poetry of Pat Parker 1961–1978* (Ithaca, N.Y.: Firebrand Books, 1990).

I must admit that when I first read Parker's books I was much more excited by the content than by the execution of her verse. *Child of Myself* contained some poems which were vague in their intentions and strained in language. The work in *Pit Stop* was generally stronger, but I was not fully aware of what Parker was accomplishing until I heard her read in person. Immediately I realized that her poems were designed, consciously or not, to be spoken. I understood that Parker was writing very much in the Black oral tradition which relies on inflection, metaphor, irony, and humor to deepen our communication and make it specifically ours. Sound and rhythm combined with the uniqueness of her subject matter to make fascinating art. I regretted that hearing her read would be for me a one-time experience. But fortunately, a new recording of both Parker's and Judy Grahn's work, "Where Would I Be Without You," has come from Olivia Records and every woman can now hear the intensity of Parker's words.

One of the most compelling aspects of Parker's work as a whole is the growth she shares with us as a woman and artist. At the beginning of her first book she debunks the Biblical creation myth of woman derived from man and asserts:

> i, woman, i
> can no longer claim
> a mother of flesh
> a father of marrow
> I, Woman must be
> the child of myself.

Her process of self-creation has many episodes, but culminates in her identity as a Black feminist dyke.

At the beginning of *Child of Myself*, for example, she is still going through changes with men, but offers an early warning:

> i will serve you no more
> in the name of wifely love
> i'll not masturbate your pride
> in the name of wifely loyalty

> Trust me no more
> Our bed is unsafe
> Hidden within folds of cloth
> a desperate slave

By the end of this book she is tentatively dealing with coming out ("Move in darkness / know the touch of a woman . . .") and concludes with several love poems to women.

Parker, it seems, has always been a nonconformist, uncomfortable with roles whether sexually or racially imposed. She calls herself a "goat child" in her long autobiographical poem and recalls:

so i settled down &
fought my way thru first grade
defending my right to
wear cowboy boots even if
i was a girl which no one
had bothered to tell me
about at home . . .

Not surprisingly, she also chafes at the requirements exacted of her as a supposedly adult female. A male lover presumptuously promises to show her "the ways of woman" and Parker bitterly admits:

& i learned
i learned hate
i learned jealousy
i learned my skills—
to cook—to fuck
to wash—to fuck
to iron—to fuck
to clean—to fuck
to care—to fuck
to wait—to fuck

Parker is saying that sexism does indeed affect Black women, rhetoric to the contrary, and that our childhood dreams are not always conventional and correct.

By the time that *Pit Stop* appears, Parker is clearly and happily woman-identified. She is fully aware, however, of the personal and political paradoxes inherent in being a Black lesbian. In "My lover is a woman" she describes the external and internal battles she must fight because she is in a relationship with a white woman. She writes that her love for this particular person makes her able to forget the brutalities visited upon her by racist whites and to transcend the distrust of white people taught by her family as a means of survival. There is also her sisters' homophobia to contend with and, if this is not enough, the disapproval of other gay people, both Black and white. Finally Parker cannot shut out these external judgments. She writes:

> I remember—
>   Every word taught me
>   Every word said to me
>   Every deed done to me
> & then i hate–
> i look at my lover
> & for an instant—doubt—

This is one of Parker's most effective works. What she claims never to think about are in fact the things you never *stop* thinking about when you're Black. Stylistically the poem works well too. Stanzas that positively describe her lover open three of the poem's four sections and function in direct opposition to the litany of abuse which follows. Her mother's question—"Lord, what kind of child is this?"—ends each of the four sections and is an amazingly resonant refrain, containing all the anxiety and love a Black woman might feel about her inexplicable daughter. Parker's reading of this poem on her record makes even more vivid the searing feelings which inspired it.

To me Parker's best poems are ones like this one in which the different elements of her identity mesh into a recognizable whole. The result is poetry with unique political impact. Parker writes the poems that only a Black feminist dyke can write. She can legitimately criticize supposedly revolutionary Black men who batter women.

Brother
    I don't want to hear
    about
    how *my* real enemy
    is the system.
i'm no genius,
    but i do know
    that system
you hit me with
    is called
        a fist.

She can also point to racism in the women's movement, a boulder which has yet to be turned over and looked at. She shouts:

SISTER! your foot's smaller
but it's still on my neck.

Parker's poetry makes sense because she has personally experienced how the major systems of oppression are linked and knows that they all must be destroyed if she or anybody else is ever going to be free. Parker's "Womanslaughter" illustrates how her identity, politics, and vision coalesce to make superb writing. In it Parker confronts the intolerable circumstances of her sister's death at the hands of her "quiet" ex-husband. The last stanza contains a declaration of the kind of commitment that will bring about the life-saving revolution:

Hear me now
it is almost three years
and i am again strong
i have gained many sisters
and if one is beaten or raped or killed
i will not come in mourning black
i will not pick the right flowers

i will not celebrate her death
and it will matter not if she is Black or white
if she loves women or men
i will come with my many sisters
and decorate the streets
with the innards of those brothers in womanslaughter
no more can i dull my rage
    in alcohol and deference to men's courts
i will come to my sisters not dutiful
i will come strong.[*]

The poetry of Pat Parker shows that by naming the unnameable, there is everything to be gained.

1978

---

[*] Transcribed from the recording.

This essay was originally presented as a paper at a conference sponsored by the Center for Twentieth-Century Studies at the University of Wisconsin, Milwaukee, in the spring of 1985. Conference participants were asked to prepare their presentations for publication in an anthology featuring the conference papers.

When the conference organizer called me to discuss my piece, her major concern was whether my essay would be "theoretical." I was surprised by her question, since she had heard me deliver my paper, but I soon understood that what she meant by *theoretical* was the European-inflected, jargonized obscurities that have now gained center stage in academic discourse. Accessible writing based upon other theoretical models has become less and less recognized as intellectually challenging and academically credible. Some other models, however, are much more likely to address the majority of people's pressing material needs and their daily struggles for dignity and justice against power structures whose purpose is to carry out *actual*, not theoretical, class, race, gender, and sexual exploitation. I did not complete the essay in time for that anthology. Several years later I was pleased for it to be included in two collections of literary criticism and political theory edited by women of color.

My primary objective in "The Truth That Never Hurts" was to confront the problems of homophobia in literature and literary criticism written by Black women, some of whom were considered to be feminists. From the vantage point of the late 1990s I might not now organize a discussion of Black lesbians in fiction around the concepts of verisimilitude and authenticity. Currently, there is a range of Black and lesbian experience and artistic representations of that experience which escapes the borders of these two terms. In 1985, however, there were very few depictions of Black lesbians in literature. My desire was to interrogate writing that was stereotypical or homophobic and that ignored the quickly changing social climate around issues of sexual orientation and sexuality in Black communities, which was being catalyzed by Black lesbians' and gays' political work.

The Truth That Never Hurts

Black Lesbians in Fiction in the 1980s

In 1977 when I wrote "Toward a Black Feminist Criticism," I wanted to accomplish several goals. The first was simply to point out that Black women writers existed, a fact generally ignored by white male, Black male, and white female readers, teachers, and critics. Another desire was to encourage Black feminist criticism of these writers' work, that is, analyses that acknowledged the reality of sexual oppression in the lives of Black women. Probably most urgently, I wanted to illuminate the existence of Black lesbian writers and to show how homophobia ensured that we were even more likely to be ignored or attacked than Black women writers generally.

In 1985 the situation of Black women writers is considerably different from what it was in 1977. Relatively speaking, Black women's literature is much more recognized, even at times by the white male literary establishment. There are a growing number of Black women critics who rely upon various Black feminist critical approaches to studying the literature. There has been a marked increase in the number of Black women who are willing to acknowledge that they are feminists, including some who write literary criticism. Not surprisingly, Black feminist activism and organizing have greatly expanded, a precondition which I cited in 1977 for the growth of Black feminist criticism. More writing by Black lesbians is available, and there has even been some positive response to this writing from nonlesbian Black readers and critics. The general conditions under which Black women critics and writers work have improved. The personal isolation we face and the ignorance and hostility with which our work is met have diminished in some quarters, but have by no means disappeared.

One of the most positive changes is that a body of consciously Black feminist writing and writing by other feminists of color actually exists. The publication of a number of anthologies has greatly increased the breadth of writing available by feminists of color. These include *Conditions: Five, The Black Women's Issue* (1979); *This Bridge Called My Back: Writings by Radical Women of Color* (1981); *All the Women Are White, All the Blacks Are Men, But Some of Us Are Brave: Black Women's Studies* (1982); *A Gathering of Spirit: North American Indian Women's Issue* (1983); *Cuentos: Stories by Latinas* (1983); *Home Girls: A Black Feminist Anthology* (1983); *Bearing Witness/Sobreviviendo: An Anthology of Native American/Latina Art and Literature* (1984); and *Gathering Ground: New Writing and Art by Northwest Women of Color* (1984). First books by individual authors have also appeared, such as *Claiming an Identity They Taught Me to Despise* (1980) and *Abeng* (1984) by Michelle Cliff; *Narratives: Poems in the Tradition of Black Women* (1982) by Cheryl Clarke; *For Nights Like This One* (1983) by Becky Birtha; *Loving in the War Years: Lo Que Nunca Pasó Por Sus Labios* (1983) by Cherríe Moraga; *The Words of a Woman Who Breathes Fire* (1983) by Kitty Tsui; and *Mohawk Trail* (1985) by Beth Brant (*Degonwadonti*). Scholarly works provide extremely useful analytical frameworks, for example, *Common Differences: Conflicts in Black and White Feminist Perspectives* (1981) by Gloria I. Joseph and Jill Lewis; *Black Women Writers at Work* (1983), edited by Claudia Tate; *When and Where I Enter: The Impact of Black Women on Race and Sex in America* (1984) by Paula Giddings; and *Black Feminist Criticism: Perspectives on Black Women Writers* (1985) by Barbara Christian.

Significantly, however, "small" or independent, primarily women's presses published all but the last four titles cited, and almost all the authors and editors of these alternative-press books (although not all of the contributors to the anthologies) are lesbians. In his essay "The Sexual Mountain and Black Women Writers," critic Calvin Hernton writes:

The declared and lesbian black feminist writers are pioneering a black feminist criticism. This is not to take away from other writers. All are blazing new trails. But especially the declared feminists and lesbian feminists—Barbara Smith, Ann Shockley, Cheryl Clarke, Wilmette Brown, and the rest—are at the forefront of the critics, scholars, intellectuals, and ideologues of our time.[1]

Yet Hernton points out that these writers are "subpopular," published as they are by nonmainstream presses. In contrast, nonlesbian Black women writers have been published by trade publishers and are able to reach, as Hernton explains, a "wider popular audience."

In an excellent essay, "No More Buried Lives: The Theme of Lesbianism in Audre Lorde's *Zami*, Gloria Naylor's *The Women of Brewster Place*, Ntozake Shange's *Sassafras, Cypress and Indigo*, and Alice Walker's *The Color Purple*," critic Barbara Christian makes a similar observation. She writes:

> Lesbian life, characters, language, values are *at present* and *to some extent* becoming respectable in American literature, partly because of the pressure of women-centered communities, partly because publishers are intensely aware of marketing trends. . . . I say, *to some extent*, because despite the fact that Walker received the Pulitzer for *The Color Purple* and Naylor the American Book Award for *The Women of Brewster Place*, I doubt if *Home Girls*, an anthology of black feminist and lesbian writing that was published by Kitchen Table Press, would have been published by a mainstream publishing company.[2]

Significantly, Christian says that "lesbian life, characters, language, values" are receiving qualified attention and respectability, but lesbian writers themselves are not. No doubt this is why she suspects that no trade publisher would publish *Home Girls*, which contains work by women who write openly as lesbians and which defines lesbianism politically as well as literarily.

The fact that there is such a clear-cut difference in publishing options for out Black lesbian writers (who are published solely by independent presses) and for nonlesbian and closeted Black women writers (who have access to both trade and alternative publishers) indicates what has *not* changed since 1977. It also introduces the focus of this essay.[3] I am concerned with exploring the treatment of Black lesbian writing and Black lesbian themes in the context of Black feminist writing and criticism.

Today, not only are more works by and about Black women available, but a body of specifically Black feminist writing exists. Although both the general category of Black women's literature and the specific category of Black feminist literature can be appropriately analyzed from a Black feminist critical perspective, explicitly Black feminist literature has a unique set of characteristics and emphases which distinguish it from other work. Black feminist writing provides an incisive critical perspective on sexual political issues which affect Black women—for example, the issue of sexual violence. It generally depicts the significance of Black women's relationships with each other as a primary source of support. Black feminist writing may also be classified as such because the author identifies herself as a feminist and has a demonstrated commitment to women's issues and related political concerns. An openness in discussing lesbian subject matter is perhaps the most obvious earmark of Black feminist writing, and not because feminism and lesbianism are interchangeable, which of course they are not.

For historical, political, and ideological reasons, a writer's consciousness about lesbianism bears a direct relationship to her consciousness about feminism. It was in the context of the second wave of the contemporary feminist movement, influenced by the simultaneous development of an autonomous gay liberation movement, that the political content of lesbianism and lesbian oppression began to be analyzed and defined. The women's liberation movement was the political setting in which antilesbian attitudes and actions were initially challenged in the late 1960s and early 1970s and where at least in theory, but more often in fact, homophobia was designated unacceptable, at least in the movement's more progressive sectors.

Barbara Christian also makes the connection between feminist consciousness and a willingness to address lesbian themes in literature. She writes:

> Some of the important contributions that the emergence of the lesbian theme has made to Afro-American women's literature are: the breaking of stereotypes so that black lesbians are clearly seen as *women*, the exposure of homophobia in the black community, and an exploration of how homophobia is related to the struggle of all women to be all that they can be—in other words to feminism.
>
> That is not to say that Afro-American women's literature has not always included a feminist perspective. The literature of the seventies, for example, certainly explored the relationship between sexism and racism and has been at the forefront of the development of feminist ideas. One natural outcome of this exploration is the lesbian theme, for society's attack on lesbians is the cutting edge of the anti-feminist definition of women.[4]

Black feminist writers, whether lesbian or nonlesbian, have been aware of and influenced by the movement's exploring of, struggling over, and organizing around lesbian identity and issues. They would be much more likely to take Black lesbian experience seriously and perhaps to explore Black lesbian themes in their writing, in contrast with authors who either have not been involved in the women's movement or are antifeminist. For example, in her very positive review of *Conditions: Five, The Black Women's Issue*, originally published in *Ms.* magazine in 1980, Alice Walker writes:

> Like black men and women who refused to be the exceptional "pet" Negro for whites, and who instead said they were "niggers" too (the original "crime" of "niggers" and lesbians is that they prefer themselves), perhaps black women writers and non-writers should say, simply, whenever black lesbians are being put down, held up, messed over, and generally told their lives should not be encouraged, *We are all lesbians*. For surely it is better to be thought a lesbian, and to say and write your life exactly as you experience it, than to be a token "pet" black woman for those whose

contempt for our autonomous existence makes them a menace to human life.[5]

Walker's support of her lesbian sisters in real life is not unrelated to her ability to write fiction about Black women who are lovers, as in *The Color Purple*. Her feminist consciousness undoubtedly influenced the positiveness of her portrayal. In contrast, an author such as Gayle Jones, who has not been associated with or seemingly influenced by the feminist movement, has portrayed lesbians quite negatively.[6]

Just as surely as a Black woman writer's relationship to feminism affects the themes she might choose to write about, a Black woman critic's relationship to feminism determines the kind of criticism she is willing and able to do. The fact that critics are usually also academics, however, has often affected Black women critics' approach to feminist issues. If a Black woman scholar's only connection to women's issues is via women's studies, as presented by white women academics, most of whom are not activists, her access to movement analyses and practice will be limited or nonexistent. I believe that the most accurate and developed theory, including literary theory, comes from practice, from the experience of activism. This relationship between theory and practice is crucial when inherently political subject matter, such as the condition of women as depicted in a writer's work, is being discussed. I do not believe it is possible to arrive at fully developed and useful Black feminist criticism by merely reading about feminism. Of course every Black woman has her own experiences of sexual political dynamics and oppression to draw upon, and referring to these experiences should be an important resource in shaping her analyses of a literary work. However, studying feminist texts and drawing only upon one's *individual* experiences of sexism are insufficient.

I remember the point in my own experience when I no longer was involved on a regular basis in organizations such as the Boston Committee to End Sterilization Abuse and the Abortion Action

Coalition. I was very aware that my lack of involvement affected my thinking and writing *overall*. Certain perceptions were simply unavailable to me because I no longer was doing that particular kind of ongoing work. And I am referring to missing something much deeper than access to specific information about sterilization and reproductive rights. Activism has spurred me to write the kinds of theory and criticism I have written and has provided the experiences and insights that have shaped the perceptions in my work. Many examples of this vital relationship between activism and theory exist in the work of thinkers such as Ida B. Wells-Barnett, W.E.B. Du Bois, Lillian Smith, Lorraine Hansberry, Frantz Fanon, Barbara Deming, Paolo Freire, and Angela Davis.

A critic's involvement or lack of involvement in activism, specifically in the context of the feminist movement, is often signally revealed by the approach she takes to lesbianism. If a woman has worked in organizations where lesbian issues were raised, where homophobia was unacceptable and struggled with, and where she had the opportunity to meet and work with a variety of lesbians, her relationship to lesbians and to her own homophobia will undoubtedly be affected. The types of political organizations in which such dialogue occurs are not, of course, exclusively lesbian and may focus upon a range of issues, such as women in prison, sterilization abuse, reproductive freedom, health care, domestic violence, and sexual assault.

Black feminist critics who are lesbians can usually be counted upon to approach Black women's and Black lesbian writing nonhomophobically. Nonlesbian Black feminist critics are not as dependable in this regard. I even question at times designating Black women—critics and noncritics alike—as feminist who are actively homophobic in what they write, say, or do, or who are passively homophobic because they ignore lesbian existence entirely.[7] Yet such critics are obviously capable of analyzing other sexual and political implications of the literature they scrutinize. Political definitions, particularly of feminism, can be difficult to pin down. The one upon which I generally rely states: "Feminism is the political theory and practice that struggles to free *all* women: women of color, working-class women, poor women, disabled women, lesbians, old women—as well as white, economically privileged, heterosexual women. Anything less than this vision of total freedom is not feminism, but merely female self-aggrandizement."[8]

A Black gay college student recently recounted an incident to me that illustrates the kind of consciousness that is grievously lacking among nonfeminist Black women scholars about Black lesbian existence. His story indicates why a Black feminist approach to literature, criticism, and research in a variety of disciplines is crucial if one is to recognize and understand Black lesbian experience. While researching a history project, he contacted the archives at a Black institution which has significant holdings on Black women. He spoke to a Black woman archivist and explained that he was looking for materials on Black lesbians in the 1940s. Her immediate response was to laugh uproariously and then to say that the collection contained very little on women during that period and nothing at all on lesbians in any of the periods covered by its holdings.

Not only was her reaction appallingly homophobic, not to mention impolite, but it was also inaccurate. One of the major repositories of archival material on Black women in the country of course contains material by and about Black lesbians. The material, however, is not identified and defined as such and thus remains invisible. This is a classic case of "invisibility [becoming] an unnatural disaster," as feminist poet Mitsuye Yamada observes.[9]

I suggested a number of possible resources to the student, and in the course of our conversation I told him I could not help but think of Cheryl Clarke's classic poem "Of Althea and Flaxie." It begins:

> In 1943 Althea was a welder
> very dark
> very butch
> and very proud
> loved to cook, sew, and drive a car
> and did not care who knew she kept company with a woman.[10]

The poem depicts a realistic and positive Black lesbian relationship which survives Flaxie's pregnancy in 1955, Althea's going to jail for writing numbers in 1958, poverty, racism, and, of course, homophobia. If the archivist's vision had not been so blocked by homophobia, she would have been able to direct this student to documents that corroborate the history embodied in Clarke's poem.

Being divorced from the experience of feminist organizing not only makes it more likely that a woman has not been directly challenged to examine her homophobia, but it can also result in erroneous approaches to Black lesbian literature, if she does decide to talk or write about it. For example, some critics, instead of simply accepting that Black lesbians and Black lesbian writers exist, view the depiction of lesbianism as a dangerous and unacceptable "theme" or "trend" in Black women's writing. Negative discussions of "themes" and "trends," which in time may fade, do not acknowledge that for survival, Black lesbians, like any oppressed group, need to see our faces reflected in myriad cultural forms, including literature. Some writers go so far as to see the few Black lesbian books in existence as a kind of conspiracy, and bemoan that there is "so much" of this kind of writing available in print. They put forth the supreme untruth that it is actually an advantage to be a Black lesbian writer.

For each lesbian of color in print there are undoubtedly five dozen whose work has never been published and may never be. The publication of lesbians of color is a "new" literary development, made possible by alternative, primarily lesbian/feminist presses. The political and aesthetic strength of this writing is indicated by its impact having been far greater than its actual availability. At times its content has had revolutionary implications. But the impact of Black lesbian feminist writing, to which Calvin Hernton refers, should not be confused with access to print, to readers, or to the material perks that help a writer survive economically.

Terms such as *heterophobia*, used to validate the specious notion that "so many" Black women writers are depicting loving and sexual relationships between women, to the exclusion of focusing on

relationships with men, arise in the academic vacuum, uninflu-
enced by political reality. "Heterophobia" resembles the concept of
"reverse racism." Both are thoroughly reactionary and have nothing to do with the actual dominance of a heterosexual white power
structure.

Equating lesbianism with separatism is another error in termi-
nology, which will probably take a number of years to correct. The
title of a workshop at a major Black women writers' conference, for
example, was "Separatist Voices in the New Canon." The workshop examined the work of Audre Lorde and Alice Walker, neither
of whom defines herself as a separatist, either sexually or racially.
In his introduction to *Confirmation: An Anthology of African American Women*, coeditor Imamu Baraka is critical of feminists who
are separatists, but he does not mention that any such thing as a
lesbian exists. In his ambiguous yet inherently homophobic usage,
the term *separatist* is made to seem like a mistaken political tendency, which correct thinking could alter. If separatist equals lesbian, Baraka is suggesting that we should change our minds and
eradicate ourselves. In both these instances the fact that lesbians
do not have sexual relationships with men is thought to be the
same as ideological lesbian "separatism." Such an equation does
not take into account that the majority of lesbians of color have
interactions with men and that those who are activists are quite
likely to be politically committed to coalition work as well.

Inaccuracy and distortion seem to be particularly frequent pitfalls when nonlesbians address Black lesbian experience because of
generalized homophobia and because the very nature of our
oppression may cause us to be hidden or "closeted," voluntarily or
involuntarily isolated from other communities, and as a result
unseen and unknown. In her essay "A Cultural Legacy Denied and
Discovered: Black Lesbians in Fiction by Women," Jewelle Gomez
asserts the necessity for realistic portrayals of Black lesbians:

> These Black Lesbian writers . . . have seen into the shadows that
> hide the existence of Black Lesbians and understand they have to

create a universe/home that rings true on all levels. . . . The Black Lesbian writer must throw herself into the arms of her culture by acting as student/teacher/participant/ observer, absorbing and synthesizing the meanings of our existence as a people. She must do this despite the fact that both our culture and our sexuality have been severely truncated and distorted.

Nature abhors a vacuum and there is a distinct gap in the picture where the Black Lesbian should be. The Black Lesbian writer must recreate our home, unadulterated, unsanitized, specific and not isolated from the generations that have nurtured us.[11]

This is an excellent statement of what usually has been missing from portrayals of Black lesbians in fiction. The degree of truthfulness and self-revelation that Gomez calls for encompasses the essential qualities of verisimilitude and authenticity that I look for in depictions of Black lesbians. By verisimilitude I mean how true to life and realistic a work of literature is. By authenticity I mean something even deeper—a characterization which reflects a relationship to self that is genuine, integrated, and whole. For a lesbian or a gay man, this kind of emotional and psychological authenticity virtually requires the degree of self-acceptance inherent in being out. This is not a dictum but an observation. It is not a coincidence, however, that the most vital and useful Black lesbian feminist writing is being written by Black lesbians who are not caught in the impossible bind of simultaneously hiding identity yet revealing self through their writing.

Positive and realistic portrayals of Black lesbians are sorely needed, portraits which are, as Gomez states, "unadulterated, unsanitized, specific." By positive I do not mean characters without problems, contradictions, or flaws, mere uplift literature for lesbians, but instead writing that is sufficiently sensitive and complex, which places Black lesbian experience and struggles squarely within the realm of recognizable human experience and concerns.

As African Americans, our desire for authentic literary images of Black lesbians has particular cultural and historical resonance,

since a desire for authentic images of ourselves as Black people preceded it long ago. After an initial period of racial uplift literature
in the nineteenth and early twentieth centuries, Black artists
during the Harlem Renaissance of the 1920s began to assert the
validity of fully Black portrayals in all art forms including literature. In his pivotal 1926 essay "The Negro Artist and the Racial
Mountain," Langston Hughes asserted:

> We younger Negro artists who create now intend to express our
> individual dark-skinned selves without fear or shame. If white
> people are pleased we are glad. If they are not, it doesn't matter.
> We know we are beautiful. And ugly too. The tom-tom cries and
> the tom-tom laughs. If colored people are pleased we are glad.
> If they are not, their displeasure doesn't matter either. We build
> our temples for tomorrow, strong as we know how, and we stand
> on top of the mountain, free within ourselves.[12]

Clearly, it is not always popular or safe with either Black or
white audiences to depict Black people as we actually are. Too
many contemporary Blacks seem to have forgotten the universally
debased social-political position Black people have occupied during all the centuries we have been here, up until perhaps the Civil
Rights era of the 1960s. The most racist definition of Black people
was that we were not human.

Undoubtedly every epithet now hurled at lesbians and gay
men—"sinful," "sexually depraved," "criminal," "emotionally mal-
adjusted," "deviant"—has also been hurled at Black people. When
W.E.B. Du Bois described life "behind the veil," and Paul Laurence Dunbar wrote:

> We wear the mask that grins and lies,
> It hides our cheeks and shades our eyes,—
> This debt we pay to human guile;
> With torn and bleeding hearts we smile,
> And mouth with myriad subtleties.

Why should the world be overwise,
In counting all our tears and sighs?
Nay, let them only see us, while
    We wear the mask. . . .[13]

what were they describing but racial closeting? For those who refuse to see the parallels because they view Blackness as irreproachably normal, but persist in defining same-sex love relationships as unnatural, Black lesbian feminist poet Audre Lorde reminds us, "Oh,' says a voice from the Black community, 'but being Black is NORMAL!' 'Well, I and many Black people of my age can remember grimly the days when it didn't used to be!'"[14] Lorde is not implying that she believes that there was ever anything wrong with being Black, but points out how distorted "majority" consciousness can cruelly affect an oppressed community's actual treatment and sense of self. The history of slavery, segregation, and racism was based upon the assumption by the powers that be that Blackness was decidedly neither acceptable nor normal. Unfortunately, despite legal and social change, large numbers of racist whites still believe the same thing to this day.

The existence of lesbianism and male homosexuality is normal, too, traceable throughout history and across cultures. It is a society's *response* to the ongoing historical fact of homosexuality that determines whether it goes unremarked as nothing out of the ordinary, as it is in some cultures, or if it is instead greeted with violent repression, as it is in ours. At a time when Acquired Immune Deficiency Syndrome (AIDS), a disease associated with an already despised sexual minority, is occasioning mass hysteria among the heterosexual majority (including calls for firings, evictions, quarantining, imprisonment, and even execution), the way in which sexual orientation is viewed is not of mere academic concern. It is mass political organizing that has wrought the most significant changes in the status of Blacks and other people of color and that has altered society's perceptions about us and our images of ourselves. The Black lesbian feminist movement simply continues that principled tradition of struggle.

A Black woman author's relationship to the politics of Black lesbian feminism affects how she portrays Black lesbian characters in fiction. In 1977, in "Toward a Black Feminist Criticism," in order to analyze a Black woman's novel with a woman-identified theme, I had to rely upon Toni Morrison's *Sula* (1974), which did not explicitly portray a lesbian relationship. I sought to demonstrate, however, that because of the emotional primacy of Sula and Nel's love for each other, Sula's fierce independence, and the author's critical portrayal of heterosexuality, the novel could be illuminated by a lesbian feminist reading. Here I will focus upon three more recent works—*The Women of Brewster Place*, *The Color Purple*, and *Zami: A New Spelling of My Name*—which actually portray Black lesbians, but do so with varying degrees of verisimilitude and authenticity, dependent upon the author's relationship to and understanding of the politics of Black lesbian experience.

Gloria Naylor's *The Women of Brewster Place* (1983) is a novel composed of seven connecting stories. In beautifully resonant language, Naylor makes strong sexual political statements about the lives of working-poor and working-class Black women and does not hesitate to explore the often problematic nature of their relationships with Black men—lovers, husbands, fathers, sons. Loving and supportive bonds between Black women are central to her characters' survival. However, Naylor's portrayal of a lesbian relationship in the sixth story, "The Two," runs counter to the positive framework of women bonding she has previously established. In the context of this novel, a lesbian relationship might well embody the culmination of women's capacity to love and be committed to each other. Yet both lesbian characters are ultimately victims. Although Naylor portrays the community's homophobia toward the lovers as unacceptable, the fate that she designs for the two women is the most brutal and negative of any in the book.

Theresa is a strong-willed individualist, while her lover, Lorraine, passively yearns for social acceptability. Despite their professional jobs, Lorraine and Theresa have moved to a dead-end slum block because of Lorraine's fears that the residents of their two other middle-class neighborhoods suspected that they were lesbians. It does not take long for suspicions to arise on Brewster Place, and the two women's differing reactions to the inevitable homophobia they face are a major tension in the work. Theresa accepts the fact that she is an outsider because of her lesbianism. She does not like being ostracized, but she faces others' opinions with an attitude of defiance. In contrast, Lorraine is obsessed with garnering societal approval and would like nothing more than to blend into the straight world, despite her lesbianism. Lorraine befriends Ben, the alcoholic building superintendent, because he is the one person on the block who does not reject her. The fact that Ben has lost his daughter and Lorraine has lost her father, because he refused to accept her lesbianism, cements their friendship. Naylor writes:

> "When I'm with Ben, I don't feel any different from anybody else in the world."
>
> "Then he's doing you an injustice," Theresa snapped, "because we are different. And the sooner you learn that, the better off you'll be."
>
> "See, there you go again. Tee the teacher and Lorraine the student, who just can't get the lesson right. Lorraine who just wants to be a human being—a lousy human being who's somebody's daughter or somebody's friend or even somebody's enemy. But they make me feel like a freak out there, and you try to make me feel like one in here. The only place I've found some peace, Tee, is in that damp ugly basement, where I'm not different."
>
> "Lorraine." Theresa shook her head slowly. "You're a lesbian— do you understand that word?—a butch, a dyke, a lesbo, all those things that kid was shouting. Yes, I heard him: And you can run in all the basements in the world, and it won't change that, so why don't you accept it?"
>
> "I have accepted it!" Lorraine shouted. "I've accepted it all my life, and it's nothing I'm ashamed of. I lost a father because I

refused to be ashamed of it—but it doesn't make me any *different* from anyone else in the world."

"It makes you damned different!"

....

"That's right! There go your precious 'theys' again. They wouldn't understand—not in Detroit, not on Brewster Place, not anywhere! And as long as they own the whole damn world, it's them and us, Sister—them and us. And that spells different!"[5]

Many a lesbian relationship has been threatened or destroyed because of how very differently lovers may view their lesbianism— for example, how out or closeted one or the other is willing to be. Naylor's discussion of difference represents a pressing lesbian concern. As Lorraine and Theresa's argument shows, there are complicated elements of truth in both their positions. Lesbians and gay men are objectively different in our sexual orientations from heterosexuals. The society raises sanctions against our sexuality that range from inconvenient to violent and that render our social status and life experiences different. On the other hand, we would like to be recognized and treated as human, to have the basic rights enjoyed by heterosexuals, and if the society cannot manage to support how we love, we would like to at least be left alone.

In "The Two," however, Naylor sets up the women's response to their identity as an either/or dichotomy. Lorraine's desire for acceptance, although completely comprehensible, is based upon assimilation and denial, while Naylor depicts Theresa's healthier defiance as an individual stance. In the clearest statement of resistance in the story, Theresa thinks:

> If they practiced that way with each other, then they could turn back to back and beat the hell out of the world for trying to invade their territory. But she had found no such sparring partner in Lorraine, and the strain of fighting alone was beginning to show on her. (P. 136)

A mediating position between complete assimilation and alienation might well evolve from some sense of connection to a lesbian/gay community. Involvement with other lesbians and gay men could provide a reference point and support that would help diffuse some of the straight world's power. Naylor mentions that Theresa socializes with gay men and perhaps lesbians at a bar, but her interactions with them occur outside the action of the story. The author's decision not to portray other lesbians and gay men, but only to allude to them, is a significant one. The reader is never given an opportunity to view Theresa or Lorraine in a context in which she is the norm. Naylor instead presents them as "the two" exceptions in an entirely heterosexual world. Both women are isolated, and although their relationship is loving, it also feels claustrophobic. Naylor writes:

> Lorraine wanted to be liked by the people around her. She couldn't live the way Tee did, with her head stuck in a book all the time. Tee didn't seem to need anyone. Lorraine often wondered if she even needed her.
>
> She never wanted to bother with anyone except those weirdos at the club she went to, and Lorraine hated them. They were coarse and bitter, and made fun of people who weren't like them. Well, she wasn't like them either. Why should she feel different from the people she lived around? Black people were all in the same boat—she'd come to realize this even more since they had moved to Brewster—and if they didn't row together, they would sink together. (P. 142)

Lorraine's rejection of other lesbians and gay men is excruciating, as is the self-hatred that obviously prompts it. It is painfully ironic that she considers herself in the same boat with Black people in the story who are heterosexual, most of whom ostracize her, but not with Black people who are lesbian and gay. The one time that Lorraine actually decides to go to the club by herself, ignoring Theresa's warning that she won't have a good time without her, is the night that she is literally destroyed.

Perhaps the most positive element in "The Two" is how accurately Naylor depicts and subtly condemns Black homophobia.

Sophie, a neighbor who lives across the airshaft from Lorraine and Theresa, is the "willing carrier" of the rumor about them, though not necessarily its initiator. Naylor writes:

> Sophie had plenty to report that day. Ben had said it was terrible in there. No, she didn't know exactly what he had seen, but you can imagine—and they did. Confronted with the difference that had been thrust into their predictable world, they reached into their imaginations and, using an ancient pattern, weaved themselves a reason for its existence. Out of necessity they stitched all of their secret fears and lingering childhood nightmares into this exis- tence, because even though it was deceptive enough to try and look as they looked, talk as they talked, and do as they did, it had to have some hidden stain to invalidate it—it was impossible for them both to be right. So they leaned back, supported by the sheer weight of their numbers and comforted by the woven barrier that kept them protected from the yellow mist that enshrouded the two as they came and went on Brewster Place. (P. 132)

The fact of difference can be particularly volatile among people whose options are severely limited by racial, class, and sexual oppression, people who are already outsiders themselves.

A conversation between Mattie Michaels, an older Black woman who functions as the work's ethical and spiritual center, and her lifelong friend, Etta, further prods the reader to examine her own attitudes about loving women. Etta explains,

> "Yeah, but it's different with them."
>
> "Different how?"
>
> "Well . . ." Etta was beginning to feel uncomfortable.
>
> "They love each other like you'd love a man or a man would love you—I guess."
>
> "But I've loved some women deeper than I ever loved any man," Mattie was pondering. "And there been some women who loved me more and did more for me than any man ever did."
>
> "Yeah." Etta thought for a moment. "I can second that but it's still different, Mattie. I can't exactly put my finger on it, but . . ."

"Maybe it's not so different," Mattie said, almost to herself. "Maybe that's why some women get so riled up about it, 'cause they know deep down it's not so different after all." She looked at Etta. "It kinda gives you a funny feeling when you think about it that way, though."

"Yeah, it does," Etta said, unable to meet Mattie's eyes. (Pp. 140–141)

Whatever their opinions, it is not the women of the neighborhood who are directly responsible for Lorraine's destruction, but six actively homophobic and woman-hating teenage boys. Earlier that day Lorraine and Kiswana Browne had encountered the toughs, who had unleashed their sexist and homophobic violence on the two women. Kiswana had verbally bested their leader, C. C. Baker, but he was dissuaded from physically retaliating because one of the other boys reminded him: "'That's Abshu's woman, and that big dude don't mind kickin' ass'" (p. 163). As a lesbian, Lorraine did not have any kind of "dude" to stand between her and the violence of other men. Although she was completely silent during the encounter, C. C.'s parting words to her were, "'I'm gonna remember this, Butch!'" That night when Lorraine returns from the bar alone, she walks into the alley which is the boys' turf. They are waiting for her and gang-rape her in one of the most devastating scenes in literature. Naylor describes the aftermath:

Lorraine lay pushed up against the wall on the cold ground with her eyes staring straight up into the sky. When the sun began to warm the air and the horizon brightened, she still lay there, her mouth crammed with paper bag, her dress pushed up under her breasts, her bloody pantyhose hanging from her thighs. She would have stayed there forever and have simply died from starvation or exposure if nothing around her had moved. (P. 171)

She glimpses Ben sitting on a garbage can at the other end of the alley sipping wine. In a bizarre twist of an ending, Lorraine crawls through the alley and mauls him with a brick she happens to find as she makes her way toward him. Lorraine's supplicating cries of "'Please. Please.' . . . the only word she was fated to utter again and again for the rest of her life," conclude the story (p. 173).

I began thinking about "The Two" because of a conversation I had with another Black lesbian who seldom comes into contact with other lesbians and who has not been active in the feminist movement. Unlike other women with whom I had discussed the work, she was not angry, disappointed, or disturbed by it, but instead thought it was an effective portrayal of lesbians and homophobia. I was taken aback because I had found Naylor's depiction of our lives so completely demoralizing and not particularly realistic. I thought about another friend who told me she had found the story so upsetting she was never able to finish it. And of another who had actually rewritten the ending so that Mattie hears Lorraine's screams before she is raped and saves her. In this "revised version," Theresa is an undercover cop who also hears her lover's screams, comes into the alley with a gun, and blows the boys away. I was so mystified and intrigued by the first woman's defense of Naylor's perspective that I went back to examine the work.

According to the criteria I have suggested, although the lesbian characters in "The Two" lack authenticity, the story possesses a certain level of verisimilitude. The generalized homophobia that the women face, which culminates in retaliatory rape and near-murderous decimation, is quite true to life. Gay and lesbian newspapers provide weekly accounts, which sometimes surface in the mainstream media, of the constant violence leveled at members of our communities. What feels disturbing and inauthentic to me is how utterly hopeless Naylor's view of lesbian existence is. Lorraine and Theresa are classically unhappy homosexuals of the type who populated white literature during a much earlier era, when the only alternatives for the "deviant" were isolation, loneliness, mental illness, suicide, or death.

In her second novel, *Linden Hills* (1985), Naylor indicates that Black gay men's options are equally grim. In a review of the work, Jewelle Gomez writes:

One character disavows a liaison with his male lover in order to marry the appropriate woman and inherit the coveted Linden Hills home. . . . We receive so little personal information about him that his motivations are obscure. For a middle-class, educated gay man to be blind to alternative lifestyles in 1985 is not inconceivable but it's still hard to accept the melodrama of his arranged marriage without screaming "dump the girl and buy a ticket to Grand Rapids!" Naylor's earlier novel [*The Women of Brewster Place*] presented a similar limitation. While she admirably attempts to portray black gays as integral to the fabric of black life she seems incapable of imagining black gays functioning as healthy, average people. In her fiction, although they are not at fault, gays must still be made to pay. This makes her books sound like a return to the forties, not a chronicle of the eighties.[16]

Gomez's response speaks to the problems that many lesbian feminists have with Naylor's versions of our lives, her persistent message that survival is hardly possible. I do not think we simply want "happy endings"—although some do occur for lesbians both in literature and in life—but an indication of the spirit of survival and resistance which has made the continuance of Black lesbian and gay life possible throughout the ages.

In considering the overall impact of "The Two," I realized that because it is critical of homophobia, it is perhaps an effective story for a heterosexual audience. But because its portrayal of lesbianism is so negative, its message even to heterosexuals is ambiguous. A semisympathetic straight reader's response might well be: "It's a shame something like that had to happen, but I guess that's what you get for being queer." The general public does not want to know that it is possible to be a lesbian of whatever color and not merely survive but thrive. And neither does a heterosexual publishing industry want to provide them with this information.

The impact of the story upon lesbian readers is quite another matter. I imagine what might happen if a Black woman who was grappling with defining her sexuality and who had never had the opportunity to read anything else about lesbians, particularly

Black ones, were to read "The Two" as a severely cautionary tale. Justifiably, she might go no further in her exploration, forever denying her feelings. She might eventually have sexual relationships with other women, but remain extremely closeted. Or she might commit suicide. Naylor's dire pessimism about our possibilities lies at the crux of the problems I, a Black lesbian reader, have with "The Two." Alice Walker's portrayal of a lesbian relationship in her novel *The Color Purple* (1982) is as optimistic as Naylor's is despairing. Celie and Shug's love, placed at the center of the work and set in a rural southern community between the world wars, is unique in the history of African American fiction. The fact that a book with a Black lesbian theme by a Black woman writer achieved massive critical acclaim, became a bestseller, and was made into a major Hollywood film is unprecedented in the history of the world. It is *The Color Purple* to which homophobes and anti-feminists undoubtedly refer when they talk about how "many" books currently have both Black lesbian subject matter and an unsparing critique of misogyny in the Black community. For Black lesbians, however, especially writers, the book has been inspirational. Reading it, we think it just may be possible to be a Black lesbian and live to tell about it. It may be possible for us to write it down and actually have somebody read it as well.

When I first read *The Color Purple* in galleys in the spring of 1982, I believed it was a classic. I become more convinced every time I read it. Besides great storytelling, perfect Black language, killingly subtle Black women's humor, and an unequivocal Black feminist stance, it is also a deeply philosophical and spiritual work. It is marvelously gratifying to read discussions of nature, love, beauty, God, good, evil, and the meaning of life in the language of our people. The book is like a jewel. Any way you hold it to the light, you will always see something new reflected.

The facet of the novel under consideration here is Walker's approach to lesbianism, but before I go further with that discussion, it is helpful to understand that the work is also a fable. The complex simplicity with which Walker tells the story, the archetypical and

timeless Black southern world in which she sets it, the clear-cut conflicts between good and evil, the complete transformations undergone by several of the major characters, and the huge capacity of the
book to teach are all signs that *The Color Purple* is not merely a novel
but a visionary tale. That it is a fable may account partially for the
depiction of a lesbian relationship unencumbered by homophobia or
fear of it and entirely lacking in self-scrutiny about the implications
of lesbian identity.

It may be Walker's conscious decision to deal with her readers' potentially negative reactions by using the disarming strategy of writing as if women falling in love with each other were
quite ordinary, an average occurrence which does not even need
to be specifically remarked. In the "real world" the complete
ease with which Celie and Shug move as lovers through a totally
heterosexual milieu would be improbable, not to say amazing.
Their total acceptance is one clue that this is indeed an inspiring
fable, a picture of what the world could be if only human beings
were ready to create it. A friend told me about a discussion of the
book in a Black writers' workshop she conducted. An older
Black woman in the class asserted: "When that kind of business
happens, like happened between Shug and Celie, you know
there's going to be talk." The woman was not reacting to *Purple*
as a fable or even as fiction, but as a "real" story, applying her
knowledge of what would undoubtedly happen in real life,
where most people just aren't ready to deal with lesbianism and
don't want to be.

Because the novel is so truthful, particularly in its descriptions
of sexual oppression and to a lesser extent racism, the reader under-
standably might question those aspects of the fable which are not
as plausible. Even within the story itself, it is conceivable that a
creature as mean-spirited as Mr. —————— might have something to say about Shug, the love of his life, and Celie, his wife,
sleeping together in his own house. For those of us who experience
homophobia on a daily basis and who often live in fear of being
discovered by the wrong person(s), like the teenage thugs in "The

Two," we naturally wonder how Celie and Shug, who do not hide their relationship, get away with it.

Another fabulous aspect of Celie's and Shug's relationship is that there are no references to how they think about themselves as lesbian lovers in a situation where they are the only ones. Although Celie is clearly depicted as a woman who at the very least is not attracted to men and who is generally repulsed by them, I am somewhat hesitant to designate her as a lesbian because it is not a term that she would likely apply to herself, and neither, obviously, would the people around her. In a conversation with Mr. —————— in the latter part of the book, Celie explains how she feels:

> He say, Celie, tell me the truth. You don't like me cause I'm a man?
>
> I blow my nose. Take off they pants, I say, and men look like frogs to me. No matter how you kiss 'em, as far as I'm concern, frogs is what they stay.
>
> I see, he say.[17]

Shug, on the other hand, is bisexual, another contemporary term that does not necessarily apply within the cultural and social context Walker has established. There is the implication that this is among her first, if it is not her only, sexual relationship with another woman. The only time within the novel when Shug and Celie make love, Walker writes:

> She say, I love you, Miss Celie. And then she haul off and kiss me on the mouth.
>
> *Um*, she say, like she surprise. I kiss her back, say, *um*, too. Us kiss and kiss till us can't hardly kiss no more. Then us touch each other.
>
> I don't know nothing bout it, I say to Shug.
>
> I don't know much, she say. (P. 109)

Despite her statement of inexperience, Shug is a wonderfully sensual and attractive woman who takes pleasure in all aspects of living, from noticing "the color purple in a field" to making love with whomever. When Shug tries to explain to Celie why she has taken up with a nineteen-year-old boy, the two women's differing perspectives and sexual orientations are obvious. Walker writes:

> But Celie, she say. I have to make you understand. Look, she say. I'm gitting old. I'm fat. Nobody think I'm good looking no more, but you. Or so I thought. He's nineteen. A baby. How long can it last?
> He's a man. I write on the paper.
> Yah, she say. He is. And I know how you feel about men. But I don't feel that way. I would never be fool enough to take any of them seriously, she say, but some mens can be a lots of fun.
> Spare me, I write. (P. 220)

Eventually Shug comes back to Celie, and Walker implies that they will live out their later years together. The recouplings and reunions that occur in the novel might also indicate that the story is more fantasy than fact. But in Celie and Shug's case, the longevity of their relationship is certainly a validation of love between women.

The day Shug returns, Celie shows her her new bedroom. Walker writes:

> She go right to the little purple frog on my mantelpiece.
> What this? she ast.
> Oh, I say, a little something Albert carve for me. (P. 248)

Not only is this wickedly amusing after Celie and Mr. ————'s discussion about "frogs," but Mr. ————'s tolerance at being described as such to the point of his making a joke gift for Celie seems almost too good to be true. Indeed, Mr. ————'s transformation from evil no-account to a sensitive human being is one of the most miraculous one could find anywhere. Those critics and readers who condemn the work because they find the depiction of men so "negative" never seem to focus on how nicely most of them turn out in the end. Perhaps these transformations go unnoticed because in Walker's woman-centered world, in order to change, they must relinquish machismo and violence, the very thought of which would be fundamentally disruptive to the nonfeminist reader's world view. It is no accident that Walker has Celie, who has become a professional seamstress and designer of pants, teach Mr. ———————— to sew, an ideal way to symbolize just how far he has come. In the real world, where former husbands of lesbian mothers take their children away with the support of the patriarchal legal system and in some cases beat or even murder their former wives, very few men would say what Mr. ———————— says to Celie about Shug: "I'm real sorry she left you, Celie. I remembered how I felt when she left me" (p. 238). But in the world of *The Color Purple*, a great deal is possible.

One of the most beautiful and familiar aspects of the novel is the essential and supportive bonds between Black women. The only other person Celie loves before she meets Shug is her long-lost sister, Nettie. Although neither ever gets an answer, the letters they write to each other for decades and Celie's letters to God before she discovers that Nettie is alive constitute the entire novel. The work joyously culminates when Nettie, accompanied by Celie's children who were taken away from her in infancy, returns home.

Early in the novel Celie "sins against" another woman's spirit and painfully bears the consequences. She tells her stepson, Harpo, to beat his wife, Sofia, if she won't mind him. Soon Celie is so upset about what she has done that she is unable to sleep at night. Sofia, one of the most exquisitely defiant characters in Black women's fiction, fights Harpo right back, and when she finds out Celie's part in Harpo's changed behavior, she comes to confront her. When Celie confesses that she advised Harpo to beat Sofia because she was jealous of Sofia's ability to stand up for herself, the weight is lifted from her soul, the women become fast friends, and she "sleeps like a baby."

When Shug decides that Celie needs to leave Mr. ————————and go with her to Memphis, accompanied by Mary Agnes

(Squeak), Harpo's lover of many years, they make the announcement at a family dinner. Walker writes:

> You was all rotten children, I say. You made my life a hell on earth. And your daddy here ain't dead horse's shit.
> Mr. ————— reach over to slap me. I jab my case knife in his hand.
> You bitch, he say. What will people say, you running off to Memphis like you don't have a house to look after?
> Shug say, Albert. Try to think like you got some sense.
> Why any woman give a shit what people think is a mystery to me.
> Well, say Grady, trying to bring light. A woman can't git a man if peoples talk.
> Shug look at me and us giggle. Then us laugh sure nuff. Then Squeak start to laugh. Then Sofia. All us laugh and laugh.
> Shug say, Ain't they something? Us say um *hum*, and slap the table, wipe the water from our eyes.
> Harpo look at Squeak. Shut up Squeak, he say. It bad luck for women to laugh at men.
> She say, Okay. She sit up straight, suck in her breath, try to press her face together.
> He look at Sofia. She look at him and laugh in his face. I already had my bad luck, she say. I had enough to keep me laughing the rest of my life. (P. 182)

This marvelously hilarious scene is one of the countless examples in the novel of Black women's staunch solidarity. As in *The Women of Brewster Place*, women's caring for each other makes life possible; but in *The Color Purple* Celie and Shug's relationship is accepted as an integral part of the continuum of women loving each other, while in the more realistic work, Lorraine and Theresa are portrayed as social pariahs.

If one accepts that *The Color Purple* is a fable or at the very least has fablelike elements, judgments of verisimilitude and authenticity are necessarily affected. Celie and Shug are undeniably authentic as Black women characters—complex, solid, and whole—but they are not necessarily authentic as lesbians. Their lack of self-consciousness as lesbians, the lack of scrutiny their relationship receives from the outside world, and their isolation from other lesbians make *The Color Purple*'s categorization as a lesbian novel problematic. It does not appear that it was Walker's intent to create a work that could be definitively or solely categorized as such.

The question of categorization becomes even more interesting when one examines critical responses to the work, particularly in the popular media. Reviews seldom mention that Celie and Shug are lovers. Some critics even go so far as to describe them erroneously as good friends. The fact that their relationship is simply "there" in the novel and not explicitly called attention to as lesbian might also account for a mass heterosexual audience's capacity to accept the work, although the novel has of course also been homophobically attacked.[18] As a Black lesbian feminist reader, I have questions about how accurate it is to identify Walker's characters as lesbians per se, at the same time that I am moved by the vision of a world, unlike this one, where Black women are not forced to lose their families, their community, or their lives because of whom they love.

A realistic depiction of African American lesbian experience would be neither a complete idyll nor a total nightmare. Audre Lorde terms *Zami: A New Spelling of My Name* (1982) a "biomythography," a combination of autobiography, history, and myth. I have chosen to discuss it here because it is the one extended prose work of which I am aware that approaches Black lesbian experience with *both* verisimilitude and authenticity. *Zami* is an essentially autobiographical work, but the poet's eye, ear, and tongue give the work stylistic richness often associated with well-crafted fiction. At least two other Black women critics, Barbara Christian and Jewelle Gomez, have included *Zami* in their analyses of Black lesbians in fiction.[19] Because *Zami* spans genres and carves out a unique place in African American literature as the first full-length autobiographical work by an established Black lesbian writer, it will undoubtedly continue to be grouped with other creative prose about Black lesbians.

The fact that *Zami* is autobiographical might be assumed to guarantee its realism. But even when writing autobiographically, an author can pick and choose details, can create a persona which has little or nothing to do with her own particular reality, or she might fabricate an artificial persona with whom the reader cannot possibly identify. A blatant example of this kind of deceptive strategy might be an autobiographical work by a lesbian which fails to mention that this is indeed who she is; of course, there are other, less extreme omissions and distortions. Undoubtedly, Lorde selected the material she included in the work, and the selectivity of memory is also operative. Yet this work is honest, fully rounded, and authentic. It is not coincidental that of the three works considered here, *Zami* has the most to tell the reader about the texture of Black lesbian experience, and that it was written by an out Black lesbian feminist. The candor and specificity with which Lorde approaches her life are qualities that would enhance Black lesbian writing in the future.

Zami is a Carriacou word for "women who work together as friends and lovers."[20] Just as the title implies, *Zami* is woman-identified from the outset and thoroughly suffused with an eroticism focusing on women. Lorde connects her lesbianism to the model her mother, Linda, provided—her pervasive, often intimidating, strength; her fleeting sensuality when her harsh veneer was lifted—and also to her place of origin, the Grenadian island of Carriacou, where a word already existed to describe who Linda's daughter would become. As in *The Color Purple* and *The Women of Brewster Place*, in *Zami* relationships between women are at the center of the work. Here they are complex, turbulent, painful, passionate, and essential to the author's survival.

Although Lorde continuously explores the implications of being a Black lesbian and she has an overt consciousness about her lesbianism which is missing from Naylor's and Walker's works, she does not define lesbianism as a problem in and of itself. Despite homophobia, particularly in the left of the McCarthy era; despite isolation from other Black women because she is gay; and despite primal loneliness because of her many levels of difference, Lorde assumes that her lesbianism, like her Blackness, is a given, a fact of life which she has neither to justify nor explain. This is an extremely strong and open-ended stance from which to write about Black lesbian experience, since it enables the writer to deal with the complexity of lesbianism and what being a Black lesbian means in a specific time and place. Lorde's position allows Black lesbian experience to be revealed from the inside out. The absence of agonized doubts about her sexual orientation and the revelation of the actual joys of being a lesbian, including lust and recognizable descriptions of physical passion between women, make *Zami* seem consciously written for a lesbian reader. This is a significant point, because so little is ever written with us in mind, and also because who an author considers her audience to be definitely affects her voice and the levels of authenticity she may be able to achieve. Writing from an avowedly Black lesbian perspective with Black lesbian readers in mind does not mean that a work will be inaccessible or inapplicable to non-Black and nonlesbian readers. Works such as *Zami*, which are based in the experiences of writers outside the "mainstream," provide a vitally different perspective on human experience and may even reveal new ways of thinking about supposedly settled questions. Or, as Celie puts it in *The Color Purple*: "If he [God] ever listened to poor colored women the world would be a different place, I can tell you" (p. 175). It would be more different still if "he" also listened to lesbians.

The fact that *Zami* is written from an unequivocally Black lesbian and feminist perspective undoubtedly explains why it is the one book of the three under discussion that is published by an alternative press, why it was turned down by at least a dozen trade publishers, including one that specializes in gay titles. The white male editor at that supposedly sympathetic house returned the manuscript saying, "If only you were just one," Black or lesbian. The combination is obviously too much for the trade publishing establishment to handle. We bring news that others do not want to hear. It is unfortunate that the vast majority of the readers of *The Women of Brewster Place* and *The Color Purple* will never have the opportunity to read *Zami*.

Lorde's description of Black "gay-girl" life in the Greenwich Village of the 1950s is fascinating, if for no other reason than that it reveals a piece of our cultural history. What is even more intriguing is her political activist's sense of how the struggles of women during that era helped shape our contemporary movement and how many of our current issues, especially the desire to build a Black lesbian community, were very much a concern at that time. The author's search for other Black lesbians and her lovingly detailed descriptions of the fragments of community she finds give this work an atmosphere of reality missing in "The Two" and *The Color Purple*. Unlike Lorraine and Theresa and Celie and Shug, Lorde is achingly aware of her need for peers. She writes:

> I remember how being young and Black and gay and lonely felt. A lot of it was fine, feeling I had the truth and the light and the key, but a lot of it was purely hell.
>
> There were no mothers, no sisters, no heroes. We had to do it alone, like our sister Amazons, the riders on the loneliest outposts of the kingdom of Dahomey.
>
> . . . .
>
> There were not enough of us. But we surely tried. (Pp. 176–177)
>
> . . . .
>
> Every Black woman I ever met in the Village in those years had some part in my survival, large or small, if only as a figure in the head-count at the Bag on a Friday night.
>
> Black lesbians in the Bagatelle faced a world only slightly less hostile than the outer world which we had to deal with every day on the outside—that world which defined us as doubly nothing because we were Black and because we were Woman—that world which raised our blood pressures and shaped our furies and our nightmares.
>
> . . . .
>
> All of us who survived these common years have to be a little proud. A lot proud. Keeping ourselves together and on our own tracks, however wobbly, was like trying to play the Dinizulu War Chant or a Beethoven sonata on a tin dog-whistle. (P. 225)

The humor, tenacity, and vulnerability which Lorde brings to her version of being in "the life" are very precious. Here is something to grab hold of, a place to see one's face reflected. Despite the daily grind of racism, homophobia, sexual and class oppression, compounded by the nonsolutions of alcohol, drugs, suicide, and death at an early age, some women did indeed make it.

Lorde also describes the much more frequent interactions and support available from white lesbians, who were in the numerical majority. Just as they are now, relationships between Black and white women in the 1950s were often undermined by racism, but Lorde documents that some women were at least attempting to deal with their differences. She writes:

> However imperfectly, we tried to build a community of sorts where we could, at the very least, survive within a world we correctly perceived to be hostile to us; we talked endlessly about how best to create that mutual support which twenty years later was being discussed in the women's movement as a brand new concept. Lesbians were probably the only Black and white women in New York City in the fifties who were making any real attempt to communicate with each other; we learned lessons from each other, the values of which were not lessened by what we did not learn. (P. 179)

Lorde approaches the meaning of difference from numerous vantage points in *Zami*. In much of her work prior to *Zami* she has articulated and developed the concept of difference which has gained usage in the women's movement as a whole and in the writing of women of color specifically. From her early childhood, long before she recognizes herself as a lesbian, the question of difference is *Zami*'s subtext, its ever present theme. Lorde writes: "*It was in high school that I came to believe that I was different from my white classmates, not because I was Black, but because I was me*" (p. 82). Although Lorde comes of age in an era when little, if any, tolerance exists for those who do not conform to white-male hegemony, her stance and that of her friends is one of rebellion and creative resistance, including political activism, as opposed to conformity and victimization. *Zami* mediates the versions of lesbianism presented in *The Women of Brewster Place* and *The Color Purple*. It is not a horror story, although it reveals the difficulties of Black lesbian experience. It is not a fable, although it reveals the joys of a life committed to women.

Since much of her quest in *Zami* is to connect with women who recognize and share her differences, particularly other Black lesbians, it seems fitting that the work closes with her account of a loving relationship with another Black woman, Afrekete. Several years before the two women become lovers, Lorde meets Kitty at a Black lesbian house party in Queens. Lorde writes:

> One of the women I had met at one of these parties was Kitty.
>
> When I saw Kitty again one night years later in the Swing Rendezvous or the Pony Stable or the Page Three—that tour of second-string gay-girl bars that I had taken to making alone that sad lonely spring of 1957—it was easy to recall the St. Alban's smell of green Queens summer-night and plastic couch-covers and liquor and hair oil and women's bodies at the party where we had first met.
>
> In that brick-faced frame house in Queens, the downstairs pine-paneled recreation room was alive and pulsing with loud music, good food, and beautiful Black women in all different combinations of dress. (P. 241)

The women wear fifties dyke-chic, ranging from "skinny straight skirts" to Bermuda and Jamaica shorts. Just as the clothes, the smells, the song lyrics, and food linger in the author's mind, her fully rendered details of Black lesbian culture resonate within the reader. I recalled this party scene while attending a dinner party at the home of two Black lesbians in the Deep South earlier this year. One of the hostesses arrived dressed impeccably in white Bermuda shorts, black kneesocks, and loafers. Her hair straightened 1980s-style, much like that of the 1950s, completed my sense of déjà vu. Contemporary Black lesbians are a part of a cultural tradition which we are just beginning to discover through interviews with older women such as Mabel Hampton and the writing of authors such as Ann Allen Shockley, Anita Cornwell, Pat Parker, and Lorde.

When she meets Afrekete again, their relationship helps to counteract Lorde's loneliness following the breakup of a long-term relationship with a white woman. The bond between the women is stunningly erotic, enriched by the bond they share as Black women. Lorde writes:

> By the beginning of summer the walls of Afrekete's apartment were always warm to the touch from the heat beating down on the roof, and chance breezes through her windows rustled her plants in the window and brushed over our sweat-smooth bodies, at rest after loving.
>
> We talked sometimes about what it meant to love women, and what a relief it was in the eye of the storm, no matter how often we had to bite our tongues and stay silent.
>
> . . . .
>
> Once we talked about how Black women had been committed without choice to waging our campaigns in the enemies' strong-holds, too much and too often, and how our psychic landscapes had been plundered and wearied by those repeated battles and campaigns.
>
> "And don't I have the scars to prove it," she sighed. "Makes you tough though, babe, if you don't go under. And that's what I like about you; you're like me. We're both going to make it because we're both too tough and crazy not to!" And we held each other and laughed and cried about what we had paid for that tough-ness, and how hard it was to explain to anyone who didn't already know it that soft and tough had to be one and the same for either to work at all, like our joy and the tears mingling on the one pil-low beneath our heads. (P. 250)

The fact that this conversation occurs in 1957 is both amazing and unremarkable. Black lesbians have a heritage far older than a few decades, a past that dates back to Africa, as Lorde herself docu-ments in the essay "Scratching the Surface: Some Notes on Bar-riers to Women and Loving."[21] Lorde's authentic portrayal of one segment of that history in *Zami* enables us to see both our pasts and our futures more clearly. Her work provides a vision of possibility for Black lesbians surviving whole, despite all, which is the very least we can demand from our literature, our activism, and our lives.

Despite the homophobic exclusion and silencing of Black lesbian writers, the creation of complex, accurate, and artistically compelling depictions of Black lesbians in literature has been and will continue to be essential to the development of African American women's literature as a whole. The assertion of Black women's rights to autonomy and freedom, which is inherent in the lives of Black lesbians and which is made politically explicit in Black lesbian feminist theory and practice, has crucial implications for all women's potential liberation. Yet far too many nonlesbian Black women who are actively involved in defining the African American women's literary renaissance as critics, teachers, readers, and writers completely ignore Black lesbian existence or are actively hostile to it.

Black women's homophobia in literary and nonliterary contexts negates any claims that they might make to honoring Black feminist principles or to respecting the even older tradition of Black women's sisterhood from which Black feminism springs. Ironically, excluding or attacking Black lesbians often marginalizes the very women who have built the political and cultural foundations that have made this renaissance possible.

Ultimately, the truth that never hurts is that Black lesbians and specifically Black lesbian writers are here to stay. In spite of every effort to erase us, we are committed to living visibly with integrity and courage and to telling our Black women's stories for centuries to come.

1985/1989

Notes

1. Calvin Hernton, "The Sexual Mountain and Black Women Writers," *The Black Scholar* 16, no. 4 (July/August 1985): 7.

2. Barbara Christian, *Black Feminist Criticism: Perspectives on Black Women Writers* (New York: Pergamon Press, 1986), 188.

3. Audre Lorde and Ann Allen Shockley are two exceptions. They have published with both commercial and independent publishers. It should be noted that Lorde's poetry is currently published by a commercial publisher, but that all of her works of prose have been published by independent women's presses. In conversation with Lorde I have learned that *Zami: A New Spelling of My Name* was rejected by at least a dozen commercial publishers.

4. Christian, *Black Feminist Criticism*, 199–200.

5. Alice Walker, "Breaking Chains and Encouraging Life," in *In Search of Our Mothers' Gardens: Womanist Prose* (New York: Harcourt Brace, 1983), 288–289.

6. In her essay "The Black Lesbian in American Literature: An Overview," Ann Allen Shockley summarizes Jones's negative or inadequate treatment of lesbian themes in her novels *Corregidora* and *Eva's Man* and in two of her short stories. Ann Allen Shockley, "The Black Lesbian in American Literature: An Overview," in *Home Girls: A Black Feminist Anthology*, ed. Barbara Smith (Latham, N.Y.: Kitchen Table: Women of Color Press, 1982), 89.

7. In her essay "The Failure to Transform: Homophobia in the Black Community," Cheryl Clarke comments: "The black lesbian is not only absent from the pages of black political analysis, her image as a character in literature and her role as a writer are blotted out from or trivialized in literary criticism written by black women." Clarke also cites examples of such omissions. In *Home Girls*, ed. Smith, 204–205.

8. Barbara Smith, "Racism and Women's Studies," in *All the Women Are White, All the Blacks Are Men, But Some of Us Are Brave: Black Women's Studies*, ed. Gloria T. Hull, Patricia Bell Scott, and Barbara Smith (New York: The Feminist Press at The City University of New York, 1981), 49.

9. Mitsuye Yamada, "Invisibility Is an Unnatural Disaster: Reflections of an Asian American Woman," in *This Bridge Called My Back: Writings by Radical Women of Color*, ed. Cherríe Moraga and Gloria Anzaldúa (Latham, N.Y.: Kitchen Table: Women of Color Press, 1984), 35–40.

10. Cheryl Clarke, *Narratives: Poems in the Tradition of Black Women* (Latham, N.Y.: Kitchen Table: Women of Color Press, 1983), 15.

11. Jewelle Gomez, "A Cultural Legacy Denied and Discovered: Black Lesbians in Fiction by Women," in *Home Girls*, ed. Smith, 122.

12. Langston Hughes, "The Negro Artist and the Racial Mountain," in *Voices from the Harlem Renaissance*, ed. Nathan Huggins (New York: Oxford University Press, 1976), 309. It is interesting to note that recent research has revealed that Hughes and a number of other major figures of the Harlem Renaissance were gay. See Charles Michael Smith, "Bruce Nugent: Bohemian of the Harlem Renaissance," in *In the Life: A Black Gay Anthology*, ed. Joseph F. Beam (Boston: Alyson Publications, 1986), 213–214 and selections by Langston Hughes in *Gay and Lesbian Poetry in Our Time: An Anthology*, ed. Carl Morse and Joan Larkin (New York: St. Martin's Press, 1988), 204–206.

13. Paul Laurence Dunbar, "We Wear the Mask," in *The Life and Works of Paul Laurence Dunbar*, ed. Lida Keck Wiggins (New York: Kraus, 1971), 184.

14. Audre Lorde, "There Is No Hierarchy of Oppressions," *The Council on Interracial Books for Children Bulletin, Homophobia and Education: How to Deal with Name-Calling*, ed. Leonore Gordon, vol. 14, nos. 3 & 4 (1983): 9.

15. Gloria Naylor, *The Women of Brewster Place* (New York: Penguin, 1983), 165–166. All subsequent references to this work will be cited in the text.

16. Jewelle Gomez, "Naylor's Inferno," *The Women's Review of Books* 2, no. 11 (August 1985): 8.

17. Alice Walker, *The Color Purple* (New York: Washington Square Press, 1982), 224. All subsequent references to this work will be cited in the text.

18. In his essay "Who's Afraid of Alice Walker?" Calvin Hernton describes the "hordes of . . . black men (and some women)" who condemned both the novel and the film of *The Color Purple* all over the country. He singles out journalist Tony Brown as a highly visible leader of these attacks. Brown both broadcast television shows and wrote columns about a book and movie he admitted neither to have read nor seen. Hernton raises the question, "Can it be that the homophobic, nitpicking screams of denial against *The Color Purple* are motivated out of envy, jealousy and guilt, rather than out of any genuine concern for the well-being of black people?" Calvin Hernton, *The Sexual Mountain and Black Women Writers* (New York: Anchor Books, 1987), 30–36.

19. Christian, *Black Feminist Criticism*, 187–210. Gomez, in *Home Girls*, ed. Smith, 118–119.

20. Audre Lorde, *Zami: A New Spelling of My Name* (Freedom, Calif.: Crossing Press, 1983), 255. All subsequent references to this work will be cited in the text.

21. Audre Lorde, *Sister Outsider* (Freedom, Calif.: Crossing Press, 1984), 45–52.

Among all of my work, I generally consider this tribute to James Baldwin, published in Boston's *Gay Community News*, my favorite. Of course I valued the opportunity to write about the person who had been so important to my development as a writer. Even more, I appreciated the chance to do something different—to describe an actual event, evoking in writing the physical space, the music, the words, the feel of a highly dramatic occurrence.

The Cathedral of St. John the Divine in New York City, where Baldwin's funeral was held, became a place I love to visit. In January 1993 I delivered a tribute from the pulpit of the Cathedral to my friend Audre Lorde at her memorial service there.

We Must Always Bury Our Dead Twice

A Tribute to James Baldwin

When I was growing up in Cleveland in the 1950s and early 1960s, there were two things I wanted, above all. One was to escape the bounds of that big midwestern city, to see wondrous places, especially New York and Paris. The other was to write.

Of all the books that I devoured during those years, it was James Baldwin's that most inspired my dreams. Fortunately, the first work I read by him was *Go Tell It on the Mountain*, which like all the Black literature my sister and I had the opportunity to read in those pre–Black Studies days, was brought home to us from the library by our Aunt LaRue. The book astounded me. For the first time I encountered somebody in fiction whose life was very much like my own, as opposed to being the polar opposite. The novel offered me the rarest gift, the gift of possibility. If John Grimes, growing up poor and Black in Harlem in the 1930s, who was as much of an outsider as I had ever been, could be a writer, then maybe so could I.

I loved James Baldwin, not only because he made me want to shape prose with a clarity and fire that gave it the power to make people change, but because his life showed me a way out. Simply because he existed, I might not have to go to a state school, get a good job working for a utility company, become a wife, keep on going to church, and always stay in Cleveland. I did not acknowledge that I had lesbian feelings until I was in my twenties, but long before that Baldwin's homosexuality was also a hopeful sign. If nothing else, it indicated his capacity to radically nonconform, to carve out his own emotional freedom, lessons that I myself would need to learn.

When I heard that he had died, just a few weeks after a death in my own family, I knew yet again how important this man had been to me. And I felt extremely lonely; someone who I only knew through his writing, but who had been a guide to me, was no longer here.

A few days later, completely exhausted from a long weekend away at a National Coalition of Black Lesbians and Gays board meeting, I decided to get up before dawn and take a train from Albany to New York so I could attend his funeral. It is his funeral that I want to focus on here, to try to convey the transcendence this public observance of James Baldwin's life brought to those of us who experienced it, and to speak also of the disappointment this same ceremony brought to those of us who are out and politically active as Black lesbians and gay men.

The funeral began at noon at the Cathedral of St. John the Divine. The cathedral sits, as if transported from another continent and century, between 110th and 112th streets and Amsterdam Avenue, at the edge of Harlem, where Baldwin was born. It is the largest Gothic cathedral in the world and for those who have seen it, the magnitude of the day's events might well be grasped from simply knowing the scale of the building in which they occurred.

At first I sat alone, but soon joined a Black lesbian artist who I'd met when I lived in New York and a friend of hers, a Black woman writer. A Black gay friend, who had also made the trip down from Albany, happened to see me and came to sit with us. Our group was typical of those that filled the cathedral beyond capacity until there was standing room only. The vast majority of the two or three thousand people who came to honor Baldwin were Black and hundreds of us were also lesbian and gay.

The very long processional began at the front of the cathedral, came up the right-hand aisle and then went down the center, accompanied by Master Babatunde Olatunji's drummers. Their sound alerted us that this "Celebration of the Life of James Arthur Baldwin" was to be a uniquely fitting mixture of African, African

American, and Anglican spiritual and cultural traditions. Following the priests and choir came a mass of Black writers and other artists, many of whom served as honorary pall bearers and many of whom were women, including Toni Cade Bambara, Paule Marshall, and Sonia Sanchez.

I had always heard about Baldwin's huge family, but to see the scores of them together, led by his mother in a wheelchair, struck a visceral emotional chord. They marched like a tribe, like the joining of many tribes in their great diversity, and they looked like everybody's Black family, including my own, in mourning.

It was of course the Black aspects of the funeral inside of the Episcopal cathedral that transported us. Although the Order of Service listed anthems, prayers, and scriptures, I felt the service begin when Odetta walked toward the microphone singing "Kumbaya," which she invited us to sing with her. She then sang three traditional Black songs, a capella: "Sometimes I Feel Like a Motherless Child," "Glory, Glory, Hallelujah, When I Lay My Burden Down," and "Let Us Break Bread Together on Our Knees." This is the music that we were raised on, just as Baldwin was. The spirit of this music as well as the spoken cadences of the Black church infused his writing and were essential to its power.

Maya Angelou's encomium/tribute set the tone for all that followed because she spoke so passionately, personally, and Blackly about her love for Baldwin. She said that it's easy for a woman to find a lover, that she could stand on any street corner or even sit in any church pew and do that, but that brothers were much harder to come by. Spontaneously, many of us clapped for her words, while wondering if we *should* be clapping at a funeral in an Anglican cathedral. By this time, however, St. John the Divine was no longer a mere cathedral. It had become a gospel church, like the ones Baldwin grew up in and like the Temple of the Fire Baptized, which he immortalized in *Go Tell It on the Mountain*. A church where spirit, pain, and joy formed a holy amalgam and were righteously acknowledged *out loud*.

Toni Morrison gave the second tribute in quite different, but no less vivid, language. She spoke about how uniquely gentle and kind Baldwin was and said his was a "tenderness and vulnerability that asked everything of us; expected everything of us. . . ." For the first time that afternoon I began to think specifically about Baldwin as a gay man and wondered if this "detail" of his being would surface here.

The three tributes, including one by the French Ambassador to the United States, were followed by "A Horn Salute," which was in fact a jazz arrangement played by Hugh Masekela on trumpet, Jimmy Owens on flugelhorn, and Danny Mixon on piano. Again, the music embodied the spirit of the life being honored and also reflected another facet of the sound of Baldwin's writing. At one point, the trio segued into a subtle jazz version of "When the Saints Go Marching In," an aural gift recognizable to those of us whose culture this music was.

Amiri Baraka's eulogy, entitled "Jimmy," went to the heart of Baldwin as a person and as an artist. By delivering his own relentless political message in Baldwin's memory, Baraka reflected and shared the activism that characterized Baldwin's true greatness as a writer. Thousands of Black people had come to commemorate Baldwin's life not just because of his remarkable literary gifts, but because, until the end, he consistently wrote about us. Unlike some writers, who the white establishment loves much more, Baldwin's constant themes were racism, oppression, and injustice, all of which are integrally linked to every nuance of Black people's personal and emotional lives. It is not possible to write accurately about how African Americans feel without also writing about the social, political, and economic context in which those feelings and individual dramas take place.

Baraka reminded us that like all great artists, Baldwin had an ethical vision. He knew that his job was to deal in "both beauty *and* truth":

> When we saw and heard him, he made us feel good. He made us feel, for one thing, that we could defend ourselves, that we were in the world not merely as animate slaves, but as terrifyingly sensitive

measures of what is good or evil, beautiful or ugly. This is the power of his spirit. This is the bond which created our love for him. This is the fire that terrifies our pitiful enemies. That not only are we alive but shatteringly precise in our songs and our scorn. You could not possibly think yourself righteous murderers, when you saw or were wrenched by our Jimmy's spirit! He was carrying it as us, as we carry him as us.

Jimmy will be remembered, even as James, for his *word*. Only the completely ignorant can doubt his mastery of it. Jimmy Baldwin was the creator of contemporary American speech even before Americans could dig that. He created it so we could speak to each other at unimaginable intensities of feeling, so we could make sense to each other at yet higher and higher tempos.

Baraka also referred to the "pre-humans" who have plagued this country's history at every turn with their vicious and violent responses to all who are not exactly like themselves. I especially appreciated, as did many others, his condemnation of the ignorant and often cruel comments about Baldwin's career in the white press upon his death. (The most pathetic example of these literary lynchings I have come across was Peter S. Prescott's in the December 14, 1987, issue of *Newsweek*.)

Baraka concluded by stating: "For Jimmy was God's Black revolutionary mouth, if there is a God, and revolution his righteous natural expression and elegant song the deepest and most fundamental commonplace of being alive." As Baraka finished, most of the Black people present rose to their feet and offered him a standing ovation.

The only voice that could adequately follow Baraka's eulogy was Baldwin's own. A recording of him singing "Precious Lord, Take My Hand" washed over the stilled crowd.

After more prayers and choral music, the recessional moved slowly back up the center aisle, this time bearing the black-shrouded coffin, again to the sound of Olatunji's roaring drums.

For me, being there was richer than any words can convey. It made me recommit myself to my work as a writer, specifically as a

Black writer who is simultaneously a political activist. I was reminded of why we do these things, when other more worn paths offer seemingly greater rewards and would certainly be a whole lot easier to walk. Memories of his funeral service and returning to Baldwin's words will undoubtedly sustain me and many others for years to come.

Although Baldwin's funeral completely reinforced our Blackness, it tragically rendered his and our homosexuality completely invisible. In those two hours of remembrance and praise, not a syllable was breathed that this wonderful brother, this writer, this warrior, was also gay, that his being gay was indeed integral to his magnificence.

If I were writing this for a straight publication with a largely heterosexual readership, undoubtedly the question would be looming now: "But what difference does it make if he was gay? Why bring it up especially at his funeral, when the point was to remember the best about him?" Well, Baldwin's being gay and having written about it with such depth and courage at a time when there was no movement nor even a few friends to back him up was definitely "the best" about him.

If all of who James Baldwin was had been mentioned at his funeral in New York City on December 8, 1987, at the Cathedral of St. John the Divine, it would have gone out on the wire services and been broadcast on the air all over the globe. Not only would this news have geometrically increased the quotient of truth available from the media that day in general, it also would have helped alter, if only by an increment, perceptions in Black communities all over the world about the meaning of homosexuality, communities where those of us who survive Baldwin as Black lesbians and gay men must continue to dwell.

The silence of his friends makes me wonder about the silence in Baldwin's life, "the price of the ticket" he paid to be accepted by the straight Black literary establishment. I wonder was it even discussed.

Although Baldwin was always frank about his homosexuality, he was not politicized about it, which means that he did not directly challenge the pantheon of African American writers and intellectuals to understand homosexuality and homophobia as significant political concerns.

For the handful of us who are out Black lesbian and gay writers, our work is obviously cut out for us. Sadly, we must always bury our dead twice. The tributes in these pages are one effort to do that with an integrity missing from the official ceremony. Undoubtedly, we will organize countless memorial gatherings in the months and years to come, where we will not be afraid to speak of James Baldwin as a Black gay brother. What galls me, finally, is that as ghettoized as we are, our efforts will be largely invisible to all but ourselves and will not have the kind of immediate and challenging impact that telling the whole truth at Baldwin's funeral could have had. Painfully, at his own funeral, among those who had the opportunity to speak, nobody knew Baldwin's full name or at least they seemed temporarily to have forgotten it for the occasion.

1987

In the summer of 1992, Fred Wasserman asked me if I would serve as one of the academic advisors for the Stonewall History Project. The project's purpose was to mount major exhibitions on lesbian and gay history at four New York City museums in commemoration of the twenty-fifth anniversary of Stonewall in 1994. My initial response was that my field was literature, not history, but Fred, a professional curator and director of the project, was persuasive and I was more than a little intrigued. Because of my lifelong love of museums, I was particularly interested in learning how an exhibit was developed from start to finish. These exhibitions also would be the first ever at mainstream institutions in the United States to focus upon lesbian and gay subject matter.

Ultimately, two of the four institutions went forward with their plans. Fred became curator (with Mimi Bowling and Molly McGarry) of the New York Public Library's landmark show, "Becoming Visible: The Legacy of Stonewall," and I was again asked to serve as an advisor. My involvement with this exhibition played an important role in my committing to do the book on Black lesbian and gay history I am currently writing. My work as a general editor of *The Reader's Companion to U.S. Women's History*, a project I joined in early 1993, as well as fruitful discussions with my literary agent, Charlotte Sheedy, about the directions I wanted to take in my writing were also important factors motivating me to do more historical work.

When I was honored as the Third Annual Kessler Lecturer by the Center for Lesbian and Gay Studies at the City

University of New York in December 1994, I decided to focus my talk upon some of the issues I anticipated facing. Three years later, after substantial primary research and some fascinating discoveries, I still find this piece a useful framework for my thinking about the book.

African American Lesbian and Gay History

An Exploration

In 1979 Judith Schwarz of the Lesbian Herstory Archives sent out a questionnaire on issues in lesbian history to women working in this just-developing field. Among the twenty-four women who responded were Blanche Wiesen Cook, Lisa Duggan, Estelle Freedman, Joan Nestle, Adrienne Rich, Carroll Smith-Rosenberg, and myself. Our responses were published in the women's studies journal *Frontiers*, in an issue devoted entirely to lesbian history.

In response to the question "How can our work be inclusive of the total lesbian experience in history, particularly given the barriers that race, class, age, and homophobia raise in many societies?" I answered as follows:

> I wanted to say something about the ways that racial and economic oppression will affect trying to do research on Black lesbian history. . . . I feel there is a gold mine of facts to find out, but the problem is that there are so few Black lesbians to do this. . . . The women who have the training and the credentials to do this kind of research don't even have feminist politics, let alone lesbian politics. . . . Many women who have the politics don't have the academic credentials, training, or material resources that would permit them to do the kind of research needed. Right now I can only think of one other Black woman besides myself who has all the resources at her disposal, and who is actively reporting on Black lesbian material she is discovering in her work: Gloria T. Hull. It's depressing, but I'm living for the day when it will change.[1]

Fifteen years later, as I research a book on the history of African American lesbians and gays, my earlier comments make my involvement in this project seem inevitable. My writing, teaching, activism, and work as a publisher have always embodied the commitment to challenge invisibility, to make a place for those of us who are unseen and unheard. Despite the building of a Black lesbian and gay political movement since the 1970s and the simultaneous flowering of Black lesbian and gay art, Black lesbians and gays are still largely missing from the historical record.

The history of African American lesbians and gays currently exists in fragments, in scattered documents, in fiction, poetry, and blues lyrics, in hearsay, and in innuendo. Ideally, what I would like to create is a chronological narrative that traces evidence of same-gender sexual and emotional connections between people of African descent in this country for as many centuries back as possible. Realistically, because of how relatively little work has been done in this field, the finished work will undoubtedly be thematically focused rather than a comprehensive chronicle of the last four hundred years of homosexual, homoemotional, and homosocial experiences in African American life. My more achievable goal is to arrive at an accurate and useful analytical and theoretical framework for understanding the meaning of Black lesbian and gay life in the United States.

Such a framework has not been developed and applied to Black lesbian and gay experience by previous researchers, the majority of whom have been European Americans, whose primary focus has not been African American subject matter. The complex scope of Black lesbian and gay history has yet to be defined by Black lesbian and gay scholars, and it has also not been written by persons who are expert in African American studies. Until now Black lesbian and gay history has largely been written in juxtaposition to the history of white lesbians and gays and has been presented in works in which the history of white gays or lesbians constitutes the dominant narrative. The fascinating examples of Black lesbian and gay life that other historians have discovered are quite useful and suggestive, but the interpretative context in which this information exists as a part of a white dominant meta-narrative leaves many questions unanswered. The most glaring omissions result from insufficient or nonexistent attention to the pervasive impact of racism and white supremacy upon the lives of all African Americans regardless of sexual orientation, and upon the attitudes and actions of whites as well.

Most of what has been written about Black lesbians and gays has attempted to understand them in relationship to other gays who are of course white. Even when a serious attempt is made to understand Black gay experience within the Black experience as a whole, analytical errors still surface. My project is to understand Black lesbian and gay life in the context of both Black history and gay history. The major questions I want to answer which have not been previously addressed are (1) How did Black lesbians and gays view their own existences within Black communities during various historical eras? and (2) How did other members of Black communities view them? In short, what has the existence of African American homosexuality meant to Black people of various sexual orientations over time?

Before looking at some examples of how Black lesbian and gay experience has been approached and avoided, I would like to explain my decision to research the history of both men and women. Because I see this as a definitional project, it seemed impossible to understand fully the history of one gender without understanding the history of the other. The kinds of questions I want to explore cannot be accurately addressed by looking at Black lesbian or Black gay experience in isolation. In the future I hope that other researchers will focus with much more clarity on the specific histories of Black lesbians, gays, bisexuals, or transgendered people because of my attempt to create a more general framework. For example, we might see separate studies concerning Black lesbian participation in Black women's clubs and sororities; Black gay men's impact upon gospel and other sacred music; Black women who passed as men; or drag performance in African and African American culture.

My own experience as a Black lesbian during the past two decades indicates that Black lesbians and gay men are linked by our shared racial identity and political status in ways that white lesbians and gays are not. These links between us are sociological, cultural, historical, and emotional and I think it is crucial to explore this new terrain together.

The amount of published historical research which focuses specifically upon African American lesbians and gays is minimal, particularly when compared to the growing body of lesbian and gay research as a whole. In the Center for Lesbian and Gay Studies of the City University of New York's first *Directory of Lesbian and Gay Studies*, for 1994–1995, which lists six hundred scholars, five individuals list an interest in Black lesbian and gay historical topics and seven more mention interest in researching African American subject matter in other disciplines.[2] It has always been obvious to me that the difficult, often hostile working conditions that Black academics face as a result of racism in white institutions would make their involvement in explicitly lesbian and gay research an even higher risk activity than it is for European American scholars. There are several courageous younger Black academics, however, some still in graduate school, who are beginning to work in this area.

I value the efforts of the handful of white historians who have made the attempt to include material concerning people of color in their work. Jonathan Ned Katz's groundbreaking documentary collections, *Gay American History*, first published in 1976, and the *Gay/Lesbian Almanac*, published in 1983, are models to this day of racial, ethnic, gender, and class inclusivity. Elizabeth Kennedy's and Madeline Davis's *Boots of Leather, Slippers of Gold*, which is based upon oral histories, also demonstrates a conscious commitment to racial and class diversity. The New York Public Library's 1994 exhibition "Becoming Visible: The Legacy of Stonewall," curated by Mimi Bowling, Molly McGarry, and Fred Wasserman, displayed a level of racial and gender diversity that is rare in cultural productions organized by European American gays and lesbians.

Other scholars have uncovered valuable evidence of Black lesbian and gay existence before Stonewall, especially during the 1920s in Harlem. The analyses of this information, however, sometimes overlook important meanings, advance inaccurate interpretations, or fail to place Black lesbian and gay experience into the context of Black American life. The most distorting error is either to ignore or give inadequate weight to the realities of racism, segregation, and white supremacy as they shape African American lesbian and gay people's existences.

Jazz Age Harlem, for example, is now recognized as the site of a vibrant Black gay cultural and social life which rivaled that of Greenwich Village. Yet there is insufficient discussion of exactly how racial segregation shaped the growth of this so-called Black lesbian and gay community. Since a large proportion of New York's Black population lived in Harlem during the 1920s, as a result of citywide housing discrimination, the gay community that arose there was obviously shaped by quite different forces than more intentional white enclaves in other parts of Manhattan. This geographic apartheid raises questions about whether the Harlem Black community's seemingly greater tolerance for visible homosexuals was evidence of more accepting attitudes about sexuality and difference or was merely a structural accommodation to the reality of segregation which forced all types of Black people to live together in one location. Perhaps it was a subtle combination of both.

We also know very little about Black lesbian and gay existence in other cities during this period. Was the manifestation of Black lesbian and gay life in Harlem and the way in which it was viewed by heterosexual African Americans an exceptional case or might parallels be drawn to what was going on in other urban centers?

Another set of assertions that needs to be investigated concerns Harlem's class composition. The issue of class identity in the Black community is exceedingly complex, often confusing, and cannot be evaluated by using measures identical to those used for whites. Racial oppression has a profoundly negative impact upon African

Americans' economic opportunities, their class and social status. To this day the average income levels of African Americans remain at or near the bottom of the U.S. scale and a tiny percentage of Blacks are in fact wealthy or upper class. When various attitudes about homosexuality are attributed to members of Harlem's upper or middle classes, there needs to be much more specific explanation of who comprised these strata and also what their numbers were relative to the population of Harlem as a whole.

An avenue of inquiry that I have wanted to pursue for some time is a revisionist history of the Harlem Renaissance itself. As I began to discover that more and more of the Harlem Renaissance's leading writers were gay, bisexual, or lesbian, I knew that the meaning of this pivotal epoch in Black culture needed to be seriously reevaluated. What does it mean that the major outpouring of Black literature, art, and cultural consciousness in this century prior to the Black Arts Movement of the sixties and seventies was significantly shaped by Blacks who were not heterosexuals? How would those who celebrate this period for its major intellectual and artistic achievements view it if they fully realized how much it was a queer production? The crucial impact of lesbian, bisexual, and gay artists and intellectuals upon the formation of the Renaissance has meaning and needs to be systematically explored.

Harlem has become a symbolic catchall for the discussion of pre-Stonewall Black lesbian and gay existence. Other regions of the country need to be studied and the Harlem experience itself needs to be revisited with a much stronger consciousness of the myriad economic, political, and social factors that shaped African American life during that era.

An example of a problem of interpretation occurs in George Chauncey's *Gay New York: Gender, Urban Culture, and the Making of the Gay Male World*. This work makes a major contribution to increasing understanding of gay life in the early part of this century and Chauncey's discussion of Harlem during the 1920s and 1930s provides significant information and insights. In one instance, however, in an effort to equalize Black and white

experience, the specificity of Black experience is not taken sufficiently into account. The author describes in detail the history of
Harlem's Hamilton Lodge Balls, the largest drag events to occur in
New York during this era. He notes that this annual event was
unique because it attracted an interracial crowd of both participants and observers at a time when racial segregation in social settings was virtually universal. Chauncey writes:

> The balls became a site for the projection and inversion of racial
> as well as gender identities. Significantly, though, white drag
> queens were not prepared to reverse their racial identity. Many
> accounts refer to African-American queens appearing as white
> celebrities, but none refer to whites appearing as well-known black
> women. As one black observer noted, "The vogue was to develop a
> 'personality' like some outstanding woman," but the only women
> he listed, Jean Harlow, Gloria Swanson, Mae West, and Greta
> Garbo, were white.[3]

Chauncey is correct to imply that white drag queens' racism
prevented them from adopting Black female personas, but my initial response to this passage was that there was in fact no compa-
rable group of Black women to be imitated. Despite the popularity
of some Black women entertainers during this period, there were
no Black women who functioned as internationally recognized
glamour icons. There were no Black women movie stars; no Black
women worked as fashion models in white contexts. White Americans simply did not see Black women as beautiful; indeed, the racist stereotypes of our physical appearances defined us as quite the
opposite. The white world certainly did not confer fame upon
Black women for either their physical attributes or outstanding
accomplishments. Josephine Baker had to leave the United States
for Paris in order to achieve stardom during this very period.
Chauncey also does not explore the racial implications of Black
men wanting not merely to be female for a night, but white as well.

    When I discussed this passage with my colleague Mattie Rich-
ardson at Kitchen Table: Women of Color Press, she pointed out

that if white males had chosen to portray Black women, they very likely would have donned blackface to complete the effect. Such a racial masquerade undoubtedly would have upset Blacks in an atmosphere that Chauncey describes as already racially charged.

An example of an analytical error that affects the entire thesis of a work occurs in Tracy Morgan's article "Pages of Whiteness: Race, Physique Magazines, and the Emergence of Gay Public Culture, 1955–1960." Although Morgan acknowledges the negative racial climate in the United States during this period, she describes the exclusion of Black men from white physique publications as a conscious strategy that white gay men pursued in order to appear more acceptable and to help neutralize their queerness. She writes:

> In thinking about race and gay community formation, it might be important to ask how patterns of white, gay racism may have been "useful," in terms of the "wages of whiteness" thesis, in assisting white gay people to attain greater social and cultural privilege as, at least, "not black" outcasts in American culture. . . .
>
> Summoning forth white-skin privilege as a salve and smoke screen in a quest for respectability, physique magazines were part of a larger phenomenon within mid-twentieth-century gay community formation that often sought individual, privatized solutions to group problems. . . .
>
> Gay maleness became synonymous with whiteness. Black, gay men became invisible—the representation of 1950s homosexuality demanded their repression.[4]

Although excluding Black men might have had the result of minimally enhancing white gay men's social position, their original motivation for such exclusion was no doubt based upon unquestioning conformity to the racial status quo. Morgan does not take into account that racism, white supremacy, and segregation were universally institutionalized, accepted, and practiced by whites of all classes, genders, sexual orientations, and geographic regions. The average white person did not have to decide to exclude Black people from every aspect of their social, economic, and personal lives. U.S. society was organized to ensure that this would always be the case. The "decision" to enforce white supremacy and to reap its benefits had been made long before white gay men in urban settings began publishing physique magazines in the mid-twentieth century. By the time these men reached maturity, unless their families were highly exceptional, complete racial segregation would have been the norm, a cherished and familiar way of life. Just as their fathers did not hire Blacks, their schools and churches did not admit them, and their neighborhoods refused to house them, their magazines did not publish physique photographs of Black men.

Morgan confuses the causes for racism with the resulting benefits. She writes, "Most lesbian and gay publications, to this very day, continue to draw on white-skin privilege as one of their main vestiges of respectability" (p. 124). If racial exclusion is primarily a strategy used by a disenfranchised group, why are straight magazines equally white in their content? Her thesis inaccurately assumes that white gays have a significantly different value system about race than other whites, and that if it were not for their attempt to enhance their credibility with white heterosexuals, they would be much more racially inclusive.

I do not want to dissuade white scholars from investigating and including material about people of color. Indeed current queer studies needs to be much more racially and ethnically inclusive, but at the same time it also needs to demonstrate a thorough consciousness of the racial and class contexts in which lesbians and gays of color actually function.

African American historical research would seem to offer more avenues into Black lesbian and gay experience. The field of Black history, which has roots in the Negro History movement of the early twentieth century, offers extensive and complex documentation of African American life. The overwhelming problem, however, is that there is virtually no acknowledgment within the confines of African American history that Black lesbians and gays ever existed.

The reasons for this silence are numerous. Homophobia and heterosexism are of course the most obvious. But there is also the reality that Black history has often served extrahistorical purposes that would militate against bringing up "deviant" sexualities. In its formative years, especially, but even today, Black history's underlying agenda frequently has been to demonstrate that African Americans are full human beings who deserve to be treated like Americans, like citizens, like men. I use "men" advisedly because until approximately twenty years ago there was little specific focus upon the history of Black women. Those who subscribe to certain strains of Afrocentric thought can be even more overtly hostile to Black lesbian and gay historical projects. The conservative agendas of some Afrocentric or Black nationalist scholarship encourage condemnation of what they define as European-inspired perversion, a conspiracy to destroy the Black family and the race. The themes of uplift, of social validation, and of prioritizing subject matter that is a "credit to the race" have burdened and sometimes biased Black historical projects. Chauncey points out that in the early part of this century "many middle-class and churchgoing African Americans grouped . . . [bulldaggers and faggots] with prostitutes, salacious entertainers, and 'uncultured' rural migrants as part of an undesirable and all-too-visible Black 'lowlife' that brought disrepute to the neighborhood and the race."⁵ "Lowlife" is exactly the image I had of the lesbian lifestyle when I was growing up in the pre-Stonewall 1950s and 1960s. I am not even sure where I got this from since sexuality in general and lesbianism in particular were seldom explicitly discussed, yet this subliminal message greatly contributed to my fear of coming out.

It is difficult to imagine traditional African American historians going out of their way to explore lesbian and gay life, or to reveal evidence of it when they happen across it while researching other topics. Arnold Rampersad's biography of Langston Hughes illustrates the opposite tendency of going out of one's way to ignore or suppress such information. It is hard to imagine Black historians combing through court and police records (as some white lesbian and gay scholars have done) to find evidence of Black homosexuality. I have weighed the implications of utilizing these kinds of sources myself, especially in today's political climate in which the right wing seeks to criminalize all people of color as part of their racist agenda.

An example of how an otherwise highly informative work can obscure Black lesbian history occurs in *Black Women in America: An Historical Encyclopedia*, whose principal editor is Darlene Clark Hine. This groundbreaking two-volume, 1,500-page reference work presents an exhaustively researched picture of Black American women. It contains interpretative articles that cover historical issues and organizations as well as hundreds of biographical entries describing individual Black women. The index alone is 150 pages long; however, there are only six entries listed under the heading "Lesbianism." Certainly the encyclopedia includes many more women who were in fact lesbian or bisexual, but because discussion of a Black woman's sexuality is not usually considered relevant, unless her orientation is heterosexual, contributors either omitted or suppressed this material. I found myself reading between the lines and trying to evaluate the work's beautiful photographic images in an effort to guess which of the many women documented might be ones I should investigate further for my study. These omissions will necessitate that others do a great deal of this primary research all over again.

Another type of omission in *Black Women in America* occurs in entries which describe women who are known to be lesbian or bisexual, especially musicians and entertainers such as Alberta Hunter and Jackie "Moms" Mabley, but who are not identified as such. The comments in the encyclopedia on the heiress A'Lelia Walker, whose legendary salons were attended by queer luminaries of the Harlem Renaissance as well as by other lesbians and gays, illustrate how reticence about sexuality can result in an incomplete portrait of an historical figure. The author, Tiya Miles, writes:

> A'Lelia Walker was not accepted by everyone in the Harlem community, however. Some begrudged the fact that she was the

daughter of a washerwoman. Some also objected to her fast-paced social life and unusual style of dress, which included turbans and jewelry. Some of her contemporaries called her the "De-kink Heiress." James Weldon Johnson's wife, Grace Nail Johnson, who was known as the social dictator of Harlem, refused to attend Walker's parties.[6]

The photograph that accompanies this article shows A'Lelia not only in a turban, but in shiny, high, black leather boots with harem pants tucked inside of them, leaning back casually with one of her legs bent and her foot propped up on the bench on which she is sitting. This is neither ladylike dress nor a ladylike pose. Walker was obviously willing to challenge the gender expectations of her time.

Mabel Hampton's description of some of A'Lelia's "less formal" parties quoted in Lillian Faderman's *Odd Girls and Twilight Lovers* offers other reasons for Walker's negative reputation:

> "[They were] funny parties—there were men and women, straight and gay. They were kinds of orgies. Some people had clothes on, some didn't. People would hug and kiss on pillows and do anything they wanted to do. You could watch if you wanted to. Some came to watch, some came to play. You had to be cute and well-dressed to get in."[7]

Probably Grace Nail Johnson and other members of the Black bourgeoisie knew about such goings-on and ostracized Walker as a result, as well as for the reasons that Miles cites.

The most painful paradoxes among the encyclopedia's entries are those that describe my contemporaries, women who I personally know to be lesbians, but who are unwilling to publicly acknowledge the fact. This is the group that will pose one of the most significant challenges for my research. The myriad closeted contemporary figures who are artists, activists, athletes, and entertainers, both male and female, constitute what I already think of as the chapter I cannot write. But I plan to write it anyway. I have no intention of outing anyone, but want to analyze instead what it means on a variety of levels that there are so many prominent African Americans whose stories are well known in lesbian and gay circles, but who I cannot include because they are unwilling to relinquish their heterosexual privilege and name themselves.

The fear of being rejected by and losing credibility in the Black community is undoubtedly one of the most significant disincentives to coming out, and this is particularly true of our closeted cultural and political leaders. Since I have personally experienced some of the difficult consequences of being honest about my sexual orientation, I will not say their fears are groundless. However, the increase in the numbers of Black people who can now be counted as allies in movements for sexual and gender freedom is the direct result of our actively challenging oppression instead of accommodating to it. It is my hope that this historical project will play a part in enlarging the space in which people of all sexualities can live and struggle.

1994

Notes

1. Judith Schwarz, "Questionnaire on Issues in Lesbian History," *Frontiers: A Journal of Women Studies* 4, no. 3 (Fall 1979): 5, 6.

2. Center for Lesbian and Gay Studies, *The CLAGS Directory of Lesbian and Gay Studies* (New York: Center for Lesbian and Gay Studies, The City University of New York, 1994), *passim.*

3. George Chauncey, *Gay New York: Gender, Urban Culture, and the Making of the Gay Male World, 1890–1940* (New York: Basic Books, 1994), 263.

4. Tracy Morgan, "Pages of Whiteness: Race, Physique Magazines, and the Emergence of Gay Public Culture, 1955–1960," *Found Object*, no. 4 (Fall 1994): 112, 123, 124. All subsequent references to this work will be designated in the text.

5. Chauncey, *Gay New York*, 253.

6. Tiya Miles. "A'Lelia Walker (1885–1931)," in *Black Women in America: An Historical Encyclopedia*, ed. Darlene Clark Hine et al. (Brooklyn, N.Y.: Carlson Publishing, 1993), 1205.

7. Lillian Faderman, *Odd Girls and Twilight Lovers: A History of Lesbian Life in Twentieth-Century America* (New York: Penguin, 1991), 76.

II

Between a Rock and a Hard Place

"Racism and Women's Studies" was delivered at the closing session of the first annual National Women's Studies Association conference in Lawrence, Kansas, in June 1979. Like all of my political writing, the ideas in the speech grew out of practice. Several years earlier, the Combahee River Collective had begun to confront actively the issue of racism in the women's movement in Boston and as a part of that work had conducted antiracism workshops at the request of various white women's organizations.

One element of the passion in this speech undoubtedly sprung from my deep involvement in the organizing around the murders of twelve Black women in Boston during a four-month period from January through May 1979. By the time I arrived in Kansas I felt as if I had been through a war. I had little patience with white women who viewed eradicating racism as a subordinate concern. Twelve Black women in Boston were dead as a result of both racism and sexism. It was past time for change.

My critique of academic feminists who are content to theorize and build careers instead of devoting a segment of their time to organizing for social and economic justice is even more relevant today than it was in the late 1970s. On a positive note, some progressive white lesbian and heterosexual feminists have been at the forefront of not only keeping antiracist struggle alive in a variety of movements, but of providing innovative antiracist leadership in the decades since this speech was made.

Racism and Women's Studies

Although my proposed topic is Black women's studies, I've decided to focus my remarks in a different way. Given that this is a gathering of predominantly white women, and given what has occurred during this conference, it makes much more sense to discuss the issue of racism: racism in women's studies and racism in the women's movement generally.

"Oh no," I can hear some of you groaning inwardly. "Not that again. That's all we've talked about since we got here." This, of course, is not true. If it had been all we had all talked about since we got here, we might be at a point of radical transformation on the last day of this conference that we clearly are not. For those of you who are tired of hearing about racism, imagine how much more tired *we* are of constantly experiencing it, second by literal second, how much more exhausted we are to see it constantly in your eyes. The degree to which it is hard or uncomfortable for you to have the issue raised is the degree to which you know inside of yourself that you aren't dealing with the issue, the degree to which you are hiding from the oppression that undermines Third World women's lives. I want to say right here that this is not a "guilt trip." It's a fact trip. The assessment of what's actually going on.

Why is racism being viewed and taken up as a pressing feminist issue at this time, and why is it being talked about in the context of women's studies? As usual, the impetus comes from the grassroots, activist women's movement. In my six years of being an avowed Black feminist, I have seen much change in how white women take responsibility for their racism, particularly within the last year. The formation of consciousness-raising groups to deal solely with this issue, study groups, and community meetings and workshops; the appearance of articles in our publications and letters in newspapers; and the beginning of real and equal coalitions between Third World and white women are all phenomena that have really begun to happen, and I feel confident that there will be no turning back.

The reason racism is a feminist issue is easily explained by the inherent definition of feminism. Feminism is the political theory and practice that struggles to free *all* women: women of color, working-class women, poor women, disabled women, Jewish women, lesbians, old women—as well as white, economically privileged, heterosexual women. Anything less than this vision of total freedom is not feminism, but merely female self-aggrandizement.

Let me make quite clear, before going any further, something you must understand. White women don't work on racism to do a favor for someone else, solely to benefit Third World women. You have to comprehend how racism distorts and lessens your own lives as white women—that racism affects your chances for survival, too, and that it is very definitely your issue. Until you understand this, no fundamental change will come about.

Racism is being talked about in the context of women's studies because of its being raised in the women's movement generally, but also because women's studies is a context in which white and Third World women actually come together, a context that should be about studying and learning about all of our lives. I feel at this point that it is not only about getting Third World women's materials into the curriculum, although this must be done. This has been happening, and it is clear that racism still thrives, just as the inclusion of women's materials in a college curriculum does not prevent sexism from thriving. The stage we are at now is having to decide to change fundamental attitudes and behavior—the way people treat each other. In other words, we are at a stage of having to take some frightening risks.

I am sure that many women here are telling themselves they aren't racists because they are capable of being civil to Black women, having been raised by their parents to be anything but. It's not about merely being polite: "I'm not racist because I do not snarl and snap at Black people." It's much more subtle than that. It's not white women's fault that they have been raised, for the most part, not knowing how to talk to Black women, not knowing how to look us in the eye and laugh *with* us. Racism and racist behavior are our white patriarchal legacy. What is your fault is making no serious effort to change old patterns of contempt—to look at how you still believe yourselves to be superior to Third World women and how you communicate these attitudes in blatant and subtle ways.

A major roadblock for women involved in women's studies to changing their individual racism and challenging it institutionally is the pernicious ideology of professionalism. That word *professionalism* covers such a multitude of sins. I always cringe when I hear *anyone* describe herself as "professional," because what usually follows is an excuse for inaction, an excuse for ethical irresponsibility. It's a word and concept we don't need, because it is ultimately a way of dividing ourselves from others and escaping from reality. I think the way to be "successful" is to do work with integrity and work that is good. Not to play cutthroat tricks and insist on being called "Doctor." When I got involved in women's studies six years ago, and particularly during my three and a half years as the first Third World woman on the Modern Language Association Commission on the Status of Women, I began to recognize what I call women's studies or academic feminists: women who teach, research, and publish about women, but who are not involved in any way in making radical social and political change; women who are not involved in making the lives of living, breathing women more viable. The grassroots/community women's movement has given women's studies its life. How do we relate to it? How do we bring our gifts and our educational privilege back to it? Do we realize also how very much there is to learn in doing this essential work? Ask yourself what the women's movement is working on in your town or city. Are you a part of it? Ask yourself which women are living in the worst conditions in your town and how your work positively affects and directly touches their lives? If it doesn't, why not?

The question has been raised here whether this should be an activist association or an academic one. In many ways, this is an immoral question, an immoral and false dichotomy. The answer lies in the emphasis and the kinds of work that will lift oppression off of not only women, but all oppressed people: poor and working-class people, people of color in this country and in the colonized Third World. If lifting this oppression is not a priority to you, then it's problematic whether you are a part of the actual feminist movement.

There are two other roadblocks to our making feminism real which I'll mention briefly. First, there is Third World women's antifeminism, which I sometimes sense gets mixed up with opposition to white women's racism and is fueled by a history of justified distrust. To me, racist white women cannot be said to be actually feminist, at least not in the way I think and feel about the word. Feminism in and of itself would be fine. The problems arise with the mortals who practice it. As Third World women we must define a responsible and radical feminism for ourselves and not assume that bourgeois female self-aggrandizement is all that feminism is and therefore attack feminism wholesale.

The other roadblock is homophobia, that is, antilesbianism, an issue that both white and Third World women still have to deal with. Need I explicate in 1979 how enforced heterosexuality is the extreme manifestation of male domination and patriarchal rule and that women must not collude in the oppression of women who have chosen each other, that is, lesbians? I wish I had time here to speak also about the connections between the lesbian-feminist movement, being woman-identified, and the effective antiracist work that is being done by many, though not all, lesbians.

In conclusion, I'll say that I don't consider my talk today to be in any way conclusive or exhaustive. It has merely scratched the surface. I don't know exactly what's going on in your schools or in your lives. I can only talk about those qualities and skills that will help you to bring about change: integrity, awareness, courage, and redefining your own success.

I also feel that the women's movement will deal with racism in a way that it has not been dealt with before in any other movement: fundamentally, organically, and nonrhetorically. White women have a materially different relationship to the system of racism than white men. They get less out of it and often function as its pawns, whether they recognize this or not. It is something that living under white-male rule has imposed on us; and overthrowing racism is the inherent work of feminism and by extension feminist studies.

1979

This article, written for a 1994 issue of the lesbian feminist journal *Sinister Wisdom* that focused upon the theme "Allies," serves as a companion piece to "Racism and Women's Studies." The fact that they were written fifteen years apart points to how deeply embedded racism is in U.S. society. Racial conditions have continued to degenerate since the 1970s as a result of the government's increasing conservatism; the shift to the right of the population as a whole; the flourishing of a militant and strategically effective right-wing movement; and deteriorating economic conditions which hit the poorest people hardest.

Because institutional racism is enforced and maintained by state power, challenging the state, demanding justice, and building new systems in which power and resources are equally distributed offer the only viable means for eradicating racism. Unfortunately, in a period of ideological confusion, backlash, and real setbacks in maintaining a minimal social safety net and basic civil rights, it is difficult for some to grasp that it is necessary to do more than think, talk, and write to alter the status quo. Examining the history of antiracist struggles that have successfully brought sweeping political change can provide a much needed antidote to pessimism and to magical thinking about how change occurs.

The Tip of the Iceberg

Before discussing how white lesbians can be allies to me as a Black lesbian, I first need to talk about what racism is and how it works. From the moment this continent was colonized, racism has been fundamental to this country's functioning on every level. To this day, racism is systematically institutionalized in every aspect of the United States' political, economic, and social life. Racism negatively affects the day-to-day lives of people of color in both devastating and "petty" ways, ranging from whether we grow up in poverty and die years earlier than whites to whether we will be waited on promptly and courteously whenever we enter a restaurant or a store.

There were two crucial events, directly tied to racism, that ensured this country's successful European settlement. The first was the wholesale theft of the land itself from the original inhabitants, the Native peoples, a process accomplished through war and other acts of genocide. The second was the importation of millions of Africans to work as slaves. The United States is built upon stolen land and stolen labor.

For racism to serve its essential purpose, which was and is the exploitation of people of color in order to maintain white economic and political power, i.e. white supremacy, a racist ideology also had to be put in place. Vicious stereotypes based upon the supposed inferiority of subhuman Indian and African "savages" were created in order to justify policies and acts that would otherwise be viewed as criminally inhumane. Racist ideology, attitudes, and beliefs, reinforced by segregation and discrimination, enable institutionalized racism to perpetuate itself.

Racism is not primarily a set of negative attitudes or behaviors on the part of individual whites. These negative attitudes and behaviors are grievous and sometimes fatal, but they are in fact symptoms of a system whose purpose is not merely to make people of color feel badly, but to maintain white power and control.

Of course there have always been people of color who have resisted white rule in every way we could. The abolition of slavery, the destruction of legal segregation, our ongoing movements that fight against racism, our very physical survival are all testaments to the resistance of people of color.

The concept of resistance brings me to how white lesbians (or anyone who is white) can be an ally to me as a Black person, a woman, and a lesbian. And that is to do political organizing with the ultimate goal of destroying the institutionalized, structural racism that oppresses all people of color, including Black lesbians. As a socialist I believe that racism will only be destroyed when capitalism is also destroyed, which means it will be a long struggle. However, there are various kinds of grassroots organizing that challenge the state which we can participate in, right now.

I consider white lesbians who do actual organizing to dismantle institutionalized racism in the society as a whole to be allies. Having a "safe space" within the lesbian community where concerned white lesbians might treat me as if I were human is all well and good, but it won't help at all when I am in my car and get pulled over by a cop who decides to crack my head open because I am Black. What would help would be for white lesbians to organize against police brutality, which is occurring in epidemic proportions against different groups of people of color all over the country. There are countless other issues to which antiracist white lesbians can bring their intelligence, activism, and support.

Doing antiracist organizing does not mean that one has to stop organizing against homophobia and sexism, as demonstrated by the multi-issued political practice of lesbian feminists of color.

Indeed, given how linked all the systems of oppression are, organizing around what may seem to be one issue should quickly lead to work around related ones. For example, lesbians and gays have a history of being mistreated by the police, so working against police brutality has direct positive consequences for our lives. Opposing the Christian right wing's homophobic campaigns logically necessitates opposing their assaults on women's reproductive freedom, their racist efforts to institute school vouchers, and their anti-immigration initiatives.

Of course I want white lesbians to treat me like a human being and there have been too many instances in the last twenty years when they have not. I also would like white lesbians to know about and respect my culture and history. But most of all I need for white lesbians to do work toward eradicating the oppression that undermines the lives of all people of color, including mine. The white lesbians who have been friends, allies, and in some cases family to me for many years all do practical political work to end racism in this country. One aspect of that work is challenging racism in lesbian contexts, but limiting one's activities to lesbian settings is to confront just the tip of the iceberg. As I wrote several years ago, I don't live in the women's movement, I live on the streets of North America.

The only way oppressed groups' situations ever change in real life as opposed to in theory is through activism. Talk doesn't do it, trainings don't do it, books don't do it, pleasant attitudes don't do it. Organizing does. The white lesbian allies I can depend upon are those who are allies in struggle.

1994

When the Simi Valley, California, jury acquitted the police officers who participated in the videotaped brutalization of Black motorist Rodney King, a spontaneous outpouring of rage led in Los Angeles to the most massive civil insurrection in U.S. history. The independent leftist weekly *The Guardian*, for which I sometimes wrote, asked if I would do a commentary on the events in Los Angeles. This article was completed less than a week after the jury's decision and appeared in the newspaper's next issue. Although it was often hectic, I liked writing for *The Guardian* and for *Gay Community News* in response to breaking news stories. It posed a different kind of challenge than doing long articles with sufficient lead time. *The Guardian*, founded in 1948, stopped publishing in 1992. Its demise left a huge gap in the quality of information and analysis available in this era of gigantic media monopolies.

Just as I predicted, the nation's short attention span soon shifted away from the lessons about race and class available from Los Angeles in the spring of 1992. Police brutality, however, is the late twentieth-century's version of lynching. What happened to Rodney King was not an isolated incident. One need only read the daily newspaper for the latest accounts of state-sanctioned terrorism or consider the summer 1997 case of Haitian immigrant and Brooklyn, New York, resident Abner Louima.*

---

* See "A Rose" in this volume.

The Rodney King Verdict

But most Americans do not yet know what anguish is.

—James Baldwin

When the verdict came down I was sitting with one of my oldest friends, Nellie McKay, in her kitchen in Madison, Wisconsin. I'd arrived a few hours earlier to visit and to speak as a guest of the Afro-American Studies Department at the University of Wisconsin, where Nellie teaches.

A Black woman friend of Nellie's called with the news, and we turned on National Public Radio. Suddenly we were thrust into the physical and emotional attitudes of grief: shoulders slumped, heads leaning on our hands, deep lines creasing our foreheads, and for me at least, tears right behind my eyes and my throat aching with a scream I could not let out.

After a while Nellie switched off the classical music that had followed the news and put on Bessie Smith. "I can't deal with Dvořák right now," she said wryly. Bessie sang "Trouble, trouble . . ." and I commented that her blues were the perfect counterpoint. Bessie knew there'd be days like this. She just didn't know that racism and poverty would be as violent and intractable at the end of the twentieth century as they were when she was alive at the century's beginning.

I said Black people should tear Los Angeles up, that we needed Watts II. As soon as I'd said it I felt the weight of those words. Besides hating violence in general, I realized that wishing for a "riot" was itself a reflection of African Americans' invisibility and powerlessness.

Watts II, however, was exactly what we got except that it spread much further than Watts, and the "rioters" were Latino and white as well as Black. The ghetto exploded and delivered the only message about racism, poverty, and despair that most of the white populace of this nation ever seems to notice. As I traveled from Wisconsin, to Ann Arbor, Michigan, to Cleveland, Ohio (where I grew up), I could catch only snatches of TV coverage but read every newspaper I could find. I soon got sick of comments that conveyed how many white people completely agreed with the verdict and were angry that we would be moved to violence in response to it. I was even more disgusted with the average whites who said that they'd never believed it when Black people "complained" about being oppressed and brutalized until now.

Quiet as it's kept, whether we are "rioting" or not, most African Americans live every day with greater or lesser amounts of rage toward white people and the system that gives them the power and privilege to decimate our lives. I know I do. When my cousin, who is not an activist or a radical, met me at the airport in Cleveland, she expressed more anger about what had happened in Los Angeles than I'd ever heard from her about anything. Although we might not have agreed on solutions, we were in almost total agreement about the problems.

What I felt at the King verdict and its aftermath was all too familiar. I felt the same gnawing in the pit of my stomach and in my chest when sixteen-year-old Yusuf Hawkins was gunned down on the streets of Bensonhurst, Brooklyn, in 1989. I felt the same impotent rage when the police murdered sixty-seven-year-old Eleanor Bumpurs with a shotgun in the process of evicting her from her Bronx apartment in 1984. I choked back the same bitter tears when I heard the verdict in the 1991 rape case involving a Black woman student and several white male students at St. John's University on Long Island. I was just as terrified when they murdered four Black school girls (my age peers) by bombing a church in Birmingham, Alabama, in 1963. And even though I was too young to understand its meaning, I learned Emmett Till's name in 1955 because of witnessing my family's anguish over his lynching in Mississippi.

So what do we do with all this fury besides burn down our own communities and hurt or kill anyone, white, Black, brown, or yellow who gets in our way? Figuring out what to do next is the incredibly difficult challenge that lies before us.

Above all, the events in Los Angeles have made it perfectly obvious why we need a revolution in this country. Nothing short of a revolution will work. Gross inequalities are built into the current system and Band-Aids, even big ones, won't cure capitalism's fundamental injustice and exploitation.

We need, however, to build analysis, practice, and movements that accurately address the specific ways that racism, capitalism, and all the major systems of oppression interconnect in the United States. It's not a coincidence that the most dramatic political and social upheavals in this country and also the most sweeping political changes have so often been catalyzed by race. In the United States, racism has shaped the nature of capitalism and of class relations.

It is our responsibility as Black activists, radicals, and socialists to create vibrant new leadership that offers a real alternative to the tired civil rights establishment and to the bankrupt "two-party" system. It is our responsibility as we build autonomous Black organizations to make the connections between all of the oppressions and to work in coalition with the movements that have arisen to challenge them.

Recognizing the leadership of radical women of color, feminists, and lesbians is absolutely critical from this moment forward. Women of color are already building a movement that makes the connections between race, class, gender, and sexual identity, a movement that has the potential to win liberation for us all.

It is past the time for talk. I really want to know how the white left, the white feminist, and the white lesbian and gay movements are going to change now that Los Angeles has burned. It's not enough to say what a shame all of this is or to have a perfect intellectual understanding of what has occurred. It's time for all the white people who say they're committed to freedom to figure out what useful antiracist organizing is and to put it into practice.

I believe the King verdict and the insurrection in Los Angeles will galvanize unprecedented organizing. In Albany, New York, where I live, there is already a community strategy meeting scheduled for later in May. It is impossible to assess all the implications of these events only days after they occurred. I only wish that a week from now most of the people who live here would not find it so easy to forget.

1992

This article was written for the issue of *Ms.* that immediately followed the October 1991 Senate confirmation hearings of Supreme Court Justice Clarence Thomas. It was also included in *The Black Scholar*'s anthology, *Court of Appeal: The Black Community Speaks Out on the Racial and Sexual Politics of Thomas vs. Hill.*

Ain't Gonna Let Nobody
Turn Me Around

Reflections on the Hill-Thomas Hearings

Early Friday evening, the day the Hill-Thomas hearings began, a friend called and said that she wasn't sure why she was so fascinated by the proceedings, she could barely tear herself away from the screen. I said it might be because we almost never see more than a few seconds of a real Black woman on television talking about *anything*, let alone the painful realities of racial-sexual politics. Both of us found it compelling simply to watch Anita Hill—bright, sincere, Black, and female—describe what had happened to her hour after hour. Here was someone we recognized, unlike the handful of Black women caricatures who populate the world of television sitcoms. Here was someone we believed.

I can think of no other situation which has commanded the nation's undivided attention that has so clearly illustrated the inextricable links between racism and sexism. It's difficult to conceive how the hearings could be understood from anything other than a Black feminist perspective, a perspective which doesn't require the shortchanging of any aspect of Black women's experience and which doesn't assume that racial oppression is more important than sexual oppression or vice versa. But of course Anita Hill's description of sexual harassment was responded to with anything but a Black feminist consciousness, which explains in part why this drama ended as it did.

As a Black feminist, I've known for nearly two decades that political analyses and strategies that take into account how racism, sexism, homophobia, and class oppression dovetail and interlock provide the clearest and most revolutionary agendas for change. Unfortunately, the outcome of the Hill-Thomas confrontation seemingly illustrates that my perspective and that of most women of color simply doesn't count, because ultimately it's the white-male power structure that gets to define reality and to call the shots.

I was furious at how Anita Hill was treated by the Senate, by the media, and by the majority of the U.S. populace (if the polls are to be believed), but I was not particularly disillusioned or surprised. I don't expect justice from either the Republicans or the Democrats, whose duplicity and ineffectualness stood out in bas-relief during the hearings. I also don't agree with the mainstream women's movement's singular solution to run as many women for office as possible. It's obvious that no matter who fills the slots in the current system, the system remains intact. Late twentieth-century U.S. capitalism cannot be fixed by adding a few new faces to the ruling class. Indeed, it was the Bush administration's cynical tactic of replacing the only other Black Supreme Court Justice, progressive and heroic Thurgood Marshall, with a Black conservative which set this whole debacle in motion in the first place.

The worst consequence of the Hill-Thomas hearings for me was not the familiar lessons they revealed about the corruption of the power elite, but what they revealed about African Americans' level of consciousness about both sexual and racial politics. It was truly demoralizing to see how the Hill-Thomas confrontation reinforced the perception that any Black woman who raises the issue of sexual oppression in the African American community is somehow a traitor to the race, which translates into being a traitor to Black men. I've always wondered how Black women (who are half the race) living free from fear and degradation and achieving their full human potential would undermine the well-being of the race as a whole.

It has always taken courage for Black and other women of color to speak out about sexism within our communities. In this instance an African American woman did so more publicly and dramatically than at any time in history, and was attacked not only by white right-wing misogynists, but by African Americans who felt that she had stepped out of line by accusing a Black man whom white racists had picked for a high public office.

It was not only Black men who succumbed to the Bush administration's calculated effort to divide and conquer the Black community via the nomination of Clarence Thomas. Black women also danced to the White House's tune. Those African American women who disassociated themselves from Anita Hill's revelation of sexual violence, and who gave their support to the man she accused, evidence a tragic degree of self-hatred. Instead of reacting with outrage, some actually had the attitude "I took it [sexual harassment, rape, battering] so why can't you?" Some Black women have so thoroughly internalized the message that Blackness and femaleness are inherently worthless that they think the only way to cancel out these "negatives" is to embrace the political agendas and values of whites and males. The Black feminist movement has worked very hard to offer Black women a more accurate perception of ourselves. Confronting our self-hatred has been a necessary prerequisite to organizing on our own behalf.

Ironically, there are probably a lot of Black people who believe Anita Hill's charges, but who still think it's more important to stand behind a Black man, even when he has utter contempt for the struggles of African Americans, than it is to support a Black woman's right not to be abused. The Monday morning polls that said that most Black Americans still support Thomas tell me how much work Black feminists still have to do to alert our communities to issues of sexual violence and also to get out the message that respecting Black women's freedom does not subtract from the freedom of Black men.

Unfortunately, the attitudes that were brought to the surface by the Hill-Thomas confrontation are not unique. In the last few years misogyny has become a growth industry in the African American community. As in the heyday of the Moynihan Report (Senator Daniel Patrick Moynihan's 1965 *The Negro Family: The Case for National Action*), Black women are once again viewed as the source of the myriad problems our people face and despite the fact that we experience sexual oppression on top of racism and class oppression, we are portrayed as being in a much better position than endangered Black men. Blaming Black women instead of racism and those who run the system and benefit from it is a political dead end, yet negative views of Black women abound whether in rap, in films, or on the street.

Recent films by Black men ridicule Black women, scapegoat us for all of the race's problems, and portray physical violence against us as perfectly justified. Rap music frequently defines Black women as shrews, with no value other than as sexual commodities. Last summer on the streets of Oakland I saw a Black male youth wearing a tee shirt with the words "SHUT UP BITCH" written on it in bold letters. Friends to whom I've mentioned it have seen the same tee shirt in other cities all over the country. I can just imagine Clarence Thomas and his cronies wearing this tee shirt underneath their three-piece suits and judicial robes.

The Hill-Thomas confrontation was incredibly depressing, but it was also politically catalytic. Although the outcome seemingly demonstrated the overarching power of white-male rule, I got a very different message. The powers that be in this country are in serious trouble. This was only the latest example of their efforts to maintain their hold upon the political economy and upon an image of power by using desperate means. And as usually occurs nowadays, whether it be the savings and loan crisis, the war in the Persian Gulf, or a failing domestic economy, they have to resort to ever more outrageous lies and deceptions just to stay in the same place.

Real political power, however, lies in the hands of the majority of people in this country who do not benefit from this system: people of color, women, lesbians, gays, workers, elders, and the differently abled. Often inspired by the multi-issued leadership of radical women of color, oppressed groups are increasingly banding together in grassroots coalitions to fight the system and to bring about fundamental political change. Feminists of color who consistently make the links between issues are building a movement whose politics have the revolutionary potential to free us all. The Hill-Thomas case illustrated why our work is so crucial and it also helped to radicalize more women. One of them, I hope, is Anita Hill.

I see numerous signs that women of color are refusing to be silenced and are on the move. African American Women in Defense of Ourselves is a grassroots network that sprang up only days after the hearings and placed ads in the *New York Times* (November 17, 1991) and in Black newspapers all over the country. Their clear analysis of the hearings signed by 1,603 Black women marks a watershed in Black feminist organizing. Never have so many Black women publicly stated their refusal to pit racial oppression against sexual oppression. The ad has elicited an outpouring of enthusiasm and support and the women who initiated it intend to create an ongoing mechanism through which Black women can organize and speak out.

Revolutionary Sisters of Color is a one-year-old organization which is building a political base both nationally and internationally. Founded at the 1990 "I Am Your Sister" conference which honored Black lesbian feminist poet Audre Lorde, RSOC has broken ground as the first autonomous group embracing all women of color in this country and abroad who are committed to an explicitly socialist and feminist action agenda.

I also find it encouraging that there were Black men who were furious about what happened to Anita Hill and who had the integrity to speak out. Many more need to do so.

I hope that white feminists have a better sense of the kinds of challenges women of color face when we make the commitment to confront sexual oppression. If white women really want to support the struggles of women of color, the best thing they can do is to clean the racism out of their own house and they can only accomplish this when they participate in political organizing that directly challenges the multiple oppressions that women of color face, oppressions which undermine their lives as well. Not only would we then have more trustworthy allies, it would also be that much harder for people in our communities to accuse us of being the dupes of unprincipled white women.

Of course as we already knew, it's going to be a long struggle. But in the aftermath of the Hill-Thomas episode my new tee shirt will display the words of the old freedom song: "AIN'T GONNA LET NOBODY TURN ME AROUND!"

1992

Leonore Gordon invited me to write this article for a special issue of the *Interracial Books for Children Bulletin*, which she guest edited on the theme "Homophobia and Education: How to Deal with Name-Calling." It is important to remember the *Bulletin's* 1983 publication date. At that time few Black lesbians or gay men had written about homophobia, especially in publications that reached Black audiences. Because the Council on Interracial Books for Children had done groundbreaking work in expanding school curricula to include materials about people of color and women, I was excited that this assignment offered me a rare opportunity to reach nonlesbian and nongay people of color, many of whom were educators.

One change that has occurred since this was written is that there are more and more portrayals of primarily white lesbians and gays in popular media. It would have been difficult to imagine the numbers of lesbian, gay, bisexual, and transgendered characters now visible in television and film in 1983. This shift is largely the result of lesbian and gay organizing, particularly organizing targeted at the media. The AIDS epidemic's impact upon the entertainment industry and the arts has also helped to heighten consciousness about lesbian and gay issues in those contexts.

Homophobia

Why Bring It Up?

In 1977 the Combahee River Collective, a Black feminist organization in Boston of which I was member, wrote:

> The most general statement of our politics at the present time
> would be that we are actively committed to struggling against
> racial, sexual, heterosexual, and class oppression and see as our
> particular task the development of integrated analysis and practice
> based upon the fact that the major systems of oppression are
> interlocking.... We ... often find it difficult to separate race from
> class from sex oppression because in our lives they are most often
> experienced simultaneously.[1]

Despite the logic and clarity of Third World women's analysis
of the simultaneity of oppression, people of all races, progressive
ones included, seem peculiarly reluctant to grasp these basic
truths, especially when it comes to incorporating an active resistance to homophobia into their everyday lives. Homophobia is
usually the last oppression to be mentioned, the last to be taken
seriously, the last to go. But it is extremely serious, sometimes
to the point of being fatal.

Consider that on the night of September 29, 1982, twenty to
thirty New York City policemen rushed without warning into
Blues, a Times Square bar. They harassed and severely beat the
patrons, vandalized the premises, emptied the cash register, and
left without making a single arrest. What motivated such brutal
behavior? The answer is simple. The cops were inspired by three

cherished tenets of our society, racism, classism, and homophobia: the bar's clientele is Black, working class, and gay. As the police cracked heads, they yelled racist and homophobic epithets familiar to every school child. The attackers' hatred of both the queer and the colored, far from making them exceptional, put them squarely in the mainstream. If their actions were more extreme than most, their attitudes certainly were not.

The Blues bar happens to be across the street from the offices of the *New York Times*. The white, upper middle-class, presumably heterosexual staff of the nation's premier newspaper regularly calls in complaints about the bar to the police. Not surprisingly, none of the New York daily papers, including the *Times*, bothered to report the incident. A coalition of Third World and white lesbians and gay men organized a large protest demonstration soon after the attack occurred. Both moderate and militant civil rights and antiracist organizations were notably absent, and they have yet to express public outrage about this verifiable incident of police brutality, undoubtedly because the Black people involved were not straight.

Intertwining "Isms"

What happened at Blues perfectly illustrates the ways in which the major "isms" *including* homophobia are intimately and violently intertwined. I have little difficulty seeing how the systems of oppression interconnect, if for no other reason than that their existence so frequently affects my life. During the 1970s and 1980s political lesbians of color have often been the most astute about the necessity for developing understandings of the connections between oppressions. They have also opposed the building of hierarchies and challenged the "easy way out" of choosing a "primary oppression" and downplaying those messy inconsistencies that occur whenever race, sex, class, and sexual identity actually mix. Ironically, for the forces on the right, hating lesbians and gay men, people of color, Jews, and women go hand in hand. *They* make connections between oppressions in the most negative ways with horrifying results. Supposedly progressive people, on the other hand, who oppose oppression on every other level, balk at acknowledging the societally sanctioned abuse of lesbians and gay men as a serious problem. Their tacit attitude is "Homophobia, why bring it up?"

There are numerous reasons for otherwise sensitive people's reluctance to confront homophobia in themselves and others. A major one is that people are generally threatened about issues of sexuality, and for some the mere existence of homosexuals calls their sexuality/heterosexuality into question. Unlike many other oppressed groups, homosexuals are not a group whose identity is clear from birth. Through the process of coming out, a person might indeed acquire this identity at any point in life. One way to protect one's heterosexual credentials and privilege is to put down lesbians and gay men at every turn, to make as large a gulf as possible between "we" and "they."

There are several misconceptions and attitudes which I find particularly destructive because of the way they work to isolate the concerns of lesbians and gay men:

1. Lesbian and gay male oppression is not as serious as other oppressions. It is not a political matter, but a private concern. The life-destroying impact of lost jobs, children, friendships, and family; the demoralizing toll of living in constant fear of being discovered by the wrong person which pervades all lesbians' and gay men's lives whether closeted or out; and the actual physical violence and deaths that gay men and lesbians suffer at the hands of homophobes can be, if one subscribes to this myth, completely ignored.

2. "Gay" means gay white men with large discretionary incomes, period. Perceiving gay people in this way allows one to ignore that some of us are women *and* people of color *and* working class *and* poor *and* disabled *and* old. Thinking narrowly of gay people as white, middle class, and male, which is just what the establishment media want people to think, undermines

consciousness of how identities and issues overlap. It is essential, however, in making connections between homophobia and other oppressions, not to fall prey to the distorted reasoning that the justification for taking homophobia seriously is that it affects some groups who are "verifiably" oppressed, for example, people of color, women, or disabled people. Homophobia is in and of itself a verifiable oppression and in a heterosexist system, all nonheterosexuals are viewed as "deviants" and are oppressed.

3. Homosexuality is a white problem or even a "white disease." This attitude is much too prevalent among people of color. Individuals who are militantly opposed to racism in all its forms still find lesbianism and male homosexuality something to snicker about or, worse, to despise. Homophobic people of color are oppressive not just to white people, but to members of their own groups—at least 10 percent of their own groups.

4. Expressions of homophobia are legitimate and acceptable in contexts where other kinds of verbalized bigotry would be prohibited. Put-downs and jokes about "dykes" and "faggots" can be made without the slightest criticism in circles where "nigger" and "chink" jokes, for instance, would bring instant censure or even ostracism. One night of television viewing indicates how very acceptable public expressions of homophobia are.

How can such deeply entrenched attitudes and behavior be confronted and changed? Certainly gay and lesbian/feminist activism has made significant inroads since the late 1960s, both in the public sphere and upon the awareness of individuals. These movements have served a highly educational function, but they have not had nearly enough impact upon the educational system itself. Curriculum that focuses in a positive way upon issues of sexual identity, sexuality, and sexism is still rare, particularly in primary and secondary grades. Yet schools are virtual cauldrons of homophobic

sentiment, as witnessed by everything from the graffiti in the bath-
rooms and the put-downs yelled on the playground to the heterosexist bias of most texts and the firing of teachers on no other basis
than that they are not heterosexual.

In the current political climate schools are constantly under hostile scrutiny from well-organized conservative forces. More than a
little courage is required to challenge students' negative attitudes
about what it means to be homosexual, female, Third World, etc.,
but these attitudes *must* be challenged if pervasive taken-for-granted
homophobia is ever to cease. I have found both in teaching and in
speaking to a wide variety of audiences that making connections
between oppressions is an excellent way to introduce the subjects of
lesbian and gay male identity and homophobia, because it offers
people a frame of reference upon which to build. This is especially
true if efforts have already been made in the classroom to teach
about racism and sexism. It is factually inaccurate and strategically
mistaken to present gay materials as if all gay people were white and
male. Fortunately, there is an increasing body of work available, usually written by Third World feminists, that provides an integrated
approach to the intersection of a multiplicity of identities and issues.

Perhaps some readers are still wondering, "Homophobia, why
bring it up?" One reason to bring it up is that at least 10 percent of
your students will be or already are lesbians and gay males. Ten
percent of your colleagues are as well. Homophobia may well be
the last oppression to go, but it will go. It will go a lot faster if
people who are opposed to *every* form of subjugation work in coalition to make it happen.

1983

Note

1. The Combahee River Collective, "A Black Feminist Statement," in
*All the Women Are White, All the Blacks Are Men, But Some of Us Are
Brave: Black Women's Studies*, ed. Gloria T. Hull, Patricia Bell Scott, and
Barbara Smith (New York: The Feminist Press at The City University of
New York, 1982), 13, 16.

This essay was written for a special issue of *The American Voice* on silencing, conceived in the wake of Congress's first attacks on the National Endowment for the Arts in the late 1980s. The endowment and artists' rights have faced continual assaults since that time. In 1997 a bill to abolish the NEA passed the House, but failed to pass the Senate. The NEA's funding remains in jeopardy, however, and has been severely cut since 1994. In contrast, military spending continues to be the highest-priced item in the federal budget.

Several artists of color have been highly visible targets of Senator Jesse Helm's rabid campaign. The firestorms surrounding Andres Serrano's *Piss Christ*, which depicts a crucifix immersed in urine; Marlon Riggs's groundbreaking film, *Tongues Untied*, about Black gay male experience; and Cheryl Dunyé's *The Watermelon Woman*, the first Black lesbian feature-length film, illustrate how threatening *and* powerful queer, sex-positive, race-conscious work by artists of color can be.

The sad reality of closeting among prominent figures in the Black community, especially artists, intellectuals, and political activists, has not altered significantly since this piece was written.

The NEA Is the Least of It

When I was growing up, I seldom spoke. My sister and I were so shy, especially when we were small, that when we were introduced to family friends they inevitably commented upon our "bashfulness" after futile efforts to get us to talk. Except at home, where I felt relatively comfortable, I spent a lot of the first eighteen years of my life seeing, thinking, feeling, but not speaking.

Of course, my shyness, my efforts to erase myself, were not solely the result of my socioeconomic status. But, looking back, I'm sure that being born Black, female, and working class in the mid-1940s affected my perception of how safe it was to speak, and made me question whether I even had the right to do so.

If it were not for political activism—the Civil Rights movement, Black student organizing, the anti–Vietnam War movement, and particularly the feminist movement—I doubt that I ever would have learned to speak out. Fortunately, when I was in high school, I discovered James Baldwin. Here was a Black person who was simultaneously angry, sensitive, and analytical and who wrote brilliantly about things that mattered to me. Whenever Baldwin appeared on television, I was mesmerized. Black people on TV were a rarity and, if we were permitted to appear, we were expected to entertain. It was unheard of for a Black person to tell millions of white viewers, not to mention a squirming white interviewer, exactly what he thought about white racism and Black freedom and dare them to disagree.

Because of his passionate activism and command of craft, Baldwin, more than any other author, fed my dreams of wanting to write. He proved that breaking silences, as a Black gay man, with both spoken and written words can make a difference, especially to people who live nearly invisible lives.

Issues of silencing, censorship, and the need to challenge them have never been abstract to me. Long before the right wing began a focused attack upon government funding of artists who counter the status quo, it was clear to those of us who are multiply oppressed that our right to speak out, to write, to dissent politically, or merely to exist are considered rebellious acts and are in constant jeopardy. Racism, sexism, homophobia, and class oppression have silenced far more people than the withdrawal of National Endowment for the Arts grants since the summer of 1989.

Of course, the campaign to place restrictions upon the content of what the NEA funds and other censorship efforts have serious repercussions, and potentially threaten the right of all individuals to express themselves. In order to effectively fight these attacks, however, it should be understood that this growing repression is inherent in the political and economic system that engenders it. Attacks on arts funding, especially the targeting of artists who create "homoerotic" art and those who are lesbian or gay, regardless of their subject matter, unequivocally signal this country's potential for fascism.

The repression of unconventional art is just one of countless tactics that the ruling class uses to frighten and disempower people, to keep the majority of the population in line as they attempt to salvage a capitalist system that is falling apart. As economic and social conditions worsen and the desperation of those in power increases, the veneer of "democracy" gets stripped away. The attempts of forces both inside and outside the government to suppress art are perfectly consistent in a historical period when all kinds of rights and freedoms are abrogated. Access to legal abortion is being curtailed; hate crimes against people of color, Jews, lesbians, gays, and women (often carried out by well-organized hate groups) are skyrocketing; laws that protect basic civil rights have been weakened or completely overturned: the First Amendment rights of radical gay,

Third World, and feminist teachers are under attack through politically motivated firings; the federal government engages in blatant union busting; and the United States sees fit to disrupt the governments of countries that it views as threatening to its imperialist hegemony, frequently ordering its military to invade other nations and to murder civilians with impunity.

White middle-class artists are discovering, as others have before them, that this system parcels out freedoms stingily and unfairly and withdraws them arbitrarily, depending upon the vagaries of the economy, foreign policy, and the electoral climate. It should surprise no one that a right-wing government would oppose the funding of work that is lesbian, gay, or sexually explicit. As Audre Lorde, one of three lesbian writers whose NEA grants have come under scrutiny from Jesse Helms and his cohorts, observes, "You can't expect the government to fund our revolution."

Most of those who are currently so incensed over this issue, however, are not revolutionaries and are not even politically involved except to protest a narrow range of issues that directly affect them. Truly revolutionary artists would make the connections between this wave of censorship and the "silencing" and literal annihilation of countless other groups. They would also understand that this system is by definition hierarchical and unjust, and that until we eradicate it and create a democracy that is socialist, feminist, and antiracist, the majority of people—people of color, women, lesbians, gays, Jews, working people, the differently abled, and elders—will not only be silenced, but oppressed in every facet of our lives.

In this society, the silencing of lesbians and gay men of color takes many forms. The censorship and repression that I and other lesbians and gay men of color find most galling is not being perpetrated by the NEA, but comes instead from *within* oppressed groups to which we supposedly belong. Racism in the lesbian, gay, and women's movements and sexism and heterosexism among people of color are "the last straws," which we nevertheless confront again and again.

A white lesbian and gay community that is up in arms about the repression of the NEA should consider how their all-white readings, exhibits, theatrical productions, conferences, and periodicals, or their token, often ill-conceived, efforts to be inclusive, effectively silence lesbians and gay men of color. Tokenizing is a form of silencing too, because even if a person of color appears, it is not possible to share the range of her or his creativity when she or he is objectified and isolated. Those of us who refuse to participate as tokens in all-white contexts are excluded and silenced by default.

Ironically, as this country moves further and further to the right, a large sector of the lesbian and gay community also becomes more conservative, focusing on electoral politics, legislative agendas, and lobbying, as opposed to fighting for genuine liberation. The upsurge in confrontational tactics and zap actions, such as "outing" apolitical and reactionary public figures, are not signs of increasing radicalism, since they generally do not spring from a multileveled analysis of oppression, nor do they challenge oppression at its roots. Given the limitations of these kinds of politics, it is not surprising that both blatant and insidious racism is on the rise within the lesbian and gay community.

Although women of color have always challenged the second wave of the women's movement to incorporate an antiracist critique and to address issues that affect all women, including women of color and working women, racism and segregation are alive and well within the feminist movement. At this late date, there are still white women's organizations that are perplexed about how to do "outreach" to women of color, and white women who resent and obstruct efforts by women of color to organize autonomously. Although there are inspiring examples of radical women of color and radical white women working together politically, the bourgeois elements that dominate the movement are still characterized by exclusivity and tokenizing.

In the area of feminist publishing, where I do much of my work, I've seen a grassroots commitment to providing a means for women to express themselves give way to women's presses as businesses in constant competition with commercial publishers and also with each other. Although these presses may publish writing by women of color, most do not incorporate women of color into other aspects of the publishing process, including editorial decision making, production, publicity, and promotion. In 1990, "ownership" of women's media is still almost exclusively in the hands of white women.

Even when the lesbian, gay, and feminist movements attempt to confront racism, a major factor which prevents them from doing it effectively is the assumption that it is feasible to address racism solely within the context of these movements, and to ignore its destruction of the society as a whole. Racism is not gender nor sexual orientation specific; it does not solely affect women, lesbians, and gay men. Indeed, racism within these movements is an indication of how thoroughly institutionalized racism is in this country's power structure, and that it inevitably manifests itself in every sector of U.S. life. When whites in these movements demonstrate a consistent commitment to speaking out and organizing offensives against racist violence, police brutality, homelessness, economic exploitation, and unequal access to quality education and health care, people of color can begin to take their antiracist *actions* seriously.

Sexism and heterosexism among people of color are even more demoralizing since our racial, ethnic, and nationality communities have usually represented home, a physical and emotional place we could rely upon to help counter the effects of white domination. Since the late 1960s, despite criticism, ridicule, and ostracism, feminists of color—American Indian, Asian American, Latina, Arab American, and Black—have spoken out about sexual oppression in our home communities. Although these problems are far from being resolved, our speaking out has made measurable differences in both male and female attitudes toward women's freedom.

There have always been elements, however, that have viewed the mere raising of sexual political issues as threatening, and, through intimidation and attacks, have attempted to silence women who do not conform to sexist expectations. In the African American community, numerous controversies have focused directly upon works by Black women writers. Reactionary forces have stated that we should not be allowed to address the realities of male chauvinism and sexual violence in our writing, that to do so is somehow disloyal to the race. Writer Ishmael Reed is probably the most vocal proponent of this position, and continues to accuse Black women writers who are critical of sexual oppression and who have achieved literary recognition of participating in a white-orchestrated conspiracy against Black men. Fortunately, most Black women writers have not been swayed by this kind of pressure.

The nineties have ushered in a resurgence of Black nationalism accompanied by, not surprisingly, more and more public expressions of misogyny. Shahrazad Ali's book *The Blackman's Guide to Understanding the Blackwoman*, the lyrics of many rap songs, and the films of Spike Lee are only three popular examples. In this climate, it is crucial for Black women writers to continue to speak out, to depict the range of our experiences, and to raise complex issues that will ultimately enable both men and women to interact with a higher level of understanding and cooperation.

As I've often stated, homophobia among all the major oppressions is "the last to go," the one form of discrimination and cruelty that many feel perfectly justified in perpetrating. Heterosexism within communities of color is undoubtedly the most volatile of the issues that lead to internal censoring and silencing. The closet itself is a form of censoring and erasure, which the heterosexual majority imposes in order to maintain its privilege. When lesbians and gay men refuse to be closeted and confront homophobia as a political issue, many nonlesbians and nongays become irate. The ones who are fascist carry out crimes of violence against us, including murder. The ones who are liberal claim that they do not mind if we exist, just so we don't call attention to that fact—in other words, just so we remain closeted.

More than for any other oppressed group, speaking out is crucial for lesbians and gay men because unless we are willing literally to articulate who we are in a variety of situations, we are assumed to be heterosexual and disappear. Speaking out and being out have been the cornerstones upon which the contemporary lesbian and gay liberation movement has been built. Act Up's slogan, "Silence = Death," is applicable not only to the AIDS crisis, but to all aspects of lesbian and gay oppression. My entire career has been affected by the reality of homophobia in my racial community, and I've devoted much of my work to challenging it. Although we still have miles to go, there is evidence of progress and increasing openness in grappling with the fact of our sexual diversity.

In early 1988, Joseph Beam and I drafted a statement that was signed by twenty Black lesbian and gay writers. We decided to go on record about the exclusion and silencing we experience at the hands of the Black literary establishment. We presented the statement at the Second National Black Writers Conference at Medgar Evers College in Brooklyn, where we circulated it widely and read it aloud at the conference's closing session. It begins as follows:

> We are Black lesbian and gay writers who are taking the opportunity of the Second National Black Writers Conference to go on record. We are well aware that despite our commitment to exploring gender roles and to challenging sexual, racial, and class oppression, work that has been essential to transforming the practice of African American literature in this era, the Black literary establishment systematically chooses to exclude us from the range of its activities. These include participation in conferences, invitations to submit work to journals and anthologies, serious and nonhomophobic criticism of our writing, positive depictions of lesbian and gay characters, inclusion in Black studies course curricula, and all levels of formal and informal mentoring and support. If we are sometimes included in token numbers, it is often amid heterosexist protest and homophobic attacks. Because we function with integrity, refuse to be closeted, and address lesbian and gay oppression as a political issue, our lives and work are made invisible.

The statement goes on to place our struggle in the context of Black lesbian and gay literary history, and concludes with the assertion that we are committed to continuing "our difficult and

much needed work." Despite our fears, our reading of this statement was met with widespread applause and a public invitation
from the conference director to work with them in planning the
next conference. We were gratified that our efforts to challenge
backward attitudes and politics were met with respect and a willingness to change. On the other hand, although we sent copies of
the statement and press releases to at least two dozen publications,
encouraging them to report our action and to reprint the statement, to our knowledge it has not appeared in any of the major
Black journals.

Confronting homophobia and sexism in our racial and nationality communities is an incredible task, but whatever the personal
pain it sometimes brings us, it is essential to continue. Heterosexism and sexism are inextricably linked. Both require the imposi-
tion of rigid gender roles, the repression of sexuality, the limiting
of reproductive choices, and the negation of women's autonomy.
The destruction of one requires the destruction of the other, and
this can only occur when capitalism, which depends upon the sub-
ordination of women and children within the nuclear family, rigid
class divisions, and surplus labor pools determined by race and
gender, is destroyed as well.

The final aspect of silencing I want to examine is that of the
closet itself. I constantly hear about prominent and productive
Black women—writers, artists, and political figures—who could
share the responsibility of changing our community's attitudes,
but who have instead chosen to hold onto the secrecy of their closets. Of course, there are real and sometimes dangerous sanctions
against being out, and there are lesbians and gays who do not have
the option, who might, for example, lose their jobs, their housing,
or custody of their children. The individuals I am referring to,
however, have secure academic positions or are successfully self-
employed, yet they still refuse to take a political stand in favor of
liberation.

It is ironic that those of us who are out, who have challenged
the heterosexist status quo, and who have helped to build the

lesbian, gay, and feminist movements, have made it a lot easier for them to have their relationships with other women "in private." A handful of out-lesbians of color have gone into the wilderness and hacked through the seemingly impenetrable jungle of homophobia. Our tools have been inadequate, our resources small, our numbers few, yet we have pressed on and come out the other side. Our closeted sisters come upon the wilderness, which now is not nearly as frightening, and walk the path we have cleared, even pausing at times to comment upon the beautiful view. In the meantime, we are on the other side of the continent hacking through another jungle.

At the very least, people who choose to be closeted can speak out against homophobia whenever it occurs. Like principled heterosexuals, they can protest the oppression without having to come out themselves. Usually, to protect their images, however, they do not even speak out in a consistent fashion.

The depth of this problem was brought home to me in November of 1989. I had been on a panel during a weekend of events celebrating the twentieth anniversary of coeducation at Yale. The next day, a Black woman graduate student drove me to the airport. I meet hundreds of students each year, but I still remember Tonnia. It wasn't only because she was so bright, had made a serious commitment to developing as an artist, and planned to use her talents in the working-class African American community from which she'd come. I remember her because of the urgent questions she put to me about how she might survive as an out Black lesbian artist in the decades that lay before her. Her questions reminded me so much of my own at her age, when there were even fewer signs that one could be a Black lesbian and live to tell about it. At one point I said, "You don't have many role models, do you?" Just saying the words made me furious because it struck me how the Black women writers, academics, and politicos who protect their closets at all costs never think about people like Tonnia. They also do not think about how their silences contribute to the silencing of others. I meet students like Tonnia all over the country: young lesbians, gay men, and those who are still questioning their sexual identities. All of them are struggling in isolation because most of the lesbian and gay adults around them are more concerned with their individual security and careers than they are with building community and working for radical political change.

From my own experience, I know that it is quite possible to provide support to students of all races, genders, and sexual orientations and still be Black and still be out. Young people respond positively to those who demonstrate integrity and courage and to those who genuinely care about them. Recent studies indicate that 30 percent of youth suicides can be attributed to turmoil about sexual orientation and the fear or actual experience of homophobia. Young lesbians and gay men of color are especially vulnerable, since there are so few adults of color who they can turn to for support. If I had to choose, I would much rather have the respect of the generation coming up than of my own. They are the ones who will shape the next century, the ones who will undoubtedly be leaders in the revolutionary struggles that will ultimately ensure every person's freedom, and that every person's voice will be heard.

1990

I wrote this article for *Gay Community News* in 1993. Unfortunately, the "great divide" between the lesbian and gay community and the Black community has not markedly improved since then. In August 1997 Alveda King, a niece of Martin Luther King Jr., denounced California legislation designed to crack down on antigay discrimination. She stated, "To equate homosexuality with race is to give a death sentence to civil rights."[1] A few weeks later gospel singers Angie and Debbie Winans released a song entitled "It's Not Natural" that condemned homosexuality as unnatural and antifamily. King's and the Winans's public homophobia was met with vigorous protests from Black lesbians and gays and from other segments of the lesbian, gay, and Black communities.

In 1995 my comment about racism in Albany's lesbian and gay community was brought home when I experienced one of the most vicious racist attacks of my life, while attempting to work with a predominantly white local group. The vast majority of white lesbians and gays here have no interest in antiracist organizing and at best seek cosmetic solutions for what they mistakenly view as interpersonal problems.

In contrast, lesbian and gay people of color organizing has flourished in the Capital Region during the same period, catalyzed in part by the racial terrorism aimed at a number of us in 1995. An umbrella coalition of four organizations, In Our Own Voices, is providing autonomous political leadership and support for people of color. Cleveland's Black lesbian and gay community has made similarly significant strides with the formation of the African American

Lesbian, Gay, and Bisexual Caucus in 1995 and the publication of a newsletter. The homophobic campaign initiated
by Black ministers in Cleveland in the summer of 1993 and
the connections I began to make there with Black lesbians
and gays in response to this crisis were important factors
in my decision to do research in Cleveland for my study of
African American lesbian and gay history.

Nationally, the National Black Lesbian and Gay Leadership Forum continues to build the scope of its critically
important work. Under its auspices, the extraordinary
activist Mandy Carter has traveled extensively as afield
organizer to work with Black lesbians and gays, especially
in areas where organized homophobic campaigns are
under way. The National Gay and Lesbian Task Force continues to work in coalition with communities of color. One
aspect of these efforts is their annual Honoring Our Allies
program which has recognized the members of the Con-
gressional Black Caucus (who have the most consistently
supportive voting record, compared to all the other members of Congress, e.g., Democrats or women, on legislation
affecting lesbians and gays); the government of South
Africa for becoming the first nation in history to protect the
rights of lesbians and gays in its constitution; and Coretta
Scott King for her decades as an ally to the lesbian, gay,
bisexual, and transgendered community.

Blacks and Gays

Healing the Great Divide

Perhaps the most maddening question anyone can ask me is "Which do you put first: being Black or being a woman, being Black or being gay?" The underlying assumption is that I should prioritize one of my identities because one of them is actually more important than the rest or that I must arbitrarily choose one of them over the others for the sake of acceptance in one particular community.

I always explain that I refuse to do political work and, more importantly, to live my life in this way. All of the aspects of who I am are crucial, indivisible, and pose no inherent conflict. They only seem to be in opposition in this particular time and place, living under U.S. capitalism, a system whose functioning has always required that large groups of people be economically, racially, and sexually oppressed and that these potentially dissident groups be kept divided from each other at all costs.

I've devoted many years to making the connections between issues and communities and to forging strong working coalitions. Although this work is far from finished, it has met with some success. In 1993, however, two aspects of my identity and two communities whose freedom I've always fought for are being publicly defined as being at war with one another.

For the first time, the relationship between the African American and lesbian and gay communities is being widely debated both within and outside of movement circles. One catalyst for this discussion has been gay leaders cavalierly comparing lifting the ban on homosexuals in the military with racially desegregating the armed forces following World War II. The National Association for the Advancement of Colored People (NAACP) and other Black civil rights organizations' decisions to speak out in favor of lesbian and gay rights and to support the April 1993 March on Washington have met with protests from some sectors of the Black community and have also spurred the debate.

Ironically, the group of people who are least often consulted about their perspectives on this great divide are those who are most deeply affected by it: Black lesbian and gay activists. Contradictions that we have been grappling with for years, namely homophobia in the Black community, racism in the lesbian and gay community, and the need for both communities to work together as allies to defeat our real enemies, are suddenly on other people's minds. Because Black lesbians and gays are not thought of as leaders in either movement, however, this debate has been largely framed by those who have frighteningly little and inaccurate information.

Thanks in part to the white lesbian and gay community's own public relations campaigns, Black Americans view the lesbian and gay community as uniformly wealthy, highly privileged, and politically powerful, a group that has suffered nothing like the centuries of degradation caused by U.S. racism. Rev. Dennis Kuby, a civil rights activist, states in a letter to the *New York Times*: "Gays are not subject to water hoses and police dogs, denied access to lunch counters, or prevented from voting." Most Blacks have no idea, however, that we are threatened with the loss of employment, of housing, and of custody of our children, and are subject to verbal abuse, gay bashing, and death at the hands of homophobes. Kuby's statement also does not acknowledge those lesbians and gays who have been subjected to all of the racist abuse he cites, because we are both Black and gay. Because we are rendered invisible in both Black and gay contexts, it is that much easier for the Black community to oppose gay rights and to express homophobia without recognizing that these attacks and the lack of legal protections affect its own members.

The racism that has pervaded the mainstream gay movement only fuels the perceived divisions between Blacks and gays. Single-issue politics, unlike lesbian and gay organizing that is consciously and strategically connected to the overall struggle for social and economic justice, do nothing to convince Blacks that lesbians and gays actually care about eradicating racial oppression. At the very same time that some gays make blanket comparisons between the gay movement and the Black Civil Rights movement, they also assume that Blacks and other people of color have won all our battles and are in terrific shape in comparison with lesbians and gays.

In an interview in the *Dallas Voice* (December 1992), lesbian publisher Barbara Grier states: "We are the last minority group unfairly legislated against in the U.S." Grier's perception is of course inaccurate. Legislation that negatively affects people of color, immigrants, disabled people, and women occurs every day, especially when court decisions that undermine existing legal protections are taken into account.

In 1991, well before the relationship between the gay community and the Black community was a hot topic, Andrew Sullivan, editor of the *New Republic* asserted the following in the *Advocate*:

> The truth is, our position is far worse than that of any ethnic minority or heterosexual women.
>
> Every fundamental civil right has already been granted to these groups: The issues that they discuss now involve nuances of affirmative action, comparable pay, and racial quotas. Gay people, however, still live constitutionally in the South of the '50s. . . .
>
> We are not allowed to marry—a right granted to American Blacks even under slavery and never denied to heterosexuals. We are not permitted to enroll in the armed services—a right granted decades ago to blacks and to heterosexual women.
>
> Our civil rights agenda, then, should have less to do with the often superfluous minority politics of the 1991 Civil Rights Act and more to do with the vital moral fervor of the Civil Rights Act of 1964.
>
> A better strategy to bring about a society more tolerant of gay men and women would involve dropping our alliance with the

current Rainbow Coalition lobby and recapturing the clarity of
the original civil rights movement. The point is to rekindle the
cause of Martin Luther King Jr. and not to rescue the career of
Jesse Jackson.

Sullivan's cynical distortions ignore that quality of life is determined by much more than legislation. Clearly, he also knows
nothing about slavery. Slaves were frequently not permitted to
marry and their marriages and family relationships were not legally
recognized or protected. Until 1967 when the Supreme Court
decided *Loving v. Virginia*, it was illegal for Blacks to marry whites
in sixteen states. The armed services were rigidly segregated until
after World War II. Racist abuse and denial of promotions and
military honors typified the Black experience in the military. Sullivan also has not noticed that joblessness, poverty, racist and sexist
violence, and the lack of decent housing, health care, and education make the lives of many "ethnic minorities" and "heterosexual
women" a living hell. But Sullivan doesn't care about these folks.
He just wants to make sure he gets what he thinks he deserves as
an upper-class white male.

Lesbians and gay men of color have been trying to push the gay
movement to grasp the necessity of antiracist practice for nigh on
twenty years. Except in the context of organizing within the wom-
en's movement with progressive white lesbian feminists, we haven't
made much progress.

I'm particularly struck by the fact that for the most part queer
theory and queer politics, which are currently so popular, offer neither substantial antiracist analysis nor practice. Queer activists'
understanding of how to deal with race is usually limited to their
including a few lesbians or gay men of color in their ranks, who are
expected to carry out the political agenda that the white majority
has already determined.

In October 1993 Lesbian Avengers from New York City traveled
to several states in the Northeast on what they called a "freedom
ride." Lesbians of color from Albany, New York, pointed out that

the appropriation of this term was offensive because the organization had not demonstrated involvement in antiracist organizing
and had made few links with people of color, including nonlesbians and nongays in the communities they planned to visit. Even
when we explained that calling themselves "freedom riders" might
negatively affect the coalitions we've been working to build with
people of color in Albany, the group kept the name and simply
made a few token changes in their press release.

These divisions are particularly dangerous at a time when the
white right wing has actually targeted people of color with their
homophobic message. As white lesbian activist Suzanne Pharr points
out in an excellent article, "Racist Politics and Homophobia":

> Community by community, the religious Right works skillfully to
> divide us along fissures that already exist. It is as though they have
> a political seismograph to locate the racism and sexism in the les-
> bian and gay community, the sexism and homophobia in commu-
> nities of color. While the Right is *united* by their racism, sexism,
> and homophobia in their goal to dominate all of us, we are *divided*
> by our own racism, sexism, and homophobia. (*Transformation*,
> July/August 1993; italics mine)

The right's divisive strategy of enlisting the Black community's
support for their homophobic campaign literally hit home for me
in June 1993. A Black lesbian who lives in Cleveland, Ohio, where
I grew up, called to tell me that a group of Black ministers had
placed a virulently homophobic article in the *Call and Post*, Cleveland's Black newspaper.

Entitled "The Black Church Position Statement on Homosexuality," the ministers condemn "HOMOSEXUALITY (including
bisexual as well as gay or lesbian sexual activity) as a lifestyle that is
contrary to the teachings of the Bible." Although they claim to have
tolerance and compassion for homosexuals, their ultimate goal is to
bring about "restoration," that is, changing lesbians and gays back
into heterosexuals in order "to restore such individuals back into

harmony with God's will." One of the several sources they cite to prove that such "restoration" is possible is the *Traditional Values Foundation Talking Points, 1993*, a publication of the Traditional Values Coalition.

The ministers also held a meeting and announced their goal to gather one hundred thousand signatures in Cleveland in opposition to the federal civil rights bill, HB 431, and to take their campaign to Detroit and Pittsburgh. A major spokesperson for the ministers, Rev. Marvin McMichol, is the minister of Antioch Baptist Church, the church I was raised in and of which the women in my family were pillars. Antioch was on a number of levels one of the most progressive congregations in Cleveland, especially because of the political leadership it provided at a time when Black people were not allowed to participate in any aspect of Cleveland's civic life.

McMichol states, "It is our fundamental, reasoned belief that there is no comparison between the status of Blacks and women, and the status of gays and lesbians." He explains that being Black or being female is an "ontological reality . . . a fact that cannot be hidden," whereas "homosexuality is a chosen lifestyle . . . defined by behavior not ontological reality."

By coincidence, I met Rev. McMichol in May when Naomi Jaffe, an activist friend from Albany, and I did a presentation on Black and Jewish relations at the invitation of Cleveland's New Jewish Agenda. Antioch Baptist Church and a Jewish synagogue cosponsored the event. My cousin had informed me that McMichol was a very important person in Cleveland and that he had just stepped down as head of the NAACP. Naomi and I were struck by his coldness to us throughout the evening in sharp contrast to the kind reception we received from both the Black and Jewish participants who were mostly elder women. We guessed that it was because of his homophobia and sexism. Little did we know at the time how right we were.

When I first got news of what was going on in my hometown I was emotionally devastated. It would have been bad enough to find out about a major Black-led homophobic campaign in any city in this country, but this place wasn't an abstraction, it was where I came from. It was while growing up in Cleveland that I first felt attraction toward women and it was also in Cleveland that I grasped the impossibility of ever acting upon those feelings. Cleveland is a huge city with a small-town mentality. I wanted to get out even before I dreamed of using the word *lesbian* to describe who I was. College provided my escape. Now I was being challenged to deal with homophobia, dead up, in the Black community at home.

I enlisted the help of the National Gay and Lesbian Task Force (NGLTF) and Scot Nakagawa who runs their Fight the Right office in Portland, Oregon, and of members of the Feminist Action Network (FAN), the multiracial political group to which I belong in Albany. Throughout the summer we were in constant contact with people in Cleveland. FAN drafted a counter petition for them to circulate and in early September several of us went there following NGLTF's and Stonewall Cincinnati's Fight the Right Midwest Summit. Unfortunately, by the time we arrived, the group that had been meeting in Cleveland had fallen apart.

We had several meetings, primarily with Black lesbians, but found very few people who were willing to confront through direct action the severe threat right in their midst. Remaining closeted, a reluctance to deal with Black people in Cleveland's inner city, and the fact that Cleveland's white lesbian and gay community had never proven particularly supportive of antiracist work were all factors that hampered Black lesbian and gay organizing. Ironically, racial segregation seemed to characterize the gay community, just as it did (and does) the city as a whole. The situation in Cleveland was very familiar to me, however, because I've faced many of the same roadblocks in attempts to do political work against racism and homophobia in my own community of Albany.

I cannot say that our effort to support a visible challenge to the ministers in Cleveland was particularly successful. The right wing's ability to speak to the concerns and play upon the fears of those it wishes to recruit; the lack of visionary political leadership among both Black and white lesbians and gays both nationally and locally; and the difficulty of countering homophobia in a Black context, especially when it is justified by religious pronouncements, makes this kind of organizing exceedingly hard. But we had better learn how to do it quickly and extremely well if we do not want the pseudo-Christian right wing to end up running this country.

Since returning from Cleveland we have been exploring the possibility of launching a nationwide petition campaign to gather at least one hundred thousand signatures from Black people who support lesbian and gay rights. One Black woman, Janet Perkins, a heterosexual Christian who works with the Women's Project in Little Rock, Arkansas, has already spoken out. In a courageous article entitled "The Religious Right: Dividing the African American Community" (*Transformation*, September/October 1993) Perkins takes on the ministers in Cleveland and the entire Black church. She calls for Black church members to practice love instead of condemnation. She writes:

> These African American ministers fail to understand they have been drawn into a plot that has as its mission to further separate, divide and place additional pressure on African Americans so they are unable to come together to work on the problems of the community. . . .
>
> What is needed in our community is a unity and bond that can't be broken by anyone. We must see every aspect of our community as valuable and worth protecting, and yes we must give full membership to our sisters and brothers who are homosexual. For all these years we have seen them, now we must start to hear them and respect them for who they are.

This is the kind of risk taking and integrity that makes all the difference. Perkins publicly declares herself an ally who we can depend upon. I hope in the months to come the gay, lesbian, and Black movements in this country will likewise challenge themselves to close this great divide, which they can only do by working toward an unbreakable unity, a bond across races, nationalities, sexual orientations, and classes that up until now our movements have never achieved.

1993

Note

1. Cassandra Sweet, "King's Niece Denounces Gay Rights," Associated Press, August 20, 1997.

I wrote "Between a Rock and a Hard Place" in 1984 for the book *Yours in Struggle: Three Feminist Perspectives on Anti-Semitism and Racism*, coauthored with Elly Bulkin and Minnie Bruce Pratt. I always describe it as the most difficult thing I ever had to write. The early 1980s were an extremely volatile time for relationships between Black and Jewish women. I had directly experienced the pain of bitter divisions and I was quite concerned about not contributing to these schisms in what I wrote on this topic. In analyzing the highly complex and emotionally weighted subject of Blacks and Jews/racism and anti-Semitism, I really wanted to "get it right."

After the book was released I was worried about how Black and Jewish women would respond to it, especially at events to publicize the book. Nearly without exception, those I met were generously supportive of my effort to encourage dialogue.

The discussion in the essay of Christianity not being a significant source of privilege for Black people brings to mind the recent wave of Black church burnings, some of which have been identified as explicitly racist attacks. During the same period the number of incidents of vandalism and arson aimed at synagogues, other Jewish buildings, and Jewish cemeteries has increased. Clearly, white racist, anti-Semitic fanatics view both Black Christians and white Jews as appropriate targets for hate crimes.

When tensions between Blacks and Jews are examined, much as in discussions focused solely upon race, it is nearly always through a male lens that severely limits the parameters of debate and the range of solutions. This essay remains one of few that looks at this important issue from a Black woman's feminist and leftist perspective.

Between a Rock and a Hard Place

Relationships between Black and Jewish Women

Our strategy is how we cope—how we measure and weigh what is to be said and when, what is to be done and how, and to whom and to whom and to whom, daily deciding/risking who it is we can call an ally, call a friend (whatever that person's skin, sex, or sexuality). We are women without a line. We are women who contradict each other.[1]

—Cherríe Moraga

I have spent the better part of a week simply trying to figure out how to begin. Every day, I've asked myself, as I sifted through files and pages of notes that were not getting me one bit closer to a start, "Why in hell am I doing this?" and when most despairing, "Why me?" Despair aside, I knew that if I could remember not just the reasons, but the feelings that first made me want to speak about the complicated connections and disconnections between Black and Jewish women, racism, and anti-Semitism, I might find my way into this piece.

The emergence in the last few years of a Jewish feminist movement has of course created the context for this discussion. Jewish women have challenged non-Jewish women, including non-Jewish women of color, to recognize our anti-Semitism and in the process of building their movement Jewish women have also looked to Third World feminists for political inspiration and support. Not surprisingly, as these issues have been raised, tensions that have characterized relationships between Black and Jewish people in this country have also surfaced within the women's movement. Jewish women's perception of Black and other women of color's indifference to or active participation in anti-Semitism, and Third World women's sense that major segments of the Jewish feminist movement have failed to acknowledge the weight of their white-skin privilege and capacity for racism, have inevitably escalated suspicion and anger between us.

To be a Black woman writing about racism and anti-Semitism feels like a no-win situation. It's certainly not about pleasing anybody, and I don't think it should be. I worry, however, that addressing anti-Semitism sets me up to look like a woman of color overly concerned about "white" issues. What I most fear losing, of course, is the political support and understanding of other women of color, without which I cannot survive.

This morning, for guidance, I turned to Bernice Johnson Reagon's "Coalition Politics: Turning the Century," because besides all the pain that has led me to examine these issues, there is also the positive motivation of my belief in coalitions as the only means we have to accomplish the revolution we so passionately want and need. She writes:

> I feel as if I'm gonna keel over any minute and die. That is often what it feels like if you're *really* doing coalition work. Most of the time you feel threatened to the core and if you don't you're not really doing no coalescing. . . . You don't go into coalition because you just *like* it. The only reason you would consider trying to team up with somebody who could possibly kill you, is because that's the only way you can figure you can stay alive.[2]

It helps to be reminded that the very misery that I and all of us feel when we explore the volatile links between our identities and the substance of our oppressions is only to be expected. If we weren't upset about the gulfs between us, if we weren't scared of the inherent challenge to act and change that the recognition of these gulfs requires, then we wouldn't "really [be] doing no coalescing."

What follows is one Black woman's perspective, necessarily affected by the generally complicated character of Black and Jewish relations in this country. This is not pure analysis. Far from it.

I am focusing on relationships between Black and Jewish women, because in my own life these relationships have both terrorized me and also shown me that people who are not the same not only can get along, but at times can work together to make effective political change. Although this discussion may be applicable to dynamics between other women of color and Jewish women, I am looking specifically at Black-Jewish relationships because of the particular history between the two groups in the United States and because as an Afro-American woman this is the set of dynamics I've experienced firsthand. Although the subject of Black and Jewish relationships cannot help but make reference to systematically enforced racism and anti-Semitism, I am emphasizing interactions between us because that feels more graspable to me, closer to the gut and heart of the matter.

Because of the inherent complexities of this subject, one of the things I found most overwhelming was the sense that I had to be writing for two distinct audiences at the same time. I was very aware that what I want to say to other Black women is properly part of an "in-house" discussion and it undoubtedly would be a lot more comfortable for us if somehow the act of writing did not require it to go public. With Jewish women, on the other hand, although we may have a shared bond of feminism, what I say comes from a position outside the group. It is impossible for me to forget that in speaking to Jewish women I am speaking primarily to white women, a role complicated by a racist tradition of Black people repeatedly having to teach white people about the meaning of oppression. I decided then to write sections that would cover what I need to say to Black women and what I need to say to Jewish women, fully understanding that this essay would be read in its entirety by both Black and Jewish women, as well as by individuals from a variety of other backgrounds.

Embedded in the Very Soil

I am anti-Semitic. I am not writing this from a position of moral exemption. My hands are not clean, because like other non-Jews in this society I have swallowed anti-Semitism simply by living here, whether I wanted to or not. At times I've said, fully believing it, that I was not taught anti-Semitism at home growing up in Cleveland in the 1950s. In comparison to the rabid anti-Semitism as well as racism that many white people convey to their children as matter-of-factly as they teach them the alphabet and how to tie their shoes, my perception of what was going on in my house is relatively accurate. But only relatively.

On rare occasions things were said about Jews by members of my family, just as comments were made about white people in general, and about Cleveland's numerous European immigrant groups in particular. My family had "emigrated" too from the rural South during the 1920s, 1930s, and 1940s and their major observation about Jewish and other white people was that they could come to this country with nothing and in a relatively short period "make it." Our people, on the other hand, had been here for centuries and continued to occupy a permanent position on society's bottom. When I was growing up there were Jewish people living in Shaker Heights, one of the richest suburbs in the United States, where Blacks were not allowed to purchase property even if they had the money, which most, of course, did not. The fact that Jews were completely barred from other suburbs and perhaps restricted to certain sections of Shaker Heights was not of great import to us. I remember vividly when my aunt and uncle (my mother's sister and brother) were each trying to buy houses in the 1950s. They searched for months on end because so many neighborhoods in the inner city including working-class ones were also racially segregated.[3] I was six or seven, but I remember their exhausted nighttime conversations about the problem of where they might be able to move, I felt their anger, frustration, and shame that they could not provide for their families on such a basic level. The problem was white people, segregation, and racism. Some Jews were, of course, a part of that, but I don't remember them being especially singled out. I did not hear anti-Semitic epithets or a litany of stereotypes. I do remember my uncle saying more than once that when they didn't let "the Jew" in somewhere, he went and built his own. His words were edged with both envy and admiration. I got the message that these people knew how to take care of themselves, that we could learn a lesson from them and stop begging the white man for acceptance or even legal integration.

Despite how I was raised, what I've come to realize is that even if I didn't learn anti-Semitism at home, I learned it. I know all the stereotypes and ugly words not only for Jews, but for every outcast group including my own. Such knowledge goes with the territory. Classism, racism, homophobia, anti-Semitism, and sexism float in the air, are embedded in the very soil. No matter how cool things are at home, you catch them simply by walking out of the house and by turning on the TV or opening up a newspaper inside the house. In the introduction to *Home Girls*, I wrote about this unsettling reality in relationship to how I sometimes view other women of color:

> Like many Black women, I know very little about the lives of other Third World women. I want to know more and I also want to put myself in situations where I have to learn. It isn't easy because, for one thing, I keep discovering how deep my own prejudice goes. I feel so very American when I realize that simply by being Black I have not escaped the typical American ways of perceiving people who are different from myself.[4]

I never believe white people when they tell me they aren't racist. I have no reason to. Depending on the person's actions I might possibly believe that they are actively engaged in opposing racism, are antiracist, at the very same time they continue to be racially ignorant and cannot help but be influenced as white people by this system's hatred of people of color. Unwittingly, antiracist whites may collude at times in the very system they are trying to fight. In her article "Racism and Writing: Some Implications for White Lesbian Critics," Elly Bulkin incisively makes the distinction between the reality of being *actively* antiracist and the illusion of being nonracist—that is, totally inno-cent.[5] She applies to racism, as I do here to anti-Semitism, the understanding that it is neither possible nor necessary to be morally exempt in order to stand in opposition to oppression. I stress this point because I want everybody reading this, and particularly Black women, to know that I am not writing from the position of having solved anything and because I have also heard other Black women, white non-Jewish women, and at times myself say, "But I'm not anti-Semitic." This kind of denial effectively stops discussion, places the burden of "proof" upon the person(s) experiencing the oppression, and makes it nearly impossible ever to get to the stage of saying: "This is an intolerable situation. What are we going to do about it?"

A Love-Hate Relationship

If somebody asked me to describe how Black and Jewish feminists, or Blacks and Jews in general, deal with each other I would say what we have going is a love-hate relationship. The dynamic between us is often characterized by contradictory and ambivalent feelings, both negative and positive, distrust simultaneously mixed with a desire for acceptance; and deep resentment and heavy expectations about the other group's behavior. This dynamic is reflected in the current dialogue about Jewish identity and anti-Semitism in the feminist movement, when Jewish women seem to have different expectations for Black and other women of color than they do for white non-Jewish women. Often more weight is placed upon the anti-Jewish statements of women of color than upon the anti-Semitism of white non-Jewish feminists, although they are the majority group in the women's movement and in the society as a whole, and have more direct links to privilege and power.

I think that both Black and Jewish people expect more from each other than they do from white people generally or from gentiles generally. Alice Walker begins a response to Letty Cottin Pogrebin's article "Anti-Semitism in the Women's Movement" by writing:

> There is a close, often unspoken bond between Jewish and black women that grows out of their awareness of oppression and injustice, an awareness many Gentile women simply do not have.[6]

Our respective "awareness of oppression" leads us to believe that each other's communities should "know better" than to be racist or anti-Semitic because we have firsthand knowledge of bigotry and discrimination. This partially explains the disproportionate anger and blame we may feel when the other group displays attitudes much like those of the larger society.

It's true that each of our groups has had a history of politically imposed suffering. These histories are by no means identical, but at times the impact of the oppression has been brutally similar— segregation, ghettoization, physical violence, and death on such a massive scale that it is genocidal. Our experiences of racism and anti-Semitism, suffered at the hands of the white Christian majority, have sometimes made us practical and ideological allies. Yet white Jewish people's racism and Black gentile people's anti-Semitism have just as surely made us view each other as enemies. Another point of divergence is the fact that the majority of Jewish people immigrated to the United States to escape oppression in Europe and found a society by no means free from anti-Semitism, but one where it was possible in most cases to breathe again. For Black people, on the other hand, brought here forcibly as slaves, this country did not provide an escape. Instead, it has been the very locus of our oppression. The mere common experience of oppression does not guarantee our being able to get along, especially when the variables of time, place, and circumstance combine with race and class privilege, or lack of them, to make our situations objectively different.

The love-hate dynamic not only manifests itself politically, when our groups have functioned as both allies and adversaries, but also characterizes the more daily realm of face-to-face interactions. I think that women of color and Jewish women sometimes find each other more "familiar" than either of our groups find Christian-majority WASPs. A Black friend tells me, when I ask her about this sense of connectedness, "We don't come from quiet cultures." There are subliminal nuances of communication, shared fixes on reality, modes of expressing oneself, and ways of moving through the world that people from different groups sometimes recognize in each other. In his collection of interviews, *Working*, Studs Terkel uses the term the "feeling tone."[7] I think that Black and Jewish people sometimes share a similar "feeling tone." Melanie Kaye/Kantrowitz corroborates this perception in her instructive article, "Some Notes on Jewish Lesbian Identity." She describes the difficulties a group of non-Jewish women had with her "style" during the process of interviewing her for a job:

> Most of the women troubled by me had been sent to expensive colleges by their fathers, they spoke with well-modulated voices, and they quaked when I raised mine. They didn't understand that to me anger is common, expressible, and not murderous. They found me "loud" (of course) and "emotional." Interestingly, I got along fine with all the women of color in the group.[8]

In a different situation a woman of color might very well feel antagonism toward a Jewish woman's "style," especially if she associates that "style" with a negative interaction—for example, if she experiences racist treatment from a Jewish woman or if she has to go through a rigorously unpleasant job interview with someone Jewish.

Nevertheless, Black and Jewish women grow up knowing that in relationship to the dominant culture, we just don't fit in. And though the chances of a Jewish woman being accepted by the status quo far exceed my own, when I'm up against the status quo I may turn to her as a potential ally. For example, on my way to an all-white writer's retreat in New England, I'm relieved to find out that the female director of the retreat is Jewish. I think she might understand the isolation and alienation I inevitably face as the only one. Feelings of outsiderness cover everything from self-hatred about features and bodies that don't match a white, blue-eyed ideal, to shame about where your father works, or how your mother talks on the telephone. These feelings of shame and self-hatred affect not just Black and Jewish women, but other women of color and white ethnic and poor women. Class can be as essential a bond as ethnicity between women of color and white women, both Jewish and non-Jewish. Chicana poet Cherríe Moraga describes her differing levels of awareness about Jewish and Black genocide in "Winter of Oppression, 1982," and also remarks on the positive link that she has felt to Jewish people:

> I already understood
> that these people were killed
> for the spirit-blood
> that runs through them.
>
> They were like us in this.
> Ethnic people with long last names
> with vowels at the end or the wrong
> type of consonants
> combined   a colored kind of white people[9]

There are ways that we recognize each other, things that draw us together. But feelings of affinity in themselves are not sufficient to bridge the culture, history, and political conditions that separate us. Only a conscious, usually politically motivated desire to work out differences, at the same time acknowledging commonalities, makes for more than superficial connection.

To Jewish Women

I was concerned about anti-Semitism long before I called myself a feminist, indeed long before there was a feminist movement in which to work. Perhaps because I was born a year after World War II ended, that whole era seems quite vivid to me, its essence conveyed by members of my family. I got a basic sense about the war years and about what had happened to Jewish people because people around me, who had been greatly affected by those events, were still talking about them. Books, films, and history courses provided facts about Jewish oppression. Being friends with Jewish kids in school provided me with another kind of insight, the perception that comes from emotional connection.

My problems with recent explorations of Jewish identity and anti-Semitism in the women's movement do not result from doubting whether anti-Semitism exists or whether it is something that all people, including people of color, should oppose. What concerns me are the ways in which some Jewish women have raised these issues that have contributed to an atmosphere of polarization between themselves and women of color. My criticisms are not of Jewish feminism in general, but of specific political and ideological pitfalls that have led to the escalation of hostility between us, and that cannot be explained away as solely Black and other women of color's lack of sensitivity to anti-Semitism.

These polarizations have directly and painfully affected me and people close to me. One major problem (which I hope this essay does not contribute to) is that far too often these battles have been fought on paper, in published and unpublished writing. Besides the indirectness of this kind of confrontation, I want to say how sick I am of paper wars, when we are living on a globe that is literally at war, where thousands of people are dying every day, and most of the rest of the world's people still grapple for the barest human necessities of food, clothing, and shelter. In *Home Girls* I wrote the following to Black women about negative dynamics between Black and Jewish women in the movement:

> I question whom it serves when we permit internal hostility to tear the movement we have built apart. Who benefits most? Undoubtedly, those outside forces that will go to any length to see us fail.[10]

I ask the same question here of Jewish women.

One of the most detrimental occurrences during this period has been the characterizing of Black and/or other women of color as being more anti-Semitic and much less concerned about combatting anti-Semitism than white non-Jewish women. Letty Cottin Pogrebin's article "Anti-Semitism in the Women's Movement," which appeared in *Ms.* magazine in June 1982, and which was widely read, exemplifies this kind of thinking. She cites "Black-Jewish Relations" as one of "the five problems basic to Jews and sisterhood," and then uses a number of quotes from Black women who are unsupportive of Jewish issues, but who also are not apparently active in the women's movement.[11] I have already referred to the social and historical circumstances that have linked our two groups and that might lead to our higher expectations for commitment and understanding of each other's situations. The desire for recognition and alliances, however, does not justify the portrayal of Black women, in particular, as being a bigger "problem" than white non-Jewish women or, more significantly, than the white-male ruling class that gets to enforce anti-Semitism via the system. Black women need to know that Jewish women can make distinctions between the differing impact, for example, of a woman of color's resentment against Jews, her very real anti-Semitism, and that of the corporate giant, the government policy maker, or even the Ku Klux Klan member. Jewish women need to acknowledge the potential for racism in singling out Black and other women of color and that racism has already occurred in the guise of countering anti-Semitism. I expect Jewish women to confront Black women's anti-Semitism, but I am more than a little suspect when such criticism escalates time and again into frontal attack and blame.

I think Jewish women's desire for support and recognition has also resulted at times in attempts to portray our circumstances and the oppressions of racism and anti-Semitism as parallel or even identical. The mentality is manifested at its extreme when white Jewish women of European origin claim Third World identity by saying they are not white but Jewish, refusing to acknowledge that being visibly white in a racist society has concrete benefits and social-political repercussions. How we are oppressed does not have to be the same in order to qualify as real. One of the gifts of the feminist movement has been to examine the subtleties of what comprises various oppressions without needing to pretend that they are all alike. As a Third World lesbian I know, for example, that although her day-to-day circumstances may look nothing like my own, a white heterosexual middle-class woman experiences sexual oppression, that she can still be raped, and that class privilege does not save her from incest.

Trying to convince others that one is legitimately oppressed by making comparisons can either result from or lead to the ranking of oppressions, which is a dangerous pitfall in and of itself. In a letter responding to the Pogrebin article, a group of Jewish women write: "We sense a competition for victim status in Pogrebin's article and elsewhere."[12] I have sensed the same thing and I know it turns off women of color more quickly than anything.

In a white-dominated, capitalist economy, white skin, and if you have it, class privilege, definitely count for something, even if you belong at the very same time to a group or to groups that the society despises. Black women cannot help but resent it when people who have these privileges try to tell us that "everything is everything" and that their oppression is every bit as pervasive and dangerous as our own. From our frame of reference, given how brutally racism has functioned politically and historically against people of color in the United States, such assertions are neither experientially accurate nor emotionally felt.

The fact that we have differing amounts of access to privilege and power can't help but influence how we respond to Jewish women's assertions of their cultural and political priorities. For example, in the last section of "Some Notes on Jewish Lesbian Identity," Melanie Kaye/Kantrowitz names Jewish women who resisted inside the concentration camps and in the Warsaw Ghetto, usually at the price of their lives. She concludes her article:

> Those were Jewish women. I come from women who fought like that.
> I want a button that says *Pushy Jew Loud Pushy Jew Dyke*.[13]

Despite the fact that this is a proud affirmation, reading the last sentence makes me wince, not because I don't understand the desire to reshape the negative words and images the society uses against those of us it hates, but because my gut response is, "I don't want to be treated like that." The positive image of Jewish women, who, like many Black women, refuse to disappear, who are not afraid to speak up, and who fight like hell for freedom, comes up against my experience as a Black woman who has, at times, felt pushed around and condescended to by women who are not just Jewish, but, more significantly, white. Because I come from a people who have historically been "pushed" around by all kinds of white people, I get upset that a traditional way of behaving might in fact affect me differently than it does a white non-Jewish woman.

Black women and other women of color are much more likely to take seriously any group which wants their political support when that group acknowledges its privilege, at the same time working to transform its powerlessness. Privilege and oppression can and do exist simultaneously. I know, because they function together in my own life. As a well-educated, currently able-bodied individual from a working-class family, who is also Black, a woman, and a lesbian, I am constantly aware of how complex and contradictory these intersections are. Being honest about our differences is painful and requires large doses of integrity. As I've said in discussions of racism with white women who are sometimes overwhelmed at the implications of their whiteness, no one on earth had any say whatsoever about who or what they were born to be. You can't run the tape backward and start from scratch, so the question is, what are you going to do with what you've got? How are you going to deal responsibly with the unalterable facts of who and what you are, of having or not having privilege and power? I don't think anyone's case is inherently hopeless. It depends on what you decide to *do* once you're here, where you decide to place yourself in relationship to the ongoing struggle for freedom.

Another extremely negative wedge that has been driven between women of color and Jewish women is the notion that white Jewish and non-Jewish women have been "forced" to confront racism while women of color have not been required to, or have been completely unwilling to confront anti-Semitism. This is, of course, untrue. There are Black women and other women of color who have taken definite stands against anti-Semitism (and our commitment to this issue cannot be measured, as I suspect it probably has been, by what is available in print). On the other hand, obviously not all white feminists or white people have sufficiently challenged racism, because if they had, racism would be a thing of the past. The implied resentment at having been "forced" to confront racism is racist in itself. This kind of statement belies a weighing mentality that has no legitimate place in progressive coalition politics. Our support for struggles that do not directly encompass our own situations cannot be motivated by an expectation of payback. Of course we're likely to choose ongoing political allies on the basis of those groups and individuals who recognize and respect our humanity and issues, but the bottom line has got to be a fundamental opposition to oppression, period, not a tit for tat of "I'll support 'your' issue if you'll support 'mine.'" In political struggles there wouldn't be any "your" and "my" issues, if we saw each form of oppression as integrally linked to the others.

A final matter that I want to discuss that can be offensive to Black women and other women of color is the idea put forth by some Jewish feminists that to be or to have been at any time a Christian is to be by definition anti-Semitic. Traditional, institutionalized Christianity has, of course, had as one of its primary missions the destruction and invalidation of other systems of religious belief, not only Judaism, but Islam, Buddhism, Hinduism, and all of the indigenous religions of people of color. Holy wars, crusades, and pogroms qualify, I suppose, as "Christian totalitarianism,"[14] but I have great problems when this term is applied to the mere practice of Christianity.

In the case of Black people, the Christian religion was imposed upon us by white colonizers in Africa and by white slaveowners in the Americas. We nevertheless reshaped it into an entirely unique expression of Black spirituality and faith, which has been and continues to be a major source of sustenance and survival for our people.

Being Christian hardly translates into "privilege" for Black people, as exemplified by the fact that most white churches do not encourage Black membership and many actually maintain tacit or official policies of racial segregation. Christian privilege becomes a reality when it is backed up by race and class privilege. It is demoralizing and infuriating to have Blacks' and other people of color's religious practices subsumed under the catchall of white Christianity or Christian "totalitarianism." If anything has been traditionally encouraged in Afro-American churches, it is an inspirational identification with the bondage of "the Children of Israel" as recounted in the Old Testament. This emphasis did not, of course, prevent anti-Semitism (during slavery there was virtually no contact between Black and Jewish people in this country), but there needs to be some distinction made between being raised as a Christian, being anti-Semitic, and the historical role of the institutionalized Christian church in promoting anti-Semitism when its powers and goals have been directly tied to the power and interests of the state.

To Black Women

Why should anti-Semitism be of concern to Black women? If for no other reason, anti-Semitism is one aspect of an intricate system of oppression that we by definition oppose when we say we are feminist, progressive, political. The Ku Klux Klan, the Christian right wing, and the American Nazi Party all promote anti-Semitism as well as racism. Lack of opposition to anti-Semitism lines us up with our enemies. People of color need to think about who our cohorts are when we express attitudes and take stands similar to those of the most dangerous and reactionary elements in this society. I'm talking here out of political principles, which can be a useful guide for approaching complicated questions. But needless to say, principles are not what any of us operate out of 100 percent of the time.

Certainly principles have only taken me so far in trying to deal with my gut responses to the ways that issues of anti-Semitism and Jewish identity have been raised in the women's movement. Like many Black feminists I could not help but notice how Jewish feminism arose just at the point that Third World feminist issues were getting minimal recognition from the movement as a whole. I saw how the feminism of women of color helped to lay the groundwork for Jewish feminists to name themselves, often without acknowledgment. I've seen how easy it has been for some Jewish women to make the shift from examining their role as racist oppressors, to focusing solely on their position as victims of oppression. I've also found the uncritical equating of the impact of anti-Semitism in the United States with the impact of racism absolutely galling.

If such "oversights" have made it difficult for us to get to the issue of anti-Semitism, continuing to experience racism from those women who seemingly want us to ignore their negative treatment of us and instead put energy into opposing an oppression which directly affects them has made commitment to the issue feel nearly impossible. The history of Black people in this country is a history of blood. It does not always dispose us to being altruistic and fair, because history has not been fair. Our blood is still being spilled. I know with what justification and fury we talk among ourselves about white people, Jews and non-Jews alike, and we will undoubtedly continue to talk about them as long as racism continues to undermine our lives.

In the case of racist Jewish people, we have something to throw back at them—anti-Semitism. Righteous as such comebacks might seem, it does not serve us, as feminists and political people, to ignore or excuse what is reactionary in ourselves. Our anti-Semitic attitudes are just that, both in the political sense and in the sense of reacting to another group's mistreatment of us. Although it isn't always possible or even logical for us to be "fair," being narrow-minded and self-serving is not part of our Black ethical tradition either. Trying as it may seem, I think we are quite capable of working through our ambivalent or negative responses to arrive at a usable Black feminist stance in opposition to anti-Semitism.

A major problem for Black women, and all people of color, when we are challenged to oppose anti-Semitism, is our profound skepticism that white people can actually be oppressed. If white people as a group are our oppressors, and history and our individual experiences only verify that in mass they are, how can we then perceive some of these same folks as being in trouble, sometimes as deep as our own? A white woman with whom I once taught a seminar on racism and sexism told me about a friend of hers, also a teacher, who used John Steinbeck's *The Grapes of Wrath* in a class that had a large number of Black students. She told me how these students were absolutely convinced that the characters in the novel were Black because their situation was so terrible. It had never occurred to them that white people could suffer like that and the instructor had quite a job to do to get them to believe otherwise. I think it was in many ways an understandable mistake on the Black students' part, given how segregated Black life still is from white life in this country; the extreme arrogance and romanticism with which white people usually portray themselves in the media; and also how lacking all North Americans are in a class analysis (economic exploitation was the major force oppressing Steinbeck's characters).

On the other hand, this incident points to a basic attitude among us that I think often operates when the issue of anti-Semitism is raised. Almost all Jews in the United States are white people of European backgrounds, and therefore benefit from white-skin privilege, which is often combined with class privilege. Our frequent attitude when this particular group of white people tells us they're oppressed is (in the words of Ma Rainey) "Prove it on me!"[15] Many Black women who I've either talked to directly or who I've heard talk about the subject of anti-Semitism simply do not believe that Jews are now or ever have been oppressed. From our perspective it doesn't add up, because in those cases where Jewish people have white skin, high levels of education, economic privilege, and political influence, they are certainly not oppressed like us. I have to admit that this is certainly the aspect of the position of Jewish people in this country that I have the most problems with and I think many other people of color do too. White skin and class privilege make assimilation possible and provide a cushion unavailable to the majority of people of color. Sometimes I actually get disgusted when I see how good other people can have it and still be oppressed. When white, economically privileged Jews admit to their privilege, as opposed to pretending that it either doesn't exist or that it has no significant impact upon the quality of their lives, then I don't feel so envious and angry.

Jewish oppression is not identical to Black oppression, but it is oppression brought to bear by the same white-male ruling class which oppresses us. An investigation of Jewish history, as well as of the current situation of Jews in countries such as Russia, reveals centuries of abuse by traditionally Christian-dominated states. Anti-Semitism has taken many forms, including physical segregation, sanctions against the practice of the Jewish religion, exclusion from certain jobs and professions, violent attacks by individuals, state coordinated pogroms (massacres), and the Nazi-engineered Holocaust which killed one-third of the world's Jews between 1933 and 1945. Anti-Semitism has been both more violent and more widespread in Europe than in the United States, but it is currently on the increase as the political climate grows ever more reactionary. Because it is not point-for-point identical to what we experience doesn't mean it is not happening or that it is invalid for people to whom it is happening to protest and organize against it.

Another instance of skepticism about whether white people can actually be oppressed sometimes occurs when Black people who do not identify with feminism are asked to consider that sexual politics affect all women. Their disbelief leads to at least two equally inaccurate responses. The first is that sexism is a white woman's thing and Black women are, of course, already liberated. The other is that it is not possible for a rich white woman, a "Miss Ann type," to be oppressed in the first place. In neither response is sexual oppression taken seriously or seen as an independently operating system. White-skin privilege is assumed to compensate for lack of power and privilege in every other sphere. All white women are assumed to be exactly alike, a monolithic group who are wealthy, pampered, and self-indulgent. However, as Third World feminists we know that sexual oppression cuts across all racial, class, and nationality lines; at the same time we understand how race, class, ethnicity, culture, and the political system under which one lives determine the specific content of that oppression. The ability to analyze complicated intersections of privilege and oppression can help us to grasp that having white skin does not negate the reality of anti-Semitism. As long as opposing anti-Semitism is narrowly viewed as defending white people's interests, we will undoubtedly be extremely reluctant to speak out about it.* We need to understand that we can oppose anti-Semitism at the very same time that we oppose white racism, including white Jewish people's racism.

In political dialogue and in private conversation, it is more than possible to attack and criticize racism and racist behavior without falling back on the stereotypes and ideology of another system of oppression. The bankruptcy of such tactics is exemplified by a front-page headline in the *Black American* newspaper (notable for its reactionary stances on just about everything) which derisively referred to New York's mayor, Edward Koch, as a faggot.[16] Koch's general misrule and countless abuses against people of color in New York are a matter of public record. Homophobia aimed at him did not directly confront these abuses, however; his racism in no way justified a homophobic put-down; and finally such tactics were transparently the weapons of the weak and weak-minded. The self-righteousness with which some individuals express homophobia parallels the self-righteousness with which some of these same individuals and others express anti-Semitism. In both instances, such attacks are not even perceived as wrong, because of the pervasive, socially sanctioned contempt for the group in question. I'm not suggesting that people merely talk nice to each other for the sake of talking nice, but that as progressive women of color

---

* It is also important to know that significant numbers of Jews outside the United States are people of color, including Jews from Ethiopia, China, India, Middle Eastern countries, and elsewhere.

it is our responsibility to figure out how to confront oppression directly. If we are not interested in being called out of our names, we can assume that other people don't want to be called out of theirs either, even when the larger white society thoroughly condones such behavior.

The disastrous situation in the Middle East is used as yet another justification for unbridled anti-Semitism, which crops up in political groupings ranging from the most reactionary to the most ostensibly radical. The fact that the left, including some Third World organizations, frequently couches its disagreements with Israel's politics in anti-Semitic terms further confuses us about how to state our criticisms effectively and ethically.[17] Too often when I've brought up the problem of anti-Semitism, a woman of color responds, "But what about the Middle East?" as if opposition to Israeli actions and support for the Palestinians' right to a homeland can only be expressed by making anti-Semitic remarks to reinforce valid political perspectives. This tactic "works" all too often because so many non-Jews do not perceive verbalized anti-Semitism as unacceptable or when confronted, they act as if it has not even occurred.

Without delving into the pros and cons of the convoluted Middle East situation, I think that it is essential to be able to separate what Israel does when it functions as a white-male-run imperialist state from what individual Jewish people's responsibility in relation to that situation can be. What do Jewish people who are not the people who run that state, by and large, actually want and stand for? There is a peace movement in Israel of which Israeli feminists are a significant part. In this country progressive groups like the New Jewish Agenda are defining a more complex political stance of supporting the continued existence of the state of Israel, while voicing grave criticisms of current policies and recognizing the rights of Palestinians to a homeland. Black and other Third World women must express our opposition to Israeli actions in the Middle East, if in fact we are opposed, without assuming that every Jewish person both there and here uncritically agrees with

Israeli actions and colludes with those policies. Can criticisms be expressed without throwing in the "obligatory" anti-Semitic remarks and attitudes? Can Jewish women hear criticisms of Israeli actions not only from women of color but also from white non-Jewish women without assuming that their rights as Jews and as human beings to continue to survive are being questioned?

Of course, there is an emotional layer to Black and Jewish women's attitudes about the Israeli-Palestinian conflict that is directly linked to who we are. Many Jewish women view Israel as a place of refuge. They support it as the only existing Jewish state, the one place where Jews were allowed to emigrate freely following the Holocaust, and where most Jews are still granted automatic citizenship.* Often Black women and other women of color feel a visceral identification with the Palestinians, because like the Vietnamese, Nicaraguans, and Black South Africans, they are people of color struggling for the liberation of their homeland. Our two groups very often have differing responses to the Middle East situation and I am not so naive as to expect total agreement between us about the best course for rectifying what has been up to now an intractable and violent situation. I am only asserting that our anti-Semitic or Jewish people's racist attacks do not comprise legitimate "criticisms" of the other group's point of view.

How we deal as Black women with anti-Semitism and with Jewish women ultimately boils down to how we define our politics, which are admittedly diverse. What I've written here are some ways to think about these vastly complicated issues, growing out of my particular political perspective. As a Black feminist I believe in our need for autonomy in determining where we stand on every issue. I also believe in the necessity for short- and long-term coalitions when it is viable for various groups to get together to achieve specific goals. Finally, there is my personal belief that political interactions and all other human connections cannot work without some basic level of ethics and respect. We don't oppose

---

* Jewish lesbians and gay men are excluded from the Law of Return.

anti-Semitism because we owe something to Jewish people, but because we owe something very basic to ourselves.

Between a Rock and a Hard Place

Some of the pitfalls that have characterized the growth of Jewish feminism can be traced to ideological tendencies in the women's movement as a whole. I want to outline several of these here, because of the effect they have had upon relationships between Black and Jewish women, as well as upon relationships between other women of different cultures, classes, and races. These tendencies have also led to numerous misunderstandings within feminism, generally, about the nature of oppression and how to fight it.

The concept of identity politics has been extremely useful in the development of Third World feminism. It has undoubtedly been most clarifying and catalytic when individuals do in fact have a combination of nonmainstream identities as a result of their race, class, ethnicity, sex, and sexuality; when these identities make them direct targets of oppression; and when they use their experiences of oppression as a spur for activist political work. Identity politics has been much less effective when primary emphasis has been placed upon exploring and celebrating a suppressed identity within a women's movement context, rather than upon developing practical political solutions for confronting oppression in the society itself.

A limited version of identity politics often overlaps with two other currents within the movement: lesbian separatism and cultural feminism (which emphasizes the development of a distinct women's culture through such vehicles as music, art, and spirituality). These approaches to dealing with being social-cultural outsiders only work when the more stringent realities of class and race are either not operative (because everybody involved is white and middle class) or when these material realities are ignored or even forcibly denied. Lesbian separatism, which might be thought of as an extreme variety of identity politics, has seldom been very useful for poor and working-class white women or for the majority of women of color, because in attributing the whole of women's oppression to one cause, the existence of men (or of patriarchy), it has left out myriad other forces that oppress women who are not economically privileged and/or white. When Jewish feminism has subscribed to or been influenced by cultural feminism, separatism, or a narrow version of identity politics, it has been limited in both analysis and strategy, since, for example, anti-Semitism does not manifest itself solely as attacks upon individuals' identities, nor does it only affect Jewish women.

Another major misunderstanding within feminism as a whole that has affected the conception of Jewish feminism is the notion that it is politically viable to work on anti-Semitism, racism, or any other system of oppression solely *within* a women's movement context. Although all the systems of oppression cannot help but manifest themselves inside the women's movement, they do not start or end there. It is fallacious and irresponsible to think that working on them internally only with other feminists is ultimately going to have a sub-stantial, permanent effect on the power structure from which they spring. I don't live in the women's movement, I live on the streets of North America. Internal women's movement solutions are just that. They have only fractional impact on the power of the state which determines the daily content of my life.

Although I've focused on relationships between Black and Jew-ish women, I do not think for a moment that the whole of our respective oppressions can be reduced to how we treat each other, which is yet another mistaken notion afloat in the movement. Yes, it helps for us as feminists to respect each other's differences and to attempt to act decently, but it is ultimately much more "helpful" to do organizing that confronts oppression at its roots in the politi-cal system as a whole.

There is a last point I want to make about the political work we do and the people we are able to do it with. My intention in addressing the issues of Black and Jewish relationships, racism, and anti-Semitism has been to encourage better understanding between us and to support the possibility of coalition work. It is obvious, how-ever, that there are substantial political differences and disagreements between us and that some of these, despite efforts to alleviate them, will no doubt remain. Ongoing coalitions are formed, in truth, not on the basis of political correctness or "shoulds," but on the pragmatic basis of shared commitments, politics, and beliefs. Some Jewish women and some women of color are not likely to work together because they are very much in opposition to each other *politically*. And that's all right, because there are other Jewish women and women of color who are already working together and who will continue to do so, because they have some basic political assumptions and goals in common.

Relationships between Black and Jewish women are the very opposite of simple. Our attempts to make personal/political connections virtually guarantee our being thrust between "the rock" of our own people's suspicion and disapproval and "the hard place" of the other group's antagonism and distrust. It is a lot easier to categorize people, to push them into little nastily labeled boxes, than time and again to deal with them directly, to make distinctions between the stereotype and the substance of who and what they are. It's little wonder that so often both Black and Jewish women first label and then dismiss each other. All of us resort to this tactic when the impact of our different histories, cultures, classes, and skins backs us up against the wall and we do not have the courage or desire to examine what, if anything, of value lies between us. Cherríe Moraga writes, "Oppression does not make for hearts as big as all outdoors. Oppression makes us big and small. Expressive and silenced. Deep and dead."[8] We are certainly damaged people. The question is, finally, do we use that damage, that firsthand knowledge of oppression, to recognize each other, to do what work we can together? Or do we use it to destroy?

1984

Notes

Portions of this essay originally appeared in a shorter version, based upon my presentation at the plenary session "Racism and Anti-Semitism in the Women's Movement" at the 1983 National Women's Studies Association conference. See "A Rock and a Hard Place: Relationships Between Black and Jewish Women," *Women's Studies Quarterly* 11, no. 3 (Fall 1983): 7–9.

1. Cherríe Moraga, "Preface," in *This Bridge Called My Back: Writings by Radical Women of Color*, ed. Moraga and Gloria Anzaldúa (New York: Kitchen Table: Women of Color Press, 1981, 1983), xviii–xix.

2. Bernice Johnson Reagon, "Coalition Politics: Turning the Century," in *Home Girls: A Black Feminist Anthology*, ed. Barbara Smith (New York: Kitchen Table: Women of Color Press, 1983), 356–357.

3. Lorraine Hansberry's classic play A *Raisin in the Sun*, written in 1958, revolves around this very dilemma of housing discrimination and a Black family's efforts to buy a house in an all-white neighborhood. Cleveland author Jo Sinclair's novel *The Changelings*, which I first read as a teenager, describes the summer when a working-class Jewish and Italian neighborhood begins to change from white to Black. The story is told from the perspective of a preteen-age Jewish girl, Vincent, and traces with more complexity and compassion than any work I know what it is that lies between us as Black and Jewish women. Despite my efforts to interest several women's presses in republishing *The Changelings*, it continues to be out of print, but is sometimes available in libraries. Jo Sinclair (Ruth Seid), *The Changelings* (New York: McGraw-Hill, 1955).

4. Barbara Smith, "Introduction," in *Home Girls*, xlii–xliii.

5. Elly Bulkin, "Racism and Writing: Some Implications for White Lesbian Critics," *Sinister Wisdom* 13 (Spring 1980), 3–22.

6. Alice Walker, "Letters Forum: Anti-Semitism," *Ms.* (February 1983): 13.

7. Studs Terkel, "Introduction," in *Working* (New York: Pantheon Books, 1972, 1974), xviii.

8. Melanie Kaye/Kantrowitz, "Some Notes on Jewish Lesbian Identity," in *Nice Jewish Girls: A Lesbian Anthology*, ed. Evelyn Torton Beck (Trumansburg, N.Y.: Crossing Press, 1981, 1984), 37.

9. Cherríe Moraga, "Winter of Oppression, 1982," in *Loving in the War Years: Lo Que Nunca Pasó Por Sus Labios* (Boston: South End Press, 1983), 73–74.

10. Smith, "Introduction," xliv.

11. Letty Cottin Pogrebin, "Anti-Semitism in the Women's Movement," *Ms.* (June 1982): 46.

12. Deborah Rosenfelt et ah, "Letters Forum: Anti-Semitism," *Ms.* (February 1983): 13.

13. Kaye/Kantrowitz, "Some Notes," 42.

14. Gloria Greenfield, "Shedding," in *Nice Jewish Girls*, 5.

15. Gertrude "Ma" Rainey, "Prove It on Me Blues" (performed by Teresa Trull), on *Lesbian Concentrate* (Oakland, Calif.: Olivia Records, 1977, LF 915).

16. "Diana Ross: The White Lady and the Faggot," *The Black American* (New York), 22, no. 29, July 14-July 20, 1983, 23 ff.

17. See for example the All African People's Revolutionary Party's Educational Brochure Number One, "Israel Commits Mass Murder of Palestinian & African Peoples: Zionism is Racism . . . It Must Be Destroyed."

18. Moraga, *Loving in the War Years*, 135.

III

Working for Liberation and Having a Damn Good Time

This article about the 1968 Democratic convention demonstrations is one of several that I wrote for the Mount Holyoke College newspaper during my senior year. I had not been involved with the newspaper previously, but a change in the paper's editorship and my political activism gave me the courage to begin to share my views in print.

One thing this article does not say is that I was one of the few Black women who participated in the Chicago demonstrations. Although I had been involved in campus antiwar organizing since my first year of college, and had heard one of Martin Luther King Jr.'s earliest speeches against the war, in front of the United Nations in the spring of 1967, many in the Black community still viewed the antiwar movement as a white issue. Consciousness about the connections between the Black struggle, anti-imperialism, the disproportionate numbers of Black men who were fighting and dying in Vietnam, and stopping the war against a Third World people increased in the years following Chicago. Those of us who had been involved in antiwar activity, which eventually grew into a mass movement, were clear that our protests had affected popular opinion and were a significant factor in curtailing U.S. military involvement.

Rereading this piece, I was struck by my surety that violence was not planned by the demonstrators nor by any of the leaders. I know that I did not hear anyone call for violence against the police, but it is conceivable that some of the demonstrators and groups there advocated violence, though I was not aware of it. The people around me in the streets practiced disciplined nonviolence in the face of what was later described by a federal commission as a "police riot."

Chicago Firsthand

A Distortion of Reality

There is something quite futile and also presumptuous about adding words to the thousands already written about the bizarre cruelty of the convention in Chicago. The world was indeed watching and the media had a special interest in reporting the events surrounding the convention, having been brutalized by the police for the first time in a northern city themselves.

There have been enough words to last a long time, or at least until the next time that people are beaten in the streets for peace and freedom. However, I can tell something that has not been told and that is what happened to me as an individual during forty-eight hours in the streets of Chicago.

Making the decision to go and participate in the demonstrations was the most difficult aspect of the experience, and once the decision was made, I found myself being fatalistic about what would probably be a physically dangerous situation. Since I had never swallowed tear gas, been maced or hit on the head with a billy club, I could not be specifically afraid of these things. On the Monday that we left Cleveland for Chicago I bought a canteen, but decided that a helmet was a capitulation to their nightmare, their distortion of reality and morality, and wore my usual head covering of hair.

When we arrived in Chicago on Tuesday morning, we circled the Amphitheatre area, which with its signs of "No Trespassing" and yards of barbwire resembled a concentration camp or perhaps a SAC missile base. As we were leaving the stockyards a policeman

stopped our car and asked us where we were going. D——
answered that he was visiting his brother who lives in Chicago and
gave the address. The policeman told us to leave there and never
come back again, and as it turned out we never did.

Tuesday was a relatively quiet day. I participated in a series of
demonstrations sponsored by the Student Health Organization and
the Medical Committee for Human Rights at the Cook County
Hospital–University of Illinois Medical School Complex. I carried
a sign that said something about admitting Black students to medical schools in a proportion that reflects the number of Black people
in the population, and was told repeatedly by a large and boisterous
woman in a pink dress that I should go to school in Russia.

That evening we heard Bobby Seale, a leader of the Black Pan-
thers, speak in Lincoln Park. It is always curious to me to see a
certain type of white person receive with such enthusiasm the
promise of the destruction of their society by Black people, but
perhaps they are so accepting because they are still naive enough to
think that it will not happen.

We went after this speech to a show in the Coliseum. It was
extraordinarily inspiring to see Jean Genet and William Burroughs
and finally Dick Gregory (a truly gentle man) on stage speaking to
us and with us. It was suggested that we proceed after the show
to Grant Park in front of the Hilton, where people from Lincoln
Park were already arriving.

This would be our first contact with the police and we were
nervous as we walked toward the Loop. Surprisingly, nothing happened that night. At one point the police pushed us back off the
sidewalk onto the grass, but this was done efficiently and without
force. At one point the singer Phil Ochs was standing near us and
we listened to him talk to someone for awhile and then drifted
away. We also spoke to some policemen who were laconic, but not
hostile. We finally went home at about 2 A.M. Wednesday. The day
of the nominations had already begun.

The rally in Grant Park the next afternoon, where the first incident of violence in which I was involved broke out, was

disappointingly small in numbers. This would not be New York and the United Nations or even Washington and the Pentagon. The police rushed us as we were sitting on benches listening to Carl Oglesby, because some persons had tried to take down the American flag and put up a revolutionary red flag. A whole section of benches was overturned, tear gas canisters were thrown, and people were beaten. A boy who had been hit in the head bled over my raincoat and shirt and I finally became scared of what was to happen.

It should be clearly understood by those people who were not there that violence was not planned by the demonstrators, in the sense that offensive tactics were never discussed. It was recognized however that the police officers would undoubtedly have orders directly from Mayor Daley to use the weapons at their disposal and many demonstrators were prepared for these assaults with helmets and wet cloths to breathe through. Vaseline was thought to be a good coating against mace, but the first-aid teams did not recommend its use. In short, violence was expected, because it was known that the police were ready to promote it. It was *never* the policy of the demonstration's leaders, however, for people to reciprocate with violence.

After the flagpole incident most people assembled to begin a nonviolent march to the Amphitheatre for which there was no permit, although repeated requests for one had been made months prior to the convention.

When we got down to the Hilton, the streets were full of people. After some minutes of indecision we sat down as a group in the center of the street and the police initiated their tactic of forming a human wedge to push us back onto the sidewalks and away from the hotel. Mace, tear gas, pepper gas, and severe beatings implemented the police action. We were in the streets for four hours. Whenever the police rushed us, we would yell to each other "WALK, WALK, WALK," so that we would not trample each other.

Sometimes we would also yell "Don't throw, don't throw," because people were mad and reacting with very human and logical anger toward an incredible situation. I do not know what was being thrown, probably rocks mostly. But a few rocks don't make a hell of a lot of difference against thousands of clubs. Other "weapons" that were found were probably planted either by the police or by "hoodlums." The fact that we could yell this advice to our comrades, however, can be considered a type of victory, a victory of conscience and of morality.

At one point, when we had been gassed very badly and pushed far back into the park, I found myself unable to stop crying from the inside because it was so difficult to accept what was happening. Children were being beaten and gassed because they wanted an alternative to war and racism. The adult establishment responded to this demand for peace and justice by exercising a kind of institutionalized hatred.

After eight hours outside we dragged ourselves home and watched with empty eyes the nomination of Hubert Humphrey. The next morning we left.

1968

The following letter that I received from writer and activist Craig G. Harris (1958–1991) explains why I dropped everything I was doing and wrote a new piece especially for the 1986 Black History Month supplement of *The New York Native*.

February 1, 1986

Dear Barbara,

Audre's off to California, Michelle's somewhere between DC and Philly, Jewelle is on tight deadlines, Betty doesn't consider herself to be a writer, Pat's OFWHC-freaked, and I'm sitting at my typewriter losing it because Gwen is the only woman who has assured me that she'll contribute something to the *Native's* Black lesbian/gay supplement.*

The boys got the same short notice that the girls did, and they're coming through (cussing me out all the way to the post office). I will certainly be the first to complain when this supplement does not portray sufficient representation. (See I'm doing it already?) I'm sure others will follow suit. I really want to avoid that situation.

My request to you, should you choose to fulfill it, is to please send me one of your articles which is timely enough to reprint. Also, if you talk to some of the other sisters, could you please ask them to do the same? I must submit edited copy to the newspaper by February 14. I'll accept manuscripts

---

* The women Craig refers to are Audre Lorde, Michelle Parkerson, Jewelle Gomez, Betty Powell, Pat Parker (who was director of the Oakland Feminist Women's Health Center, OFWHC), and Gwen Rogers.

from lesbian writers up until the very last minute. Please help me out with this one, Barbara.

I look forward to seeing you again, probably in New York during the March 22 NCBLG [National Coalition of Black Lesbians and Gays] board meeting. Until then, be well, and keep doing your wonderful work.

Sincerely,
Craig

Who could resist Craig's energy and wit? I also wanted to support his efforts to build stronger links between Black lesbians and gay men. In the twelve years since I wrote this, my connections to my brothers have continued to expand. Tragically, many of those dearest to me are no longer here: Joseph F. Beam, Craig, Donald Woods, Assotto Saint, and Essex Hemphill, all gone too soon because of the AIDS epidemic. Their passion and vision continue to be a blessing in my life.

Working for Liberation and
Having a Damn Good Time

I have never been very comfortable around men. Although I had male lovers when I was straight, they were few and far between. My major recollection of these relationships, besides how painful and humiliating they were, was that I never really understood what was going on. I am frankly amazed when some lesbians say how easy it was for them to handle men and even to run their relationships with them during their heterosexual youths. I did not understand men, period.

By the time my twin sister and I were born, all the men in my family, with the exception of two uncles, had vanished. My grandmother and one of her sisters were widowed. Another of her sisters was divorced, and yet another, whom I now think may have been a lesbian, never married at all. My mother's sister, Aunt LaRue, was married, but Uncle Bill left the year I was nine. My own father was a total mystery. The official story was that he and my mother had separated before or soon after our birth. He was never discussed. Recently, I've wondered what actually happened, but in any case I never met him, never even saw a picture of him. Whenever I look in the mirror, I see a face I can only partially explain.

When I was growing up during the *Donna Reed Show, Father Knows Best* 1950s, I often wished that I lived in a regular family with a father, a mother who stayed home, a big house, desserts at every meal, and so on. But "regular" was of course white. Not every kid in my neighborhood had a father; most of the mothers went to work as mine did. And then, exactly a month before my tenth birthday, she died. Because I had no father, I became, to my mind, more definitively an orphan; but as years passed and most of the other family members who raised me also died, I felt much more longing for the women I had known than for the man I never met. What I feel now is tremendous curiosity, intensified perhaps by being a writer. I want to know my whole "story," including the missing facts about my father. It's unlikely I ever will.

Long before I came out I was most familiar and comfortable with a world of women. Although I was intrigued by males' sexual potential when I reached adolescence and found some boys attractive, I found girls attractive, too. Men were in general scary and unknown and the older I got the more frightening and incomprehensible they became. It was apparent that they wanted women, but they did not seem to like women. Although I never experienced physical violence, the loud-talking on the street and the mental games men played reminded me that the potential was always there. They were also the means by which one might get pregnant and thereby ruin everything. What a relief it was to come out finally and be done with the whole mess.

As a feminist and lesbian, some things about my prior relationships with men became clearer. I found out that it wasn't just me, but that sexism had basically stacked the deck against me from the start. As I got more and more involved in specifically Black feminist organizing, I was always conscious of how significant race was in shaping my experience as a Black lesbian. Although the politics of feminism were empowering, the white women's movement was no haven. My racial identity and North America's response to it—i.e., racism—kept my fate directly linked to that of every Black person alive, including Black men. Race assigns to us a shared status, certain common experiences, and a rich history and culture, despite differences in gender, sexual orientation, and class. To put it another way, being Black puts us in a great deal of danger here, no matter what variety of Black person we are or how much running we may do to try to prove otherwise. If Thomas Sowell's car breaks down on a back road in Mississippi or a dead-end street in Philadelphia, South Boston, or Bay Ridge, his ass is just as likely to be grass as is any other Black person's who is not neoconservative, upper middle class, straight, and/or male.

Blackness is an inestimable bond. My having established a positive relationship to mine years ago is a major reason that I'm still alive. Even as a baby I suffered as a result of racial oppression and I had to learn to cope with it long before I had any inkling of what it might mean to be a woman or a lesbian. This does not mean that racism is more important than other oppressions. But as I've often stated, it is the most pervasive and dangerous oppression in *my* life.

My perceptions about race are not something I have to explain to activist Black gay men, nor do I need to delineate the challenge of being queer in the Black community. I also don't have to explain the talk I talk, why I cannot get into white women's music, why I do not call Black persons past a certain age by their first names, or why I am so worried about our youth. It's all understood. We share language, culture, values, the African genius, family ties—in short, we share Blackness.

My appointment to the board of the National Coalition of Black Lesbians and Gays (NCBLG) last year has given me the opportunity to work with and to know many more of my brothers and the experience has been for the most part wonderful. Of course, I am blessed to be in contact with highly progressive and aware Black gay men who have chosen to define their situation politically and not merely as a lifestyle. I am not saying that our differences never cause problems or that sexism never enters in, but I've observed a great deal of willingness to grapple with these issues. If there's one thing that most impresses me about our interactions, it is how much kindness there is between us. Perhaps because sexual and romantic agendas are suspended, we can all just relax and treat each other like folks. I often imagine what our heterosexual sisters and brothers might think if they could see us, supposed man- and woman-haters, steadily working for our and their liberation and having a damned good time in the process.

Our relationships with each other are objectively different from those that white lesbians have with white men, gay or straight.

Most white women have been raised to identify with a dominant and privileged racial group as opposed to an embattled subordinate one. Unless they come from ethnic, nationality, or religious groups that are not WASP and not assimilated, or from the working class, white women do not consciously share a specific culture or the experience of oppression with white men. White lesbians' relationships with white gay men frequently break down when the men identify more strongly with their privileges as white, often affluent, males, than with their lack of privilege as homosexuals.

The different content of their relationships with white men does not fully explain however, why some white women adamantly refuse to acknowledge the historical and political status that links Black lesbians to the other members of our race, especially to those members who are gay. Because the most outspoken Third World lesbian activists have not generally advocated a "men are the root of all evil" position, we have been accused of being hopelessly male-identified and viciously attacked by white lesbian separatists in particular. What these women never bother to examine is how their intransigent racism leads them to invalidate our legitimate concern about the destruction of all people of color.

A letter from a woman named Ruth in the recently revived *Lesbian Inciter* cites seven disturbing "trends," including working on issues that do not solely affect white lesbians. She writes:

4. Using ALL your time, energies, and whatever material resources you may have, on everything but the Lesbian cause; Nicaragua, apartheid, etc., etc. Of course we should all be for an end to U.S. and contra involvement and apartheid. . . . But to drop what affects women for what affects men as well as women, is just going right back to humanism.

5. Very tough, but must be addressed—Julia Penelope has had the courage to do so—the attitude of many Black Lesbian[s], who say "if you want us you must take our men, too."[1]

(See also Julia Penelope's articles "The Mystery of Lesbians: I, II, and III" in *Lesbian Ethics*.)

This writer has distorted a major point of Black feminist analysis. We never asked white women to "take" either us or Black men. We have demanded repeatedly, however, that the white women's movement seriously confront racism, which minimally requires the understanding that it grievously affects all people of color—women and men, heterosexuals and homosexuals, old and young all over the globe. It does not merely crop up from time to time among wimmin at womyn's events. It also beats me how one can "be for" an end to the crimes of intervention in Latin America and apartheid in South Africa without *working* toward same. Perhaps one just loafs and invites the goddess to fix it all. Fortunately, this brand of apolitical purism does not dominate the lesbian/feminist movement. And in any case it is highly inappropriate for any white people to dictate what kinds of relationships we should have with our people.

During Black History Month 1986, Black lesbians and gay men have something special to celebrate: the growing cohesiveness and vitality of our movement, coupled with our growing love and respect for each other. We are definitely progressing. I only wish I could tell Michael.

I met Michael in the mid-1970s, when he was a medical student at Boston University. He was my first Black gay friend after I came out. He was also no doubt the first man to tell me somewhat wistfully, upon observing our early organizing efforts, "You women seem like you have it all together." I probably assured him that it only looked that way and that historical conditions were also in our favor because the feminist movement, for all its problems, provided a stronger base from which to build as Black lesbians, than the more narrowly defined white-male-dominated gay rights movement possibly could.

Michael was brilliant, politically active, a lover of Black culture, and the soul of wit. He was also a home boy, whose family, like mine, came from Georgia. When he completed his internship and residency at Harlem Hospital, he returned there to practice psychiatry in a rural community health center. Years passed and we sometimes got news of each other from our mutual friend, Alyce, also a doctor.

In 1983 I visited Michael in Georgia and we finally took a trip we had often talked about, to see some relatives of mine in Dublin. I had not seen Aunt Viola for almost thirty years, since she and her first husband (my grandmother's brother) had come up to Cleveland for my mother's funeral. I joked that having Michael along might throw them off my trail, queer though we were. Aunt Viola was lovely, but her new husband, a farmer and traveling country preacher, definitely picked up on something. As we were getting ready to leave, he actually took down the Bible and read us the verse that warns women not to put on things that pertain to a man and vice versa. Thunderstruck, but trying to remain composed, I asked him if he read that because I was wearing pants and he said, "Yes." He admitted that the secretary at one of his churches also insisted upon wearing pants and that when they argued about it she pointed out that the pants she wore were made for women. I thought, "Well, I sure can't tell that lie, since the ones I have on came from the men's store at A&S."

Michael and I said our good-byes, then stopped for fried chicken. On the drive back, we talked about how rough it was to be who we were, especially for him, without a support system or community. But thank goodness, he certainly was my support system that day. If he hadn't been with me, I might have keeled right over when the Reverend started in with his little sermon. To thank him, I sent him a package of my own and other books by lesbians of color. I also told him about organizations like Black and White Men Together and NCBLG and encouraged him to try to find folks when he commuted to Atlanta to see friends and go to the bars.

Last October, Alyce called to tell me Michael had died, not from the scourge of AIDS, but from the complications of diabetes. He was thirty-four. This then is for Michael. Like all my work, it is indebted to those who have made the work possible—the members of my family.

1986

Note

1. Letter in *Lesbian Inciter* (December 1985): 5.

Like many activists, I have been frustrated by how little written material there is about what it takes to do political work. I wanted to address that need when I wrote this article in 1995 for a Black lesbian anthology in which it ultimately did not appear. "Doing It from Scratch" complements the dialogue, "Black Lesbian/Feminist Organizing: A Conversation," which I did with three other women in 1982, for my book *Home Girls: A Black Feminist Anthology.*

Doing It from Scratch

The Challenge of Black Lesbian Organizing

For Audre Lorde and Pat Parker

As I grow older, I am more and more convinced that coming of age in the 1960s was one of the luckiest coincidences of my life. I graduated from high school in 1965 and from college in the class of 1969. The incredible intensity and political ferment of that decade perfectly coincided with the time when I was personally discovering who I was, testing my intellect, leaving home, exploring my sexuality, and meeting more and more people who cared about the same things I did: writing, art, and making political change.

I am well aware that the sixties often take on the proportions of a myth, a myth which does injustice both to the achievements and the failings of that era. From the vantage point of the 1990s, however, I realize that one of the sixties' greatest gifts was providing a living, breathing sense of radical political possibility for those of us who were open to embracing it.

Simply switching on the television or picking up a newspaper could provide that day's object lesson about this society's incredible contradictions, its moral and material wrongs. The useless carnage in Vietnam; the violence that whites visited upon Black human beings who wanted to do outrageous things like attend school, ride public transportation, and vote; and eventually not being able to distinguish news footage of Newark and Detroit burning from Soweto and Saigon served to raise popular consciousness and to heighten a sense of urgency. Current events provided dramatic illustrations of a system on the edge, a country in grave need of repair.

My political education and commitments were profoundly shaped by this history. The iconoclasm and hopefulness of those times inspire me still. One of the most important things I learned was that actual power lies in the hands of "ordinary" people who come together to challenge authority and to make a difference; that effective grassroots organizing can transform consciousness, policies, laws, and most importantly the quality of individual people's daily lives. I learned that the measure of successful organizing lies not in the size of a group's budget, but in how clear its goals are, how consistently its members carry out the tasks they have taken on, how deep their analysis goes of what is really wrong with this system, and finally how much they care about and love other human beings. The political ferment of that era provided me with a school for life.

I often explain that the reason I am an activist is that for me *not* being one is tantamount to saying "Yes massa, yes boss, whatever you say. It's fine with me that your heavy foot is planted directly on my neck." Of course it takes courage to speak out and any organizer who is really doing the work sometimes gets scared, but to me the alternative of unchecked racism, homophobia, sexual and class oppression is a hundred times worse.

The only activity that has ever altered oppression and transformed disenfranchised people's powerlessness is collective grassroots organizing. The abolition of slavery, the overturning of Jim Crow, the victories of the labor movement, ending the war in Vietnam, the ongoing struggles against racism and imperialism, and the fight for lesbian, gay, and women's liberation are all examples of what people can achieve when we band together to take control of our lives. On the other hand, getting politicians to listen, passing needed legislation, creating positive media images, and individually earning a decent living at a workplace that would not have hired you a generation ago are the *result* of effective organizing, not the ultimate goals of liberation itself.

The former examples have revolutionary potential because of how they alter power relationships in the society and challenge the status quo. The latter examples are essentially reforms, which although beneficial and needed, do not get to the root of our problems and transform the system. The so-called democracy that we have under capitalism can accommodate numerous reforms without diminishing the power of the ruling class. As a socialist and an alert Black woman, it is clear to me that it is not possible to achieve justice, especially economic justice, and equality under capitalism because capitalism was never designed for that to be the case. When I do political work, it is always important to be able to distinguish between issues and actions that have the potential ultimately to change the system and those that address symptoms of oppression more than causes. The assaults from the present system necessitate that most activists work for reforms, but those of us who are radicals understand that it is possible to do so at the very same time that we work for fundamental change—a revolution.

Recognizing capitalism's fundamental limitations and inequalities, I have no illusions that individual financial success (which I have never experienced) is a substitute for real freedom because I am not merely concerned about what I possess. Of course I want to be able to pay my bills, but I also want to live in a world where no one and nothing suffers because of violence, exploitation, and poverty. I cannot really be free if I live in a context where wrong is being carried out in my name, and as a U.S. citizen, this government's inhumane domestic and foreign policies constantly place me in this undesired position, unless I counter them by speaking out and fighting back. The financial success of a few, even if they are members of racially and sexually oppressed groups, is not justice, but merely privilege.

I have brought the practical lessons and the passionate optimism of my political awakening in the sixties to my organizing as a Black lesbian feminist. Activism, like the deepest learning or an art form that one hones for a lifetime, can stay with you forever if you keep it alive through constant use. Because I still work for peace, I cannot forget going to New York one Saturday in the spring of 1967, marching to the United Nations to protest the

Vietnam War, and hearing Martin Luther King Jr. speak out against the war at a time when most Blacks still saw it as a white issue. Nor will I forget being on the streets of Chicago during the Democratic convention in the summer of 1968, when the Chicago police rioted and brought the war home. Because of my devotion to Black women's freedom, I will never forget meeting Fannie Lou Hamer at a basement party in Cleveland in 1965 following a rally at which she had spoken. What struck me most about her was how much she resembled the women in my family who I would return home to later that night: her southern voice, her ample figure, her difficulty walking, and her great kindness to me simply because I was young.

I have received an incredible amount of joy from activism. I suppose it is in my nature always to question, to want to shake things up, to be generally "contrary" as my grandmother would have put it. It gives me great pleasure and a feeling of pride to hear, for example, that Indian peasants rebelled in Chiapas, Mexico, on the day that the North American Free Trade Agreement (NAFTA) went into effect or that Black lesbians and gays had the courage to organize the Bayard Rustin Memorial contingent at the thirtieth anniversary of the 1963 March on Washington. I feel good whenever I hear that those who are not rich, not white, not male, and not straight have stood up to our enemies and triumphed. Whatever the outcome, the ultimate triumph lies in the fact that they chose to stand up.

Because of where I have come from I find it difficult to accept that many Black lesbians who are so multiply oppressed are not involved in organizing on behalf of their own liberation during this period. As we wrote in the Combahee River Collective statement in 1977:

> The most general statement of our politics at the present time would be that we are actively committed to struggling against racial, sexual, heterosexual, and class oppression, and see as our particular task the development of integrated analysis and practice

based upon the fact that the major systems of oppression are interlocking. The synthesis of these oppressions creates the conditions
of our lives. As Black women we see Black feminism as the logical
political movement to combat the manifold and simultaneous
oppressions that all women of color face.[1]

Although we acknowledged the difficulty of organizing as Black
women against myriad forms of systematic oppression, we nevertheless asserted:

We might use our position at the bottom, however, to make a
clear leap into revolutionary action. If Black women were free, it
would mean that everyone else would have to be free since our
freedom would necessitate the destruction of all the systems of
oppression.[2]

Obviously Black women, including Black lesbians, have a
remarkable tradition of struggle. But the great potential for vibrant
political leadership embodied by the work of Combahee and the
unprecedented, energetic coalitions of a variety of feminists of
color at the beginning of the 1980s seem to have all but disappeared in the 1990s. Of course there are lesbian of color activists
who are doing wonderful organizing on a range of issues in the
United States and Canada and it is gratifying that many of them
are also younger women. Nevertheless, my impression is that the
majority of Black lesbians are not politically active and this
includes women who only a decade ago would probably have
become dynamic organizers. I do not pretend to know all of the
reasons why more Black lesbians do not get involved in doing
political work, but I am aware of several roadblocks that seem to
prevent people from becoming active.

Probably the most serious deterrent to Black lesbian activism is
the closet itself. It is very difficult and sometimes impossible to
organize around Black lesbian issues, such as homophobic violence, child custody, and right-wing initiatives, when you do not
want people to know who you are. Not only does staying closeted

keep women from becoming involved in specifically lesbian activism, but I have seen it deter them from being politically involved in any issue. In Albany, where I have lived for the last ten years, very few Black lesbians are out and politically active, which means that they not only avoid lesbian and gay activities, but they also steer clear of feminist organizing, antiracist organizing, antiwar organizing, et cetera. I have often wondered if they are afraid that if they are seen participating in any progressive cause, it might make them more visible as lesbians, so they avoid political involvement completely.

The repercussions of being out can indeed be quite serious, but I have found that the benefits of being honest, of loving one's self, of building a supportive community where you can be all of who you are, and the empowerment and sense of freedom that come from not being in hiding, far outweigh the negatives.

Another roadblock for potential Black lesbian activists, which results from being closeted, is a lack of visible models of what effective Black lesbian (and gay) organizing looks like. To this day Black women ask me how to get in touch with the Combahee River Collective, which disbanded in 1981. Clearly, the collective's words communicate a practical vision that continues to inspire. I wish that I could fully convey to them what it was like to do Black feminist and lesbian organizing in the mid-1970s when we certainly had no specific role models. As one of our cofounders, Demita Frazier, said at one of our early meetings, "This is not a mix cake. We have got to make it up from scratch." Not only did Combahee do consciousness raising and political work on a multitude of issues, we also built strong friendship networks, community, and a rich Black women's culture where none had existed before.

I believe that another serious roadblock to activism is the ideological content of much of current theory, especially in the academy. Black lesbians who have been in school recently have often been exposed to the airless, inaccessible abstractions that dominate literary studies, women's studies, and queer studies. The varieties of academic theory that are most popular have little to say about collective struggle and less to say about the inhumane material conditions that motivate people to want to make change.

Despite the largely incomprehensible arguments that proponents of such theories offer when challenged about the political usefulness of their ideas, most of these modes of thought are frighteningly effective in maintaining the political status quo. Very little is said about why and under what conditions people begin to move, about how successful movements happen. One criterion I often rely upon for assessing the revolutionary content of ideas and actions is to ask the question originally posed by the visionary poet and activist Sonia Sanchez, which is, "But how do it free us?" Sanchez is asking about collective strategies, not individualized solutions. When most popular theoretical models are interrogated in this way, they do not have much to offer.

Other deterrents to effective organizing are the negative attitudes and behaviors that substitute for activism among some Black lesbians and gay men themselves. These individuals operate with unfortunate, even dangerous misperceptions of what organizing actually is. Their actions ignore one of the most basic principles for a successful organizer, which is that she must have a sufficient capacity to work with other people so that a job can get done without emotionally annihilating those with whom she works. Sometimes it seems that people actually measure the success of their activities and the righteousness of their politics by how thoroughly they can attack and tear down the efforts of others, in short, how lousy they can make others feel.

Humor, cooperation, reliability, humility, and kindness work better than arrogance, cruelty, manipulation, and divahood any day. Real leaders know this. They also know that being in the limelight or up on the stage is a by-product of effective organizing not the goal. The best organizing is not ego driven, power tripping, or top down. It is egalitarian, fair, humane, and damned hard work.

In assessing reasons for the diminishing of dynamic Black lesbian organizing during this period, it is crucial to take into account the overall political climate in which we must operate—the blows to progressive organizing that all of our movements have experienced in the eighties and the nineties. Reactionary politics not only have dominated the government for more than a decade, but hold more and more sway among the population as a whole, as illustrated by the huge popularity of media hatemongers such as Rush Limbaugh and Howard Stern. The increasing power of the well-organized right wing makes this a difficult and challenging time to be an activist. The problems we face such as drugs, homelessness, and violence seem so overwhelming and complicated that cocooning and focusing on one's personal life and career seem so much easier than figuring out what to do politically. In this situation the lack of visible models of successful activism becomes particularly debilitating to movement building.

Our lack of political activism is dangerous at a time when the right wing is flourishing and has placed homophobic campaigns against lesbian and gay rights at the top of their agenda. In the last two years, the white pseudo-religious right wing has specifically targeted communities of color nationwide with their hate-filled, protofascist message. They are successfully passing homophobic initiatives or rescinding existing gay rights legislation in cities all over the country and too often doing so with the help of Black ministers, Black church members, and Black voters. This is the first time in history that some segments of the African American community have made alliances with groups that have always been our enemies. The right's divisive tactics are exemplified by the vicious propaganda film *Gay Rights, Special Rights* which is explicitly aimed at Black audiences.

In most of the places where the right has run these campaigns, Black lesbians and gay men have not visibly mobilized to counter their attacks. Often the right wing has had complete carte blanche in targeting the Black community in a particular locale because Black lesbians and gays have not previously organized around any issue. When national right-wing groups begin to mobilize in their home town, they are unprepared to respond to a crisis situation that requires organizational infrastructures and strategic political expertise that are impossible to acquire overnight. In most cases countercampaigns against the right are led by white gays and lesbians who have little idea how to communicate with and work effectively with members of the Black community. The racism, white solipsism, and élitism that traditionally dominate the mainstream white gay male political agenda spell absolute disaster when what is at stake is changing our own communities' attitudes about issues of sexual orientation and civil rights.

I see the need for specifically Black-lesbian-led organizing more than ever. Not only do we have the potential to counter homophobic and heterosexist attacks within the Black community, but we also can provide much needed leadership in all kinds of struggles. Despite the challenges I have outlined there are in fact Black lesbians who are engaged in incredibly effective organizing all over the country. Knowing that these courageous women exist plays a major role in keeping me sane. When I feel discouraged and alone I think of them and know that there are other sisters out there doing the work.

There are sisters like Skye Ward in the Bay Area who was a founding editor of the Black lesbian magazine *Aché* and who is now doing groundbreaking work in the African American community to counter homophobia and attacks from the right wing; Stephanie Smith who coordinates the Lesbian of Color Project of the National Center for Lesbian Rights and is organizing against the right wing both locally in the Bay Area and nationally; Kathleen Saadat in Portland, Oregon, who has been a Black lesbian feminist activist for two decades and who worked exhaustively to defeat the Oregon Citizens' Alliance's Proposition Nine; Cathy Cohen in Brooklyn who did organizing against police brutality in Ann Arbor, Michigan, and who cofounded New York's Black AIDS Mobilization; N'Tanya Lee who works with People Advocating Change in Education (PACE) in New York City, an organization which played a pivotal role in the struggle to establish the Children of the Rainbow curriculum and which is now developing a school curriculum about lesbians and gay men of color; Tamara Jones in Brooklyn who is currently working to build the first organization for Caribbean American lesbians and gay men; Tania Abdulahad in Washington, D.C., who was a founder in the 1970s of Sapphire Sapphos and who has done years of organizing to challenge violence against women; Mandy Carter of the Human Rights Campaign Fund who worked on Harvey Gantt's historic campaign against Senator Jesse Helms in North Carolina in 1990 and who now coordinates a national project cosponsored by the National Black Lesbian and Gay Leadership Forum to mobilize the Black community against the right wing's homophobic initiatives; Ivy Young of the National Gay and Lesbian Task Force in Washington, D.C., who is a longtime political and cultural organizer and who coordinates the task force's annual Creating Change conference; Pat Hussain who was a national coordinator for the 1993 March on Washington for Lesbian, Gay, and Bi Equal Rights and who is now working to develop strategic lesbian organizing in the south; and Candice Boyce, Maua Flowers, and many other women in New York City who founded and are still committed to African American Women United for Societal Change, the oldest Black lesbian organization in the United States. Of course there are countless sisters I have not mentioned, but whose political energy is apparent even in these hard times.

I want to pay particular tribute to Black women in Albany, the "home girls" with whom I do political work. Sheila Stowell coordinated the first Grassroots Organizing Track at the 1994 National Black Lesbian and Gay Leadership Forum Conference with Suzanne Shende from New York. This two-day series of keynotes and workshops offered an explicitly progressive political focus at the conference and established a base for an ongoing activist presence. Mattie Richardson is the associate publisher of Kitchen Table: Women of Color Press and in her less than two years in Albany has worked for reproductive rights, organized against homophobia and the right wing in the Black community, run writing workshops for women who are HIV positive or who are living with AIDS, and been an active member of the Feminist Action Network (FAN).

I always describe Vickie Smith as a natural organizer because of the quality and quantity of the work she does. She has played a key role in the Capital District's Coalition Against Apartheid and Racism, served on Albany's Police/Civilian Relations Commission, done AIDS organizing in the Black community, was actively involved in our area's organizing against the Gulf War, was a cofounder in 1989 of FAN, and has provided transforming leadership as president of the board of Holding Our Own, Albany's women's foundation. One of Vickie's longtime dreams, finally realized in 1993, was to bring the Lavender Light gospel choir to Albany. Not only was the concert a highly successful cultural event, but it was consciously organized as a unique opportunity to bring various constituencies together, especially the African American and lesbian and gay communities.

Albany, New York's state capital, is a small, conservative city which means that the organizing we do here must overcome some of the same obstacles that challenge activists who work outside of east and west coast urban centers. Before I moved here, I had never tried to do political work in so inhospitable a context. But through the years we have continued to do whatever we could to link issues and communities and to offer an alternative vision to the electoral and legislative campaigns that dominate the politics of this city's racially exclusive white lesbian, gay, and women's communities. Soon after I moved to Albany I realized two things. First, that you cannot have everything, for example, a lower cost of living and less hectic lifestyle at the same time as the stimulation of an intellectually and politically diverse big city. Second, I learned that you have to brighten the corner where you are, which meant to me that I had to do the most effective and needed political work I could in the situation where I was. The conditions for making social and political change are never perfect. If they were you would not need the change to begin with. Serious activists know that they are a part of the struggle for their entire lives which means that success can be measured with a very long yardstick. Committed organizing guarantees not just a lifetime of very hard work, but the most incredible triumphs. Nelson Mandela's election to the presidency of South Africa after decades as a political prisoner is a stellar example.

Personally, despite my initiation into organizing during the remarkable political ferment of the 1960s, I cannot explain all of the reasons I became so committed to political work. Sometimes students ask me if my parents were activists. I smile at the image of the women in my family, who spent almost all of their time working so that our family could survive, being "activists." But then I remember their daily discussions about what was in the news, their conversations about race and Black history. I recall how seriously they took voting, a right which most of them only began to exercise as elders after moving up north. My grandmother worked at the polls regularly and attended ward meetings. My family was also very active in our church, which played a significant political role in Cleveland's Black community during a period when Blacks were excluded from participation in the city's government and civic life. Obviously, I learned some important lessons about struggle at home, for which I am eternally grateful.

I have also learned most of what I know about organizing from working with other activists. When I was growing up it was activists and writers who I most admired and since it was the Civil Rights era, many Black activists were clearly heroic. There are two Black lesbians who I was privileged to learn from who made a great difference in my life: Audre Lorde and Pat Parker. Not only were they out as lesbians in their writing in the early 1970s, but they were incredibly political women who did not have the illusion that it was enough for them just to pursue their individual artistic careers and let the rest of the world go hang. Both Pat, who died of breast cancer in 1989, and Audre, who died of breast cancer in 1992, were people I could count on for inspiration and in Audre's case, as we were personal friends, direct support.

In the early 1980s there was a Black feminist writers' conference in Eugene, Oregon, that all three of us attended. On Saturday afternoon we were going around the room discussing how we defined Black feminism and saw our work. I will never forget what Pat said. She stated that she saw herself as a revolutionary, that this was a word that people used to say all of the time in the sixties and seventies, but that we did not hear much any more. She told us that what she was working for as a Black feminist and lesbian was a revolution. What Pat said reminded me of how highly we had defined the stakes just a few years before. I vowed to myself from that day on not only to use the word revolution when I described my political goals, but always to be conscious in doing the work that this was what we were in fact fighting for.

The contradictions, privation, and inhumanity of these times tell me that we need a revolution more than ever. And who better to forge it than radical lesbians of color?

1995

Notes

1. The Combahee River Collective, *The Combahee River Collective Statement: Black Feminist Organizing in the Seventies and Eighties* (New York: Kitchen Table: Women of Color Press, 1986), 9.

2. *Ibid.*, 15.

I wrote "Where's the Revolution?" for the July 5, 1993, issue of *The Nation*, which was the first in its 128-year history to be devoted to lesbian and gay writing. The issue was conceived by the late Andrew Kopkind. I found it a pleasure to work with guest editor Ann-christine d'Adesky, who suggested the topic to me and offered incisive comments that sharpened my thinking and writing.

Since this was written, I have grown even more disenchanted with the mainstream gay movement at the same time that I am heartened by the increased visibility and organizing of lesbians, gays, bisexuals, and transgendered people of color.

In 1997 Ellen DeGeneres's coming out episode made television history, but it also illustrated how the struggle for lesbian and gay liberation can be reduced to a media event, even a consumer product. In an interview in the April 14, 1997, issue of *Time* magazine, Bruce Handy asks DeGeneres if she is "mad that X or Y in the entertainment industry isn't out too." She replies:

> "No, no. I don't care what X or Y does. I didn't do it to make a political statement. I did it selfishly for myself and because I thought it was a great thing for the show, which desperately needed a point of view. If other people come out, that's fine. I mean, it would be great if for no other reason than just to show the diversity, so it's not just the extremes. Because unfortunately those are the people who get the most attention on the news. You know, when you see the parades and you see dykes on bikes or these men dressed as women. I don't want to judge them. I don't want to come off like I'm attacking them—the whole point

of what I'm doing is acceptance of everybody's differences. It's just that I don't want them representing the entire gay community, and I'm sure they don't want me representing them. We're individuals."

The "extreme" "individuals" she describes, however, do not have their own network television shows. Handy's last comment is, "It must be odd having your sexuality a subject of national debate." DeGeneres responds:

"Yeah. That's why I want to get beyond this. I mean, I understand the curiosity and I understand the not understanding of it. Because I didn't understand for a long time, and I'm still struggling to—I have the same problems that a lot of people do. But let's get beyond this, and let me get back to what I do. Maybe I'll find something even bigger to do later on. Maybe I'll become black."

The interview concludes with DeGeneres's "joke" which I am sure amused other Black readers of various sexual orientations as much as it did me. "Where's the revolution?" Judging from Ellen's statements, it is obvious that it will not be televised.

Where's the Revolution?

When I came out in Boston in the mid-1970s, I had no way of knowing that the lesbian and gay movement I was discovering was in many ways unique. As a new lesbian I had nothing to compare it with, and there was also nothing to compare it with in history. Stonewall had happened only six years before and the militance, irreverence, and joy of those early days were still very much apparent.

As a Black woman who became politically active in the Civil Rights movement during high school and then in Black student organizing and the anti–Vietnam War movement as the sixties continued, it seemed only natural that being oppressed as a lesbian would elicit the same militant collective response to the status quo that my other oppressions did. Boston's lesbian and gay movement came of age in the context of student activism, a visible counterculture, a relatively organized left, and a vibrant women's movement. The city had always had its own particularly violent brand of racism and had become even more polarized because of the crisis over school busing. All of these overlapping influences strengthened the gay and lesbian movement, as well as the political understandings of lesbian and gay activists.

Objectively, being out and politically active in the seventies was about as far from the mainstream as one could get. The system did not embrace us, nor did we want it to. We also got precious little support from people who were supposed to be progressive. The white sectarian left defined homosexuality as a "bourgeois aberration" that would disappear when capitalism did. Less doctrinaire leftists were also homophobic even if they offered a different set of excuses. Black power activists and Black nationalists generally viewed lesbians and gay men as anathema—white-minded traitors to the race. Although the women's movement was the one place where out lesbians were permitted to do political work, its conservative elements still tried to dissociate themselves from the "lavender menace."

Because I came out in the context of Black liberation, women's liberation, and—most significantly—the newly emerging Black feminist movement that I was helping to build, I worked from the assumption that all of the "isms" were connected. It was simply not possible for any oppressed people, including lesbians and gay men, to achieve freedom under this system. Police dogs, cattle prods, fire hoses, poverty, urban insurrections, the Vietnam War, the assassinations, Kent State, unchecked violence against women, the self-immolation of the closet and the emotional and often physical violence experienced by those of us who dared leave it made the contradictions crystal clear. Nobody sane would want any part of the established order. It was the system—white supremacist, misogynistic, capitalist, and homophobic—that had made our lives so hard to begin with. We wanted something entirely new. Our movement was called lesbian and gay *liberation*, and more than a few of us, especially women and people of color, were working for a *revolution*.

Revolution seems like a largely irrelevant concept to the gay movement of the nineties. The liberation politics of the earlier era, which relied upon radical grassroots strategies to eradicate oppression, have been largely replaced by an assimilationist "civil rights" agenda. The most visible elements of the movement have put their faith almost exclusively in electoral and legislative initiatives, bolstered by mainstream media coverage, to alleviate *discrimination*. When the word "radical" is used at all, it means confrontational, "in your face" tactics, not strategic organizing aimed at the roots of oppression.

Unlike the early lesbian and gay movement, which had both ideological and practical links to the left, Black activism, and feminism, today's "queer" politicos seem to operate in a historical and ideological vacuum. "Queer" activists focus on "queer" issues, and racism, sexual oppression, and economic exploitation do not qualify, despite the fact that the majority of "queers" are people of color, female, or working class. When other oppressions or movements are cited, it's to build a parallel case for the validity of lesbian and gay rights or to expedite alliances with mainstream political organizations. Building unified, ongoing coalitions that challenge the system and ultimately prepare a way for revolutionary change simply isn't what "queer" activists have in mind.

When lesbians and gay men of color urge the gay leadership to make connections between heterosexism and issues like police brutality, racial violence, homelessness, reproductive freedom, and violence against women and children, the standard dismissive response is, "Those are not our issues." At a time when the gay movement is under unprecedented public scrutiny, lesbians and gay men of color and others committed to antiracist organizing are asking: Does the gay and lesbian movement want to create a just society for everyone? Or does it only want to eradicate the last little glitch that makes life difficult for privileged (white male) queers?

The April 1993 March on Washington, despite its historical importance, offers some unsettling answers. Two comments that I've heard repeatedly since the march are that it seemed more like a parade than a political demonstration and that the overall image of the hundreds of thousands of participants was overwhelmingly Middle American, that is, white and conventional. The identifiably queer—the drag queens, leather people, radical faeries, dykes on bikes, and so on—were definitely in the minority, as were people of color, who will never be Middle American no matter what kind of drag we put on or take off.

A friend from Boston commented that the weekend in Washington felt like being in a "blizzard." I knew what she meant. Despite the fact that large numbers of lesbians and gay men of color were present (perhaps even more than at the 1987 march), our impact upon the proceedings did not feel nearly as strong as it did six years ago. The bureaucratic nineties concept of "diversity," with its superficial goal of assuring that all the colors in the crayon box are visible, was very much the strategy of the day. Filling slots with people of color or women does not necessarily affect the politics of a movement if our participation does not change the agenda, that is, if we are not actually permitted to lead.

I had had my own doubts about attending the April march. Although I went to the first march in 1979 and was one of the eight major speakers at the 1987 march, I didn't make up my mind to go to this one until a few weeks before it happened. It felt painful to be so alienated from the gay movement that I wasn't even sure I wanted to be there; my feelings of being an outsider had been growing for some time.

I remember receiving a piece of fund-raising direct mail from the magazine *Outlook* in 1988 with the phrase "tacky but we'll take it" written next to the lowest potential contribution of $25. Since $25 is a lot more than I can give at any one time to the groups I support, I decided I might as well send my $5 somewhere else. In 1990 I read Queer Nation's manifesto, "I Hate Straights," in *Outweek* and wrote a letter to the editor suggesting that if queers of color followed its political lead, we would soon be issuing a statement titled, "I Hate Whiteys," including white queers of European origin. Since that time I've heard very little public criticism of the narrowness of lesbian and gay nationalism. No one would guess from recent stories about wealthy and "powerful" white lesbians on TV and in slick magazines that women earn 69¢ on the dollar compared with men and that Black women earn even less.

These examples are directly connected to assumptions about race and class privilege. In fact, it's gay white men's racial, gender, and class privileges, as well as the vast numbers of them who identify with the system rather than distrust it, that have made the politics of the current gay movement so different from those of other identity-based movements for social and political change. In the seventies, progressive movements—especially feminism—positively influenced and inspired lesbians' and gays' visions of struggle. Since the eighties, as AIDS has helped to raise consciousness about gay issues in some quarters of the establishment, and as some battles against homophobia have been won, the movement has positioned itself more and more within the mainstream political arena. President Clinton's courting of the gay vote (at the same time as he did everything possible to distance himself from the African American community) has also been a crucial factor in convincing the national gay and lesbian leadership that a place at the ruling class's table is just what they've been waiting for. Of course, the people left out of this new gay political equation of mainstream acceptance, power, and wealth are lesbians and gay men of color.

Our outsider status in the new queer movement is made even more untenable because supposedly progressive heterosexuals of all races do so little to support lesbian and gay freedom. Although homophobia may be mentioned when heterosexual leftists make lists of oppressions, they do virtually no risk-taking work to connect with our movement or to challenge attacks against lesbians and gays who live in their midst. Many straight activists whose politics are otherwise righteous simply refuse to acknowledge how dangerous heterosexism is, and that they have any responsibility to end it. Lesbians and gays working in straight political contexts are often expected to remain closeted so as not to diminish their own "credibility" or that of their groups. With so many heterosexuals studiously avoiding opportunities to become enlightened about lesbian and gay culture and struggle, it's not surprising that nearly twenty-five years after Stonewall so few heterosexuals get it. Given how well-organized the Christian right is, and that one of its favorite tactics is pitting various oppressed groups against one another, it is past time for straight and gay activists to link issues and work together with respect.

The issue of access to the military embodies the current gay movement's inability to frame an issue in such a way that it brings various groups together instead of alienating them, as has happened with segments of the Black community. It also reveals a gay political agenda that is not merely moderate but conservative. As long as a military exists, it should be open to everyone regardless of sexual orientation, especially since it represents job and training opportunities for poor and working-class youth who are, disproportionately, people of color. But given the U.S. military's real function of acting as the world's police force, implementing this country's imperialist foreign policy, and murdering those who stand in its way (e.g., the quarter of a million people, mostly civilians, who died in Iraq as a result of the Gulf War), a progressive lesbian and gay movement would at least consider the political implications of frantically organizing to get into the mercenary wing of the military-industrial complex. A radical lesbian and gay movement would of course be working to dismantle the military completely.

Many people of color (Colin Powell notwithstanding) understand all too well the paradox of our being sent to Third World countries to put down "rebellions" which are usually the efforts of indigenous populations to rule themselves. The paradox is even more wrenching when U.S. troops are sent to quell "unrest" in this country's internal colonies, such as South Central Los Angeles. Thankfully, there were some pockets of dissent at the April march expressed in slogans like: "Lift the Ban—Ban the Military" and "Homosexual, Not Homocidal; Fuck the Military." Yet it seemingly has not occurred to movement leaders that there are lesbians and gays who have actively opposed the Gulf War, the Vietnam War, military intervention in Central America, and apartheid in South Africa. We need a politics complex enough and principled enough to talk about nondiscrimination at the same time that it provides a critique of why a military and weapons arsenal of the type that the U.S. government maintains negates any possibility of justice and world peace.

The movement that I discovered when I came out was far from perfect. It was at times infuriatingly racist, sexist, and elitist, but also not nearly so monolithic. There was at least ideological room to point out failings, and a variety of allies willing to listen who wanted to build something better.

I think that homosexuality embodies an innately radical critique of the traditional nuclear family, whose political function has been to constrict the sexual expression and gender roles of all of its members, especially women, lesbians, and gays. Being in structural opposition to the status quo because of one's identity, however, is quite different from being consciously and actively opposed to the status quo because one is a radical and understands how the system works.

It was talking to radical lesbians and gay men that finally made me decide to go to the march. Earlier in the month, I attended an extraordinary conference on the lesbian and gay left in Delray Beach, Florida. The planners had made a genuine commitment to racial and gender parity; 70 percent of the participants were people of color and 70 percent were women. They were also committed to supporting the leadership of people of color and lesbians—especially lesbians of color—which is almost never done outside of our own autonomous groupings. The conference felt like a homecoming. I got to spend time with people I'd worked with twenty years before in Boston as well as with younger activists from across the country.

What made the weekend so successful, aside from the humor, gossip, caring, and hot discussions about sex and politics, was the huge relief I felt at not being expected to cut off parts of myself that are as integral to who I am as my sexual orientation as the price for participating in lesbian and gay organizing. Whatever concerns were raised, discussions were never silenced by the remark, "But that's not our issue." Women and men, people of color and whites, all agreed that there desperately needs to be a visible alternative to the cut-and-dried, business-as-usual agenda of the gay political mainstream. Their energy and vision, as well as the astuteness and tenacity of radical lesbians and gays I encounter all over the country, convince me that a different way is possible.

If the gay movement ultimately wants to make a real difference, as opposed to settling for handouts, it must consider creating a multi-issue revolutionary agenda. This is not about political correctness, it's about winning. As Black lesbian poet and warrior Audre Lorde insisted, "The master's tools will never dismantle the master's house." Gay *rights* are not enough for me, and I doubt that they're enough for most of us. Frankly, I want the same thing now that I did thirty years ago when I joined the Civil Rights movement and twenty years ago when I joined the women's movement, came out, and felt more alive than I ever dreamed possible: freedom.

1993

This open letter to the lesbian, gay, bisexual, and transgendered movement about the Millennium March was written during the first week of May 1998. It was initially circulated via e-mail all over the country. Within days of its appearance I received requests to reprint it in the *Washington Blade*, *Sojourner: The Women's Forum*, and *Gay Community News*. I also received dozens of e-mails in response, almost all of them positive.

Because the controversy over the Millennium March so perfectly illustrates the issues that I address in "Where's the Revolution?" I thought it was important to include my letter here.

In an article profiling Elizabeth Birch, executive director of the Human Rights Campaign, in the April 1998 issue of *Out* magazine, reporter J. Jennings Moss describes a joking exchange in which Birch assesses her role in the l/g/b/t movement. Moss, however, takes her statement more seriously.

> "This is what you should write," she [Birch] joshed to a reporter, her big hazel eyes brightening and a smile creasing her fine, angular features. "In the 1990s there had to be a meeting of minds between the raw activist spirit and the communications and marketing techniques that define a new voice for gay America. It came together in the person of Elizabeth Birch."
>
> It's a presumptuous view but quite genuine.[*]

Later in the article Birch states, "Imagine what you would have done if three years ago you woke up and found that

---

[*] J. Jennings Moss, "Capitol Gains," *Out*, no. 58 (April 1998): 113–114.

someone had handed you the movement. . . . I'll bet you would have made most of the same decisions I've made."

Thanks to racism and élitism, progressive people of color are barely allowed to *share* movement leadership, let alone control it. Rest assured, if we did get to decide movement agendas, they would be a lot different from what they are now. Middle-of-the-road and conservative corporate-inspired strategies automatically marginalize huge sectors of the l/g/b/t movement, a movement that thousands of us built together with "raw activist spirit" long before Birch imagined that it had been "handed" to her on a silver platter.

It is no coincidence that the first protests about the Millennium actions have been led by Black lesbian feminists Mandy Carter and Nadine Smith and by a Black organization, the National Black Lesbian and Gay Leadership Lorum. As of this writing town meetings are being held in various cities to discuss the Millennium organizers' blatant disregard for a democratic and inclusive process. Progressive and radical grassroots activists are also utilizing this great opportunity to develop meaningful and innovative political alternatives to the élitist and reactionary corporate monster that the mainstream lesbian and gay movement has become.

Where's the Revolution? Part II

Dear Sisters and Brothers,

I want to share my criticisms of the proposed Millennium March on Washington and of the march planners' process of excluding grassroots participation of people of color and other constituencies. It is clear to me at this point in the lesbian, gay, bisexual, and transgendered movement's history that we need to prioritize doing organizing where we live. The proposal to carry out coordinated simultaneous actions in the fifty state capitals is a much more useful and strategic plan and one that I thoroughly support.

Another march on Washington organized by conservative and moderate white forces, which have the single-issue agenda of petitioning the establishment to extend a few gay rights, will do little to address the pressing needs of l/g/b/t people of color. We don't simply need gay rights. We need social, political, and economic justice, which means at the very least that we need to work with those who have been and continue to be "actively" committed to eradicating racism, sexism, and class oppression as well as homophobia.

Elizabeth Birch, executive director of the Human Rights Campaign, is quoted in the April 17 issue of the *Washington Blade* as stating: "We have not always done our best. We have not always been a good neighbor. But this year, you will see us at the Black Lesbian and Gay Pride weekend and at other major events."

Being "a good neighbor" and showing up at Black events is beside the point. What is to the point is the articulation of a serious, antiracist activist platform that would lay out specific strategic actions for challenging racism both in the society as a whole and within the white l/g/b/t movement. With such a platform HRC would have been one of the first voices we heard when Haitian immigrant Abner Louima was brutalized by the Brooklyn police last summer or when African immigrant Oumar Dia was murdered by a white skinhead in Denver last November. Birch's statements sound frighteningly similar to those made by Ralph Reed and other members of the pseudo-Christian right wing when numerous Black churches were being burned a couple of years ago. In both cases the leaders of organizations that previously showed little or no concern about challenging racism have responded to a racial crisis in language that minimized the magnitude of the problem and their culpability in perpetuating it. Both leaders also act as if by simply showing up at places where Blacks are gathered and throwing a little money their way, their organizations' long histories of attacking or ignoring Black struggles will be magically erased. Institutionalized white supremacy is hardly a problem of good and bad "neighbors."

The *Blade* article also cites the e-mail campaign started on March 30 by the Rev. Troy Perry, founder of the Universal Fellowship of Metropolitan Community Churches (UFMCC), which is the other initiator of the Millennium March, to pressure the National Black Lesbian and Gay Leadership Forum and the National Gay and Lesbian Task Force to endorse the march without ever seeking the input of the Forum. Perry is quoted in the article as stating, "Ask them to come on board and to endorse the march. Let them know how much we want and need and *expect* their support." The fact that the National Black Lesbian and Gay Leadership Forum and other people of color were not communicated with from the very beginning when the Millennium March was being conceived, but are now expected to sign on after the fact, is the epitome of undemocratic tactics as well as of racism.

I believe this is a crucial time for the Forum and all l/g/b/t people of color to stand firm on principle and not to be bought off. We have an opportunity to demonstrate that we demand consistent respect, that we refuse to be tokenized, and are committed to total liberation for all people, not merely to getting a few rights, that is, crumbs—whether they come from the table of HRC and UFMCC or society at large. We have a great opportunity to define our movement, to honor our heritage of struggle, and to establish our place in history. I sincerely hope we will take it.

In solidarity and struggle,

Barbara Smith
Albany, New York

1998

IV

A Rose

I wrote "A Rose" to conclude this book. I often imagined that I would write about what it meant to be responsible for Kitchen Table: Women of Color Press after I stopped being its publisher. I took the opportunity to do so here.

I have always been struck by how oblivious most white people are to the actual substance of Black people's lives, how consistently they ignore our humanity as well as deny the waking nightmare of racial oppression. Even those who care about racial justice do not always recognize that the kind of brutality experienced by Abner Louima at the hands of the Brooklyn police in the summer of 1997 *directly* impacts the lives of other Black people, including the ones they know, in deeply demoralizing ways. Less conscious whites view racist violence as atypical, isolated incidents. The majority of whites, however, barely register that such violence and other acts of institutionalized racism occur in this country millions of times every single day. This mass denial accounts in part for racism's virulent persistence more than five hundred years after European contact.

A few weeks after I completed "A Rose," Oumar Dia, a political refugee from West Africa, was murdered by Nathan Thill, a white skinhead, while he waited for a bus in Denver. The white woman who tried to help him was also shot and permanently paralyzed from the waist down. Thill, who confessed, stated, "In a war, anybody wearing the enemy's uniform . . . should be taken out." The "enemy's uniform" he refers to is Black skin. Thill also commented about the shootings, "Didn't seem like much to me."*

---

* Andrew Murr, "'Didn't Seem like Much,'" *Newsweek*, December 1, 1997, *Newsweek* Archive/*Newsweek* Interactive, America on Line.

A Rose

On the evening of Friday, August 8, 1997, Abner Louima, a Brooklyn resident and Haitian immigrant, went to a Haitian nightclub after a long week at work to hear one of his favorite bands. Although Mr. Louima has a degree in electrical engineering, he worked as a licensed security guard. As the club was closing, a fight started between other patrons and Mr. Louima intervened to stop it. When the white police officers arrived he was arrested.

On the way to the precinct, the police beat Mr. Louima repeatedly. When he arrived at the station house they made him strip from the waist down in full public view. They then took him into a bathroom and proceeded to torture him using the wooden handle of a bathroom plunger rammed up his rectum. Next they forced the filthy handle of the plunger into his mouth, breaking two of his teeth. His bladder and colon were torn up. They then placed him in a cell. After several hours of hemorrhaging nearly to death, another prisoner was able to persuade the police to get Mr. Louima medical help. Even after an ambulance was called, it took several more hours for it to leave because the officers refused to accompany Mr. Louima to the hospital, a required procedure for anyone held in custody.

For the first four days that he was in the hospital in critical condition following extensive surgery, Mr. Louima was handcuffed to his bed and members of his family, including his wife, were not permitted to see him. Eventually all charges against him were dropped. It is apparent that the police did everything they could to cover up their sadistic and criminal actions. A nurse, who is also of Caribbean heritage, refused to falsify a report about Mr. Louima's condition and courageously helped to bring public attention to the atrocity. Two months later, Mr. Louima is still hospitalized. He has undergone surgery several times. A recent, potentially life-threatening blood clot has proven difficult to treat because of the severity of his other injuries.

For nights after learning what had happened to Abner Louima, it was difficult for me to sleep. Every time I awoke I thought about him and felt the horror once again. Day or night, I was near tears whenever I focused upon what he and his family were going through. The despair and fury I felt were nothing new. Since childhood I have been forced to live this nightmare again and again. In 1955, although I was too little to know what it meant, I learned fourteen-year-old Emmet Till's name when he was lynched in Mississippi for whistling at a white woman. In 1957, when I was ten, I watched nine Black students attempt to enter Little Rock High School while a mob of screaming white adults attacked them verbally and physically.

In 1963 four Black girls near my own age, Addie Mae Collins, Denise McNair, Carole Robertson, and Cynthia Wesley, were murdered when the Sixteenth Street Baptist Church was bombed in Birmingham, Alabama. More than any of the others, their deaths taught me the measure of my life in the great white scheme of things. Somebody's daughter, somebody's neighbor girl, somebody's child, someone with carefully plaited hair and a crisply ironed blouse, someone whose people saw to it that she got to church every Sunday, someone like me was in the end worth nothing, was a creature to be hunted down, obliterated, and killed.

On none of these occasions, nor in response to the countless other atrocities which occurred when the Black freedom movement was at its height, did the white media run stories about how to comfort children as they do now following tragic events, since the only children suffering from the aftermath of these acts of terrorism were Black ones.

During the 1980s New York State, where I have lived since 1981, spawned some of the nation's most notorious acts of racial violence. These include the mob attack on three Black men at Howard Beach in which one of them, Michael Griffith, died; Bernhard Goetz's shooting of four Black youths on the subway; the murders of Eleanor Bumpurs, Michael Stewart, and Yusuf Hawkins; and the series of racially motivated murders of six Black men in Buffalo. Shortly before I moved to Albany in 1984, an unarmed Black man, Jessie Davis, was murdered by the police in his apartment a few blocks from where I now live. The "weapons" the police claimed they saw in his hand turned out to be a key case and a toy truck. Days after Abner Louima's torture and attempted murder, two white men in Virginia burned alive a Black man, Garnett Paul Johnson, and then beheaded him.[1]

In 1995 the Oklahoma City bombing was orchestrated by sociopaths who were not merely antigovernment, but white supremacist, a fact ignored by most of the white media. One supporter of the bombing commented on the internet: "It's a real injustice that White children had to be injured and killed in this attack on the ZOG's [Zionist Occupation Government's] Okla H.Q."[2]

When I confront the ongoing reality of racist hatred it affects me not only politically, but personally. These acts serve as unequivocal reminders of how thoroughly *I* am hated here because I was born Black instead of white. As long as I am alive in the United States of America I cannot assume that a similar act of terrorism will not happen to me. I have had my car run off the road in Watertown, Massachusetts, by a white male driver who repeatedly rammed my car from behind, and who I am sure would have been delighted if I had crashed into the utility pole a few inches away from where I managed to stop. When I drove to the police station in Cambridge to report the incident, still shaking, the white police officers' attitude was one of barely disguised amusement. They told me there was nothing they could do. Eight years ago on a cold January night in Philadelphia, as I left my friend Joseph Beam's memorial service, two white male strangers slammed their bodies full force into mine, simply because I was there and Black.

Like every Black person who lives in this nation's racist cauldron, I know I am lucky still to be alive. I take it personally that from the moment of my birth my life has been consistently viewed as less valuable than a white life. Even if I am fortunate enough to escape an act of direct physical violence, my "natural" life expectancy is years less than that of a white woman simply because I am Black. I also take it personally that most of the "decent" white people in this country have never lifted a finger to make absolutely certain that what happened to Abner Louima will never happen again and will never happen to me. Celebrating "diversity" and attending multicultural events will not do it.

As usual, in the aftermath of a racist atrocity that makes international headlines, the white women's movement and the white lesbian and gay movement have had nothing to say about this latest incident, except for some interest in the fact that the police tried to cover up their attack by attributing Mr. Louima's injuries to a homosexual encounter at the in fact straight nightclub he visited that night.

I have mentioned a mere handful of examples of the war against body, mind, and spirit that we have had to endure for centuries since our involuntary arrival in the Americas as slaves. In the last days of the twentieth century it is staggering to realize how little general regard there is for our humanity, to be reminded so bitterly that racism is as alive and well as ever.

Until this summer, whenever a tragedy like Abner Louima's torture occurred, whether caused by race hatred, misogyny, or any permutation of "man's inhumanity to man," I could always talk to Lu. My friend Lucretia Medina Diggs was born in 1926. It was a particular relief to say whatever was on my mind to a Black woman who was old enough to be my mother. Lu would often tell me how exceedingly weary she was as an elder to have to face yet more racism after so many decades of not merely facing it, but fighting it. We had countless conversations tinged with fury, grief, and at times sardonic humor about the public manifestations of racial violence and injustice.

What I remember most, however, are the times Lu recounted the individual cruelties and insults she experienced simply because she was a Black woman trying to live in a white world: the nasty waitress at the pancake house where she and her two daughters had gone for brunch, the abusive teenagers who made her refuse to shop at our area's largest mall, the salesman at the luxury car dealership, who when she asked the price of one of their models, snidely told her, "If you have to ask, you obviously can't afford it." Hearing these stories made me livid. I thought, "Here is one of the best persons I have ever met and look at how she gets treated!" And of course there was little I could do except attentively listen. My commitment to antiracist organizing is about changing the big picture, the macrocosm, but in the microcosm of everyday life, both Lu and I were at the potential mercy of any white person who needed to show us who was the boss.

One of the many things I learned from Lu, however, was that at times there was something you could do about the ordinary racist encounters of daily life. You *could* talk back or at the very least write a letter. I always marveled when Lu repeated to me the sharp and elegant put-downs she came up with on the spot when highly imperfect strangers saw fit to disrespect her. She put that waitress in her place and wrote a scorching letter to the car salesman's employer. One day when a young white man at the supermarket where she was a regular customer continually pushed up against her in line, Lu said in a strong, clear voice, "Young man, if you get any closer to me, I'm afraid we will have to get married." He turned beet red and stopped pushing.

After knowing Lu for a while, whenever I experienced similar acts of racist rudeness, I would think to myself, "Now what would Lu do in this situation?" and then would attempt to speak up on my own behalf. This was not something I had learned at home, perhaps because all of my family, except my sister and myself, had been born in rural Georgia at a time when Georgia had more lynchings than any other state in the union including Mississippi. They knew all too well the dire consequences of talking back to white people. Lu, on the other hand, unlike most Black men and women of her generation, had been born in the North (New York City) and spent most of her childhood in Princeton, New Jersey. Lu's mother was from Virginia, however, and Lu had spent a lot of time there with her maternal grandparents and other relatives. Perhaps Lu's capacity to speak up was not geographically determined at all, but in the end was just Lu. Whatever the source of her outspokenness, her behavior inspired me. Talking back to white strangers was a hard and frightening thing to do, but when I did I always felt better. Even when those white men slammed into me on the streets of Philadelphia, my sister and I both yelled back at them at the top of our lungs, our anger momentarily blunting our fear in what could have become a much more dangerous situation.

I think it is possible to learn courage. I have learned most of what I know about it from older Black women—the members of my family, my Boston friend Marlene Stephens, Audre Lorde, and Lu. Lu's courage became apparent soon after we met because of a daunting task I brought to her. But I need to go back and say how our friendship began.

In the spring of 1986 an arts organization sponsored a one-day book fair in Albany. Because I had to attend another conference for Kitchen Table: Women of Color Press the same weekend, I decided to try to find other women who could staff our table in my absence. I had moved to Albany less than two years before and did not know very many people. I called a woman of color I hardly knew and when I told her why I was calling she said, "You have got to call Lucretia Diggs." My acquaintance told me that Lu was familiar with the Press and had read some of our books. I called Lu and without hesitation she agreed to work with the other women at the book fair.

What I recall about that initial conversation is that we spoke with the kind of humor, candor, and depth that seldom occurs between people who do not know each other. One of the topics we discussed that day was racism and anti-Semitism and by the time we got off the phone I had promised to send Lu a copy of *Yours in Struggle*. A few days later she was at the meeting I'd arranged at my apartment to explain to the volunteers how to sell Kitchen Table books. Lu was a few inches shorter than my 5 feet 7½ inches. She had warm coppery skin that beautifully contrasted with her once dark, now mostly gray hair. She usually wore her hair natural and also straightened and curled it for special occasions. Her most striking features were her dark, penetrating eyes, which I came to believe could see everything. Lu had a round, ample figure about which she had always felt self-conscious. Sometimes when we talked about our struggles with weight she would say, "I've always been a fatty." This comment, expressed in the language of a school-yard taunt, always shocked me. I thought Lu looked fine. We shared a similar taste in clothes—well-tailored, conservative classics that never went out of style. When I met Lu, the impression that I had gotten over the telephone was reconfirmed. She seemed familiar to me. She seemed like someone I would like.

Soon after the book fair Lu invited me to dinner at her home in Latham, a suburb of Albany. It was the first of many superb meals that she prepared for me and at times for other family members and friends. A few weeks after we met I invited her to a meeting that I had helped to organize at Blue Mountain Center in the Adirondacks to discuss the formation of a Women of Color Institute for Radical Research and Action. The institute never materialized, but at the end of the weekend when we were going around the circle saying our good-byes, Lu hugged me and said, "I love you so much." By that time I loved her too. As years passed Lu referred to me as one of her "daughters." Since I had ceased to be a daughter at the age of nine, when my mother died at age thirty-four, there was nothing more precious that Lu could have given me.

By the late spring of 1986 it was apparent that Kitchen Table Press was in very serious trouble. Although my closest friends were extremely worried about the emotional and physical toll that my efforts to save the Press would take on me, I decided to move the Press, which was still in New York City, to Albany. Several women made the move possible. Papusa Molina took over as interim administrator that summer while the Press was still in New York. I asked my new friends Vickie Smith and Lu if they would help me bring the Press to Albany. Lu had just taken early retirement from her job at the state department of social services in June and told me she would do "whatever she could." I am sure in many ways that Lu was always a feminist in the decisive way she moved through life. Through her job she had become actively involved with domestic violence groups, she was a volunteer speaker for Planned Parenthood, and she was the first woman of color to be president of the board of Albany's YWCA. Lu loved what Kitchen Table stood for, knew how important the Press was to me, and did not want to see it die.

Her promise to do "whatever she could" was a vast understatement. If it were not for Lucretia Diggs, Kitchen Table would have ceased to exist in the mid-1980s. For nearly four years Lu worked at Kitchen Table as if it were a paying job, which needless to say it was not. She was from a tradition of race women who understood that they had a responsibility to use their talents to help their communities and not merely to serve themselves. She would often speak angrily about some of the younger women in New York who had been paid staff and who had let the Press fail. I felt the same way.

I was very concerned in the early 1980s when the Press shifted quickly from being a "collective" of women who did at least some of the necessary work voluntarily to being an organization in which everyone (except for me) got paid for their time. I was afraid that the Press would not be able to sustain itself with this level of paid staffing, at least not at that early stage. I also viewed the Press as a movement commitment, but the increasingly conservative political climate of the early 1980s, the extremely high cost of living in New York, a new generation of women who had minimal connections to earlier movements for social change, and the withdrawal of founding members from the Press's day-to-day work all contributed to the Press's change in direction. As I feared, the attempt to maintain several paid staff positions, as well as other negative factors, led by 1986 to the Press's crisis.

By the time the Press's physical belongings arrived in Albany I had temporarily relocated to Minneapolis for the fall where I was a visiting professor in women's studies at the University of Minnesota. Albany's Social Justice Center, located in a small storefront, allowed us to move some of our equipment into an area in the back. There was space for one desk and a couple of filing cabinets and that was it. There was literally no room to turn around. When we had work to do that required more space, such as packing books or doing mailings, we would move to a meeting area with tables, also in the back. I made one trip back to Albany in October and continued, as usual, to do Kitchen Table work from my apartment in Minneapolis, including a large review copy mailing.

The years 1986 and 1987 were undoubtedly the most dire period in the Press's history. When the Press's New York bank account was transferred to Albany it had two dollars and forty-six cents in it. Lu told me she showed the statement to Vickie Smith, who continued to volunteer a great deal of time, and said, "Read this. Shouldn't there be at least one more zero here?" But the statement was correct. We had less than three dollars in the bank and tens of thousands of dollars in debt, owed mostly to our printer. It never occurred to either Lu or myself to renege on our bills, but through hard work, faith, and sheer tenacity we paid them off so that the Press could continue to function. Both Lu and I had learned the habits of thrift in our working-class families and these habits served the Press quite well.

People who live outside of Albany have often asked me, "Where is Latham, New York?" Latham is less than ten miles from the center of Albany. The reason our address was in Latham is that Lu lived there and since she was handling all of the Press's daily functions following the move, she set up the post office box, bank account, and storage room where it would be convenient for her.

One freezing cold winter day in early 1987 Lu and I needed to get a shipment of *Home Girls* ready to send to one of our distributors. Despite the cold we might have labeled and reinforced the boxes with tape at our storage room and taken them directly to United Parcel Service, which was also in Latham. However, we had changed the cover price of *Home Girls*, which meant that every single one of the several hundred books we were shipping that day had to be taken from the boxes so that we could place a sticker with the correct price over the old price printed on the book. Even if we had wanted to do this work from the unheated storage room, we could not, because it was so cold that the adhesive on the tiny price stickers that I had typed myself would not stay on. So Lu and I loaded the cartons of books into our two cars and drove to her nearby apartment. Because she lived on the second floor and there was no elevator, we set up a card table in the ground-floor stairwell and, wearing coats and hats, worked for several hours repricing, repacking, and then taping and labeling the boxes for shipping. We then loaded them back into our cars and drove them to UPS.

This is just one example of the kind of work it took to keep Kitchen Table's doors open, the kind of work both of us were willing to do without compensation. During that period I had the equivalent of four jobs: my unpaid work as publisher of Kitchen Table; a part-time teaching job in the English Department of Hobart and William Smith Colleges in Geneva, New York, a four-hour commute each way; numerous speaking engagements; and a women's writing course I taught every Saturday at the "Y" as a requirement for a small grant I had received from the New York State Council on the Arts. I was also living in a motel because the new house a friend had helped me to buy, designed for low-to-moderate income first-time homeowners in Albany's Black community, Arbor Hill, was not completed in time for my return from Minneapolis. These were really hard times for those of us who were committed to Kitchen Table. Sometimes Lu and I disagreed about the best way to allocate our small resources, but the bottom line was that we both had the Press's survival as our highest goal.

Despite our twenty-year age difference, Lu and I shared many values. We both had lived through de facto segregation and this country's continual devaluing of anything or anyone Black. Our fury at being so constantly threatened, dehumanized, and erased had been galvanized into action by the Civil Rights movement. Black power and Black pride offered us more positive ways to see ourselves in a white supremacist nation. The feminist movement helped explain the ways we had been trivialized and victimized just because we were female and offered strategies for empowerment and change. But in both the Black and women's movements, with their sexism, racism, and élitism, we were still poor relations. For us, Black feminism was a lifeline and Kitchen Table Press was one of its few visible outposts. Fighting to save Kitchen Table was in some ways fighting for our own lives. And we knew if we needed the Press, other women of color did too.

I think our capacity to work so hard had a lot to do, finally, with rage. Every single day our people—people of color, women, lesbians, gays, poor people, children, and elders—were being physically and emotionally annihilated. Every single day, Lu and I got the message delivered personally, whether from rude waiters, store clerks who refused to put our change in our hands, or the daily hate crimes report, also known as the six o'clock news, that our lives were worth nothing. Each of us had concluded long before we met each other that we could either self-immolate with fury and grief or figure out pragmatic ways to fight back. Every day we kept the Press open was one more day that the annihilators, the hate-mongers had not won. Gradually, the Press began to pull out of debt and became productive once again.

Early in 1987, Lu said that she thought we could afford to hire a part-time office manager. Through one of her friends who worked for the state we met Wanda Carríon Mejías, a Puertorriqueña, who began working with the Press in the winter. Wanda was divorced, had a preschool-age daughter, and wanted a job that required less than forty hours of work a week. When all three of us were at the office, there was no room for all of us to sit down. We often wore our coats and hats because it was so cold at the back of the store-front. But despite the physically inadequate conditions and the constant worry about money and bills, we had fun working together. I appreciated how Wanda in particular could always find the humor in our straitened circumstances.

By the summer of 1987 we had relocated to a slightly bigger space in another storefront, that belonged to the Women's Build-ing. When they were ready to move to much larger, partially reno-vated quarters, Lu had a number of misgivings about moving with them, not the least of which was that we would be on an upper floor in a building with no elevator. At her urging, I was able at the last minute to find us a space at Albany's Urban League, a few blocks down the street from my home. Our location was conve-nient and our rent for two small rooms was well under one hun-dred dollars a month. I also liked our feminist and lesbian of color organization being associated with one of the oldest Black civil rights groups in the nation.

Near the end of 1987 Lu and I interviewed a potential intern, Sheilah Sable, who had enrolled in the women's studies internship seminar at the State University at Albany. Sheilah was a white Jew-ish woman and in the past we had prioritized working with other women of color. Both Lu and I were impressed with Sheilah and as Lu pointed out, "We could really use the help." Sheilah joined us in January 1988 and did such an excellent job that we offered her the part-time office manager position after Wanda returned to full-time work. Like Wanda, Sheilah had a wonderful sense of humor, an unwritten job requirement for dealing with the chal-lenge of working at the Press. Wanda continued to come in on Saturdays and two years after the Press had hit its lowest point, we now had a team of four devoted women.

The Press's situation, although always incredibly difficult, had improved. Eventually, Lu decided to cut back on the volunteer time she gave to several organizations, including Kitchen Table. In 1990 I moved the Press to the first floor of my two-family house. Sheilah worked with the Press until the early summer of 1990. By then I was able to hire Lillien Waller, who came to the Press with previous publishing experience, full time. Mattie Richardson, a recent Dartmouth graduate, joined the Press full time in 1992 and over the years we continued to have a number of excellent interns. As I look back, I think that the Press's hardest time was in some ways its best time. Wanda, Sheilah, Lu, and I were not merely co-workers, but friends, and Lu in many ways was at the center. All of our friendships outlasted our time together at Kitchen Table.

On a number of levels how we treated each other embodied the vision of Kitchen Table itself. Here were four women of different races, ethnicities, sexual orientations, and ages, who held each other in high regard, who came to love each other. When I would sing Lu's praises to friends outside of Albany, they would sometimes ask if she was a lesbian or simply made that assumption without asking. When I explained that Lu was heterosexual, they marveled that she would associate herself with me and with an organization which was known for its lesbian leadership and support of lesbians of color nationwide.

Lu's opposition to homophobia was in some ways remarkable, but it was so consistent with her character and her capacity to respect the humanity of her huge and diverse circle of colleagues and friends, I came to take it for granted. Sometimes I would ask her for suggestions about contacts with other Black women for political work in which I was involved, such as the Feminist Action Network's AIDS organizing in the Black community. She might give me a few suggestions, but would add with much disgust, "Most of the Black women in Albany are so homophobic!"

As our friendship continued past her involvement in the Press, I could see that Lu could be genuinely conservative about some matters. For example, she expressed her skepticism about Eleanor Roosevelt's documented relationships with lesbians. She thought the ideal home situation was a traditional two-parent family. Lu had been fortunate to have a strong and loving marriage. Yet when I was considering adoption, she was completely supportive and helpful. She expressed admiration for Blacks who achieved in any context, including mainstream politics, the corporate world, and the military. Usually I stated my views, but sometimes I just nodded, feeling little need to clash about matters we viewed quite differently. I respected Lu as an elder, but more importantly I also trusted that we were in agreement on the most important issues, that we had far more commonalities than differences.

One thing that upset me after we stopped working together was that Lu almost never phoned me. I always called her. I do not know if she had an aversion to talking on the telephone (although we had many a lively conversation) or if she thought it was more appropriate for me as the younger person to call her. Whatever the reason, I would often feel guilty when several months went by and I had not gone out to visit her. My workload at the Press, the necessity to earn my living doing other work, and my travel schedule continued to be overwhelming. Eventually, I decided to give myself a break about this and since Lu was obviously so glad to hear from me and to see me whenever we did get together, I gradually stopped worrying about it.

Often I would go to see her after doing some Kitchen Table errands out in Latham. Those afternoon visits were a joy. She would make tea, usually accompanied by some delicious treat. Our conversations covered every conceivable topic including the latest things we had read. Lu loved to read, as much as I do, and her love for books had drawn her to the Press before we ever met. Going to Lu's apartment for a visit or for a homemade meal was always an oasis of calm in my otherwise hectic life.

Kitchen Table's most serious difficulties were always financial, which caused a host of other problems, most significantly drastic understaffing. Usually, I had no choice but to work to the point of exhaustion, day after day. Even more debilitating than the work was the constant worry about money. How was I going to pay my coworkers and the huge printer's bills? How was I going to pay my own bills and what would I have to live on next week? This constant anxiety often awoke me in the middle of the night. After lying in the dark going over and over the impossible situation in

my mind, I would get up and work. It was always so frustrating to
know that there were so many tasks left undone, especially the
Press's and my own voluminous correspondence. Once I told my
sister, Beverly, that on a weekend, without other Press business
interrupting, I could still only answer ten or fifteen pieces of mail
in one day. She exclaimed, "But that's a lot!" I replied, "But it
doesn't even make a dent in the amount I actually receive."

The most demoralizing aspect of running Kitchen Table, however, was those occasions when other women of color, usually potential or actual authors, were unsupportive or hostile to the Press as a
direct result of the Press's poverty, which prevented us from always
functioning as quickly and efficiently as I so much wanted. When
these extremely painful, though fortunately not typical, incidents
occurred, I wished that those who were undermining our work
could see our tiny, apartment-sized office, which did not even have a
photocopier. I also wished that they could watch me work in the
middle of the night and on weekends, as well as every week day, to
keep the Press alive. Because of the quality of our work, few would
have guessed the conditions under which it was produced. Lu, much
like Audre before her, understood what I was up against. Long after
she had stopped working at the Press I was always able to depend
upon her for the emotional support I needed to face one more day.

Sometimes Lu and I went on outings together, for example, to
see the Boys Choir of Harlem, one of Lu's particular favorites, or
to take a picnic to Tanglewood in Lenox, Massachusetts. Once we
drove there to see Jessye Norman. Lu loved opera and I never really
let on that I was not a fan. I was of course excited to see Jessye Norman perform. Unfortunately, she was ill that evening and a substitute sang instead. We were both disappointed and promised
ourselves that we would go see Jessye Norman together wherever
she appeared within a two-hundred-mile radius of Albany. She
returned to Tanglewood in the summer of 1996 and we finally got
to hear her incredible voice in person.

In early June 1992 I had just returned, exhausted, from the
American Booksellers Association convention. It was a Friday and

everyone at Kitchen Table had the day off. When I checked the messages on the office machine there was one for me from someone at Wanda's office. Wanda still did some work for the Press and every so often we would reconnect on the telephone. When I called her office they gave me the stunning news that Wanda had died suddenly a few days before. I was in shock. Wanda was only thirty-five and her little girl was ten. The parallels with my own mother's death made Wanda's loss even more devastating. I knew that I needed to tell Lu in person. I drove out to Latham hating the thought of what I had to do.

That afternoon we cried together and talked for hours, still in disbelief, about what Wanda had meant to us. Lu had gone out of her way to help her as a "young mom" long after she stopped working at the Press. A few days later, Lu and I went together to the wake and to Wanda's funeral the following morning. We were both glad that we had each other to lean on during a terrible time.

I had learned that I could always depend upon Lu for something that was not always so easy to obtain from other Black women, that is, open-hearted and compassionate emotional support. I shared many of my personal burdens with Lu and even when they could not be instantly solved I always felt better for the telling. During the time I knew Lu, some of my closest friends and several members of my family died. I could always turn to her for understanding. I loved how she noticed what was going on with me without my having to say anything; she would mention when I had circles of exhaustion under my eyes or comment on my new pair of shoes. Once she even complimented me on my posture!

Undoubtedly, the difficult personal situation that Lu helped me with the most was my relationship to my twin sister. Lu had met Beverly when she had visited me in Albany. In December 1987, I was eagerly planning my first Christmas in my new home and Beverly was supposed to come for the holiday. On December 22 she called to say she had decided to stay in Boston, which meant that my holiday was ruined. I was devastated. I told Lu what had happened and she immediately invited me to share Christmas Eve

with her and her family. I spent most of Christmas Day in my car
driving to Philadelphia to have dinner with Joe Beam.

Throughout my life Beverly had often stopped speaking to me for
periods of time and when we were in contact she was emotionally
unpredictable. Our relationship was made more intense by the fact
that we were each other's only sibling and also because the members
of our family who had raised us had died many years before. I often
wonder how my sister's and my relationship might have been different if one of our significant family members had survived into our
adulthoods, our mother or our Aunt LaRue who raised us after
our mother died. I imagine that if my aunt, who died in 1971 at the
age of fifty-seven, were alive, she would have been very upset by Beverly's withdrawal from me and from our remaining family and
would have made an effort to help resolve the situation. Even if she
could have done nothing to change Beverly's behavior, she would
have offered me emotional support and also the link to my family
and past that Beverly's absence has so painfully deprived me of.

The last time I saw Beverly was in June of 1990. In early 1991 I
spoke to her on the telephone about a serious health problem I was
having and that was our last conversation. For many years I continued to call and to write her, but it became apparent that it was
futile. Lu was aware of what was going on and of how painful
it was for me. Every so often she would ask me if I had heard
from Beverly. Most of my other, younger friends had never even
met Beverly and even if they had, they did not ask about her.

One day when I was visiting, several years after I had last talked
to Beverly, Lu asked me again if I had heard anything from her. I
shook my head. Lu looked me directly in the eye and said, "Barbara, you have got to know that you've done everything you could."
She added other words of solace. I never forgot that moment. It was
with those words that a burden I had carried for a lifetime began to
lift. Because she had actually met Beverly, because of her age and
wisdom, because she was Lu, I knew that I could believe her. I
think at that moment Lu said what a mother might have said. She
knew the exact words that would allow me to move forward and to

begin to heal. She also knew me well enough to know that whatever the situation, I was always capable of blaming myself for it. That day I received a rare gift from a rare human being.

In early 1995, Lu's heart condition had become so serious that she had to undergo valve replacement surgery. By mid-February of that year I had relinquished my duties as publisher of Kitchen Table, the Press had moved to Brooklyn, and I was ecstatic at the prospect of what felt like a whole new life. Fortunately, Lu survived the surgery and began the slow months of recovery. Every time I visited her she was a bit stronger. By the summer she was a lot better. But in the autumn of 1995, Lu was diagnosed with cancer of the colon. She had to have more surgery, but since she was still recovering from the valve replacement, this operation posed a high level of risk. Shortly after her surgery for cancer, Lu's lungs began to fill with fluid and she almost died. The fact that her cardiologist happened to be in the hospital seeing other patients as her crisis peaked probably saved her life.

Lu made the difficult decision to do chemotherapy, "just to make sure," although there was no indication of spread. She told me that if the cancer later recurred she wanted the peace of mind of knowing that she had done everything possible to fight it. Thus began almost a whole year of treatments, each one of course making her weaker and weaker. In December 1995, Lu had to return to the hospital for minor surgery on her vocal cords, which had been damaged during the crisis with her lungs. Miserably, she had to spend Christmas Eve and Christmas Day in the hospital, a trying circumstance for her and her family.

During 1996, Lu's spirits seldom seemed to flag. She was able to cope with most of the side effects of the chemotherapy, including her hair loss. In the spring, in the midst of treatment, she did a quite remarkable thing. Lu had befriended two children who lived in her building. They often came downstairs to visit when I was there and it was clear that Lu and the kids had formed a mutual admiration society. Once when Jennifer was reading, she came across a description of an English tea which mentioned scones. When Jennifer asked Lu what they were, Lu told her about the kinds of things served at a formal tea. Then Lu decided to host a full-fledged high tea in honor of Jennifer, to which she invited all of her women friends. Lu mailed out beautifully handwritten invitations and had her two daughters, Margaret and Susan, and her daughter-in-law, Jeanette, help her with the food. She used her silver tea service and prepared a magnificent repast which included homemade scones, watercress and cucumber sandwiches, cookies, cakes, fresh strawberries dipped in chocolate, and other delicacies too numerous to name. I came with my friend Sybil and Sybil's nine-month-old baby, Sayeed, who became the star of the show for the afternoon. It was an unforgettable event, bringing together Lu's family and her eclectic circle of friends. And she accomplished all of this in the midst of forty-eight weeks of chemotherapy.

Sometimes when Lu, Vickie, and I got together, Lu would remark on our three different generations. The tea brought together five or six generations and was a gift especially for those younger guests who had never attended a similar event and likely might never attend a formal tea again. It also delighted me that Lu brought together Jennifer, who was Korean American, members of Jennifer's family, and friends who were African American and white. Given how persistently segregated this country continues to be, Lu's gathering would have been unique even if we had all merely gotten together and sent out for pizza!

In both the academic years 1995–1996 and 1996–1997, I had fellowships which required me to be away from Albany even more than usual. I had also begun to make long research trips to various locations for my book on the history of African American lesbians and gays. I hated the fact that I had to be away from home so much, especially while Lu was ill, but I tried to write her once a week from wherever I was and would also call. Long before, I had gotten into the habit of calling Lu from the airport or the train station before I left Albany and I called her long distance from hotel rooms all over the map.

In November 1996, just before Thanksgiving, Lu completed chemotherapy and her tests indicated that there was still no sign of spread. She was so relieved that it was done, that her prognosis was so positive, and jubilant at the fact that she would be able to celebrate Christmas at home, unlike the year before. I went to see her a few days before Christmas and brought her a present, a Christmas CD by the Boys Choir of Harlem. She needed to buy a gift certificate at a bookstore for Jennifer, and I offered to drive her so that she did not have to deal with the holiday traffic.

The second week in January I had to go to Cambridge, but before I left Vickie and I made a plan to visit Lu together on Sunday, January 19. The temperature was in the single digits that day. Vickie and Lu joked about whether I would actually make it because they knew how thoroughly I (and my asthma) despised the cold. Tired as I was from returning to town the day before, I did not consider canceling, especially since Lu was making brunch. Vickie brought a third guest, Sheila Ambrose, who had never met Lu before. As usual we had a great time. Lu had "thrown together" a feast: eggs scrambled with cheese on a platter framed with delicately sliced cantaloupe and oranges, homemade popovers, and creamed chipped beef. For dessert Lu had baked gingerbread, which she served with whipped cream. I told her that I had never tasted creamed chipped beef before and that my Aunt LaRue refused to eat it after World War II because she had had to eat so much of it during the war. Lu kidded me that I was implying that she was old because she had served a dish that I thought was really old-fashioned, from the era before I was born. I protested that that was not what I meant at all. Our laughter filled the room—four Black women aged 70, 50, 37, and 27; three of us lesbians, one of us not; three of us bonded by "the Kitchen Table years"; all of us still working to shape better lives for ourselves and for our communities than the power structure said we deserved.

A few days after our brunch a pipe froze in my home and I thought about calling Lu to ask her advice about whether I should go ahead and call a welder since the plumber could not seem to fix it.

It turned out that a water main had broken a few blocks away and that my own pipes were fine. On Friday, January 24, when I returned home at about six o'clock, I had a message from Lu's daughter, Margaret. Since Margaret only called me when Lu was ill, I was immediately apprehensive. I called Margaret and reached her partner who told me that Lu had died suddenly of a heart attack that afternoon.

There are no words to describe adequately what I felt at that moment, except perhaps to say that I felt like I had lost a mother once again. I still do, although the raw pain of those first days has dulled with time.

Lu's family asked me to speak at her memorial service, a signal honor. Somehow I managed to do it. The funeral chapel was filled to standing room only and, like at Lu's social gatherings, there were all varieties of people present. Although Lu was not a member of any religious congregation, both the Episcopal and Catholic bishops spoke because of their friendships with her formed many years before when Lu worked tirelessly as a community activist on behalf of the children and families of Arbor Hill. I spoke that night about Kitchen Table. Because Lu had numerous lesbian and gay friends, many of whom were also my friends, who had come to the service, I felt I also needed to speak about Lu's unique capacity to treat us as human beings.

I learned a lot from Lu. I hope that others might learn from her as well. If she were here today we would speak with incredulity and sorrow about what they did to Abner Louima. I would most likely mention that the Haitian and African American communities in New York have mobilized against police brutality following his attack and organized several demonstrations to which many participants brought bathroom plungers. As so often occurred, she might offer an observation about this horror that I never would have thought of myself, an assessment shaped by her expansive intelligence and experience.

If Lu were here I would tell her about my trip last weekend to a meeting of Black leftists in Atlanta. For the first time I was in a room with my age peers in the struggle who I had never met because antifeminism and homophobia continue to keep me and other Black lesbians and gays cordoned off from so many in the Black community. I would tell her that she would have much to teach those seasoned activists who, with a few exceptions, avoided both eye contact and conversation. She could give them pointers on how to challenge homophobia and misogyny simply by how she lived, not merely by what she said.

I would undoubtedly mention "the largest gathering of Black women writers ever held" (as described in *Essence*) in New York a few weeks from now to which I was not invited and describe the hell I have gone through to be permitted to speak there.

I would tell her that Sayeed is both walking and talking and that her grandson, Jason, graduated from high school in June and is starting college. I would definitely tell her about getting together a few days ago with my friend Naomi, her son, Lonnie, and his best friend, Keaon, so that I could contribute to my friends' collective efforts to help Keaon acquire the skills that will make his dream of college possible. I would share the news that I am finally going to publish a collection of my own writing. I might *not* tell her that Kitchen Table closed this past summer and has not reopened.

Finally, I would tell Lu that I am still here, that my work is going well, that I continue to scrape by financially, that I am feeling good, and that I am so much better able to face what life puts before me, both the brambles and the roses, because of knowing her.

1997

Notes

1. In June 1998 James Byrd Jr. was lynched in Jasper, Texas, when three white men chained him to the back of a truck and dragged him until he was dismembered. A few days later, three white men in Belleville, Illinois, abducted another Black man, Baron Manning, and attempted to murder him in a similar fashion, but Manning survived the dragging attack.

2. Erik Davis, "Barbed Wire Net," *The Village Voice*, May 2, 1995, 28.

Organizations to Contact

Much of the writing in this collection focuses on political issues, activism, and organizing. The following are organizations that challenge many types of oppression, most from a multi-issue perspective. I encourage readers to find out more about these groups. All of them offer effective strategies for change, have a wealth of information to share, and need your material support to survive.

AMERICAN FRIENDS SERVICE COMMITTEE (AFSC)
Works internationally on issues of peace and justice, ranging from projects on lesbian and gay youth to women's health in Haiti to Indigenous rights throughout the world.
Publications: Regional, U.S., and international. Visit website for newsletter.
1501 Cherry St.
Philadelphia, PA 19102
(215) 241-7000
Website: http://afsc.org/
E-mail: afscinfo@afsc.org

THE AUDRE LORDE PROJECT
A community center for lesbian, gay, bisexual, two-spirit, trans, and gender nonconforming people of color in the New York City area that organizes for progressive social and economic justice.
(718) 596-0342
Website: https://alp.org/

BLACK FEMINIST FUTURE (BFF)
A member-centered organization whose members help inform
its work, campaigns, and initiatives. BFF centers leadership
development, community care, and joy to build political and
social power.
Website: https://blackfeministfuture.org/
E-mail: members@blackfeministfuture.org

BLACK WOMEN RADICALS
A Black feminist advocacy organization dedicated to uplifting
and centering Black women's and gender-expansive people's
radical political activism.
Website: http://blackwomenradicals.com/
E-mail: blackwomenradicals@gmail.com

BYP100 (BLACK YOUTH PROJECT 100)
A member-based organization of Black youth activists creating
justice and freedom for all Black people. It engages in direct-
action organizing, advocacy, and education through a Black,
queer, feminist lens.
Website: http://byp100.org/
E-mail: info@byp100.org

CENTER FOR THIRD WORLD ORGANIZING
Through a number of projects, the center assists grassroots
organizing in communities of color.
1714 Franklin St.
Oakland, CA 94612
Website: http://ctwo.org/
E-mail: comms@ctwo.org; trainings@ctwo.org

DREAM DEFENDERS
A group of young Black and Brown people that formed in 2012 in response to the killing of seventeen-year-old Trayvon Martin. Based in Florida, it is now a national organization committed to abolitionist, Black feminist, socialist, and internationalist work.
Website: https://www.dreamdefenders.org/
E-mail: info@dreamdefenders.org

ESPERANZA PEACE AND JUSTICE CENTER
A multi-issue social justice and cultural organization that is especially supportive of the leadership and concerns of lesbian, gay, bisexual, and transgender people of color.
Publication: *La Voz de Esperanza*
922 San Pedro Ave.
San Antonio, TX 78212
(210) 228-0201
Website: http://esperanzacenter.org/
E-mail: esperanza@esperanzacenter.org

HIGHLANDER RESEARCH AND EDUCATION CENTER
The "cradle of the Civil Rights movement," founded in 1932, continues to support collective action to achieve economic and social justice.
1959 Highlander Way
New Market, TN 37820
Website: http://highlandercenter.org/
E-mail: hrec@highlandercenter.org

INCITE!
A network of radical feminists of color organizing to end state violence and violence at home and in communities.
Publications: https://incite-national.org/blog/
Website: http://incite-national.org/
E-mail: Incite.natl@gmail.com

MOBILIZATION 4 MUMIA
Fights for Mumia Abu-Jamal's freedom and for his right to proper
health care.
Website: http://mobilization4mumia.com/
E-mail: Mobilization4Mumia@gmail.com

THE MOVEMENT FOR BLACK LIVES (M4BL)
An ecosystem of individuals and organizations creating a shared
vision and policy agenda to win rights, recognition, and resources
for Black people. In doing so, the movement makes it possible for
Black people and everyone to live healthy and fruitful lives.
Website: https://m4bl.org/

NATIONAL LGBTQ TASK FORCE
Builds power, takes action, and creates change to achieve
freedom, justice, and equity for LGBTQ+ people.
1050 Connecticut Ave. NW, Suite 65550
Washington, DC 20035
(202) 393-5177
Website: http://thetaskforce.org/

NATIONAL NETWORK OF ABORTION FUNDS
Builds power with members to remove financial and logistical
barriers to abortion access by centering people who have abortions
and organizing at the intersections of racial, economic, and
reproductive justice.
Website: https://abortionfunds.org/

POLITICAL RESEARCH ASSOCIATES (PRA)
The preeminent progressive think tank that monitors and
challenges the U.S. right wing. As a social justice research and
strategy center, it supports the organizing efforts of those targeted
as scapegoats of right-wing attacks.
Publication: *The Public Eye*
Website: http://politicalresearch.org/
E-mail: contact@politicalresearch.org

SHOWING UP FOR RACIAL JUSTICE (SURJ)
A national organization that brings hundreds of thousands of
white people into fights for racial and economic justice. SURJ
seeks to bring more white people into racial justice work and to
find mutual interest with movements led by Blacks and persons of
color.
Website: https://surj.org/

SISTERSONG
SisterSong's mission is to strengthen and amplify the collective
voices of Indigenous women and women of color to achieve
reproductive justice by eradicating reproductive oppression and
securing human rights.
P.O. Box 94408
Atlanta, GA 30377
(404) 756-2680
Website: https://www.sistersong.net/
E-mail: info@sistersong.net

SOUTHERNERS ON NEW GROUND (SONG)
A home for LGBTQ liberation across all lines of race, class, abilities, age, culture, gender, and sexuality in the South. SONG works to build, sustain, and connect a southern regional base of LGBTQ people to transform the region through strategic projects and campaigns.
561 W. Whitehall St.
Atlanta, GA 30310
(404) 549-8628
Website: http://southernersonnewground.org/
E-mail: kindred@southernersonnewground.org

SOUTHERN POVERTY LAW CENTER (SPLC)
A catalyst for racial justice in the South and beyond, working in partnership with communities to dismantle white supremacy, strengthen intersectional movements, and advance the human rights of all people.
Publications: See website for their various publications
400 Washington Ave.
Montgomery, AL 36104
(888) 414-7752
Website: http://splcenter.org/

SYLVIA RIVERA LAW PROJECT
Works to guarantee that all people are free to self-determine gender identity and expression regardless of income or race and without facing harassment, discrimination, or violence. They help through facilitating access to legal services at low/no cost for things like name changes, IDs, immigration, and more.
Publications: https://srlp.org/allnews/
147 W. 24th St., 5th Floor
New York, NY 10011
(212) 337-8550
Website: https://srlp.org/
E-mail: DST@srlp.org (legal support); FFT@srlp.org (finance & fundraising); MBT@srlp.org (movement building and membership)

WOMEN'S MARCH
The mission of Women's March is to harness the political power of diverse women and their communities to create transformative social change. It is committed to dismantling systems of oppression through nonviolent resistance and building inclusive structures guided by self-determination, dignity, and respect. Website: https://www.womensmarch.com/

Selected Bibliography

Abu-Jamal, Mumia. *Death Blossoms: Reflections from a Prisoner of Conscience.* Farmington, Pa.: Plough Publishing, 1997.

————. *Live from Death Row.* Reading, Mass.: Addison-Wesley Publishing, 1995.

Beam, Joseph F., ed. *In the Life: A Black Gay Anthology.* Boston: Alyson Publications, 1986.

*Bethel, Lorraine, and Barbara Smith, eds. *Conditions: Five, The Black Women's Issue* 2, no. 2 (Autumn 1979).

Black Scholar, The, eds. *Court of Appeal: The Black Community Speaks Out on the Racial and Sexual Politics of Thomas vs. Hill.* New York: Ballantine Books, 1992.

*Bulkin, Elly, Minnie Bruce Pratt, and Barbara Smith. *Yours in Struggle: Three Feminist Perspectives on Anti-Semitism and Racism.* Ithaca, N.Y.: Firebrand Books, 1984, 1988.

Gay Community News. 29 Stanhope Street, Boston, MA 02116.

Hemenway, Robert E. *Zora Neale Hurston: A Literary Biography.* Urbana: University of Illinois Press, 1980.

Hemphill, Essex, ed. *Brother to Brother: New Writings by Black Gay Men.* Boston: Alyson Publications, 1991.

*Hull, Gloria T., Patricia Bell Scott, and Barbara Smith, eds. *All the Women Are White, All the Blacks Are Men, But Some of Us Are Brave: Black Women's Studies.* New York: The Feminist Press at The City University of New York, 1982.

---

* These titles are coauthored or coedited by Barbara Smith.

Hurston, Zora Neale. *Dust Tracks on a Road: An Autobiography.* New York: HarperCollins Publishers, 1991.

——. *Jonah's Gourd Vine.* New York: HarperCollins Publishers, 1990.

——. *Moses, Man of the Mountain.* New York: HarperCollins Publishers, 1991.

——. *Mules and Men.* New York: HarperCollins Publishers, 1990.

——. *Seraph on the Suwanee.* New York: HarperCollins Publishers, 1991.

——. *Spunk: The Selected Stories of Zora Neale Hurston.* San Francisco: Turtle Island Foundation, 1985.

——. *Tell My Horse.* New York: HarperCollins Publishers, 1990.

——. *Their Eyes Were Watching God.* Urbana: University of Illinois Press, 1991.

Lorde, Audre. *The Collected Poems of Audre Lorde.* New York: W. W. Norton, 1997.

——. *Sister Outsider: Essays and Speeches.* Freedom, Calif.: Crossing Press, 1984.

——. *Zami: A New Spelling of My Name.* Freedom, Calif.: Crossing Press, 1984.

*Mankiller, Wilma, Gwendolyn Mink, Marysa Navarro, Barbara Smith, and Gloria Steinem, eds. *The Reader's Companion to U.S. Women's History* Boston and New York: Houghton Mifflin, 1998.

Moraga, Cherríe, and Gloria Anzaldúa, eds. *This Bridge Called My Back: Writings by Radical Women of Color.* New York: Kitchen Table: Women of Color Press, 1981, 1983.

Morrison, Toni. *The Bluest Eye.* New York: Alfred A. Knopf, 1993.

——. *Sula.* New York: Alfred A. Knopf, 1973.

Naylor, Gloria. *The Women of Brewster Place.* New York: Viking Penguin, 1983.

---

* These titles are coauthored or coedited by Barbara Smith.

Ng, Vivien. "Race Matters." In *Lesbian and Gay Studies: A Critical Introduction*, edited by Andy Medhurst and Sally R. Munt. London: Cassell Publishing, 1997.

Parker, *Pat. Jonestown & Other Madness*. Ithaca, N.Y.: Firebrand Books, 1985.

———. *Movement in Black*. Ithaca, N.Y.: Firebrand Books, 1990.

Pharr, Suzanne. *Homophobia: A Weapon of Sexism*. Berkeley, Calif.: Chardon Press, 1997.

———. *In the Time of the Right: Reflections on Liberation*. Berkeley, Calif.: Chardon Press, 1996.

Pratt, Minnie Bruce. *Rebellion: Essays 1980–1991*. Ithaca, N.Y.: Firebrand Books, 1991.

Radical Teacher, The. Boston Women's Teachers Group, Box 383316, Cambridge, MA 02138-3316.

Reddy, Maureen T. *Crossing the Color Line: Race, Parenting, and Culture*. New Brunswick, N.J.: Rutgers University Press, 1994.

———, ed. *Everyday Acts Against Racism: Raising Children in a Multiracial World*. Seattle, Wash.: Seal Press, 1996.

Segrest, Mab. *Memoir of a Race Traitor*. Boston: South End Press, 1993.

———. *My Mama's Dead Squirrel: Lesbian Essays on Southern Culture*. Ithaca, N.Y.: Firebrand Books, 1985.

Shockley, Ann Allen. *The Black and White of It*. Tallahassee, Fla.: Naiad Press, 1987.

———. *Loving Her*. Boston: Northeastern University Press, 1997.

———. *Say Jesus and Come to Me*. Tallahassee, Fla.: Naiad Press, 1987.

Sinclair, Jo. *The Changelings*. New York: The Feminist Press at The City University of New York, 1985.

Smith, Barbara. "'Feisty Characters' and Other People's Causes': Memories of White Racism and U.S. Feminism." In *The Feminist Memoir Project: Voices from Women's Liberation*, edited by Rachel Blau DuPlessis and Ann Snitow. New York: Crown Publishing, 1998.

———, ed. *Home Girls: A Black Feminist Anthology*. New York: Kitchen Table: Women of Color Press, 1983.

———. "Where Has Gay Liberation Gone? An Interview with Barbara Smith." In *Homo Economics: Capitalism, Community, and Lesbian and Gay Life*, edited by Amy Gluckman and Betsy Reed. New York and London: Routledge, 1997.

Sojourner: The Women's Forum. 42 Seaverns Avenue, Jamaica Plain, MA 02130.

Walker, Alice. *The Color Purple.* New York: Harcourt Brace, 1982.

———. *In Love & Trouble: Stories of Black Women.* New York: Harcourt Brace, 1974.

———. *In Search of Our Mothers' Gardens: Womanist Prose.* New York: Harcourt Brace, 1983.

———, ed. *I Love Myself When I Am Laughing: A Zora Neale Hurston Reader.* New York: The Feminist Press at The City University of New York, 1979.

About the Author

BARBARA SMITH is an author and independent scholar who has played a groundbreaking role in opening a national cultural and political dialogue about the intersections of race, class, sexuality, and gender. In her work as a critic, teacher, activist, lecturer, and publisher, Smith was among the first to define an African American women's literary tradition and to build Black women's studies and Black feminism in the United States.

She is editor of *Conditions: Five, The Black Women's Issue* with Lorraine Bethel; *All the Women Are White, All the Blacks Are Men, But Some of Us Are Brave: Black Women's Studies* with Akasha (Gloria) Hull and Patricia Bell-Scott; and *The Reader's Companion to U.S. Women's History* with Wilma Mankiller, Gwendolyn Mink, Marysa Navarro, and Gloria Steinem. She is coauthor of *Yours in Struggle: Three Feminist Perspectives on Anti-Semitism and Racism* with Elly Bulkin and Minnie Bruce Pratt, and she is the editor of the anthology *Home Girls*, featuring writings by Black feminists and lesbians. *Ain't Gonna Let Nobody Turn Me Around: Forty Years of Movement Building with Barbara Smith*, coedited by Alethia Jones and Virginia Eubanks with Barbara Smith, was published in 2014 by SUNY Press. In 2015, it won the Lambda Award for Lesbian Memoir/Biography and the Judy Grahn Award for Lesbian Nonfiction from the Publishing Triangle.

From 2006 until 2013, she served two terms as a member of the Albany Common Council. In 2005, she was nominated for the Nobel Peace Prize.